TEN YEARS WITH THE BENGALS

TRUMP

TEN YEARS WITH THE BENGALS
TRUMP

By Bob Trumpy
With Bill Mefford

Donning
Virginia Beach/Norfolk

Library of Congress Cataloging in Publication Data

Trumpy, Bob, 1945-
    Trump!
  1. Cincinnati Bengals (Football club) I. Mefford, Bill,
joint author. II. Title.
GV956.C54T78   796.33'264'0977178   79-20367
ISBN 0-89865-019-4

Printed in the United States of America

To Pat
Matt
Jason
Marn
Allyssa
and Michael

FOREWORD

I suppose I could have selected the 1968 season, our first; or the surprise division winning years of '70 and '73, or even my final season in '77.

But I didn't.

As a backdrop for this collection of memories, flashbacks and vignettes I chose the 1975 season. Why? Because it was the finest season the Bengals ever had, 11-3, missing the playoffs by a mere thirty-four yards in Oakland. It was also the year in which the rag-tag team that had first taken the field seven seasons earlier showed for the first time that it had, finally, matured into a *legitimate* powerhouse in the NFL.

There was something else, too. We didn't know it at the time, of course, but this was to be the final year of head coaching for a fella by the name of Brown. It was Paul's last hurrah after forty-plus years in the business. Pro football was *his* game: he led it, designed it, overhauled it and manipulated it as no other man before or since.

But this book is not so much a chronicle of a single season as it is an inside look into a decade of football with the Bengals. I was there when it began, in 1968, with our roving band of misfits, castoffs and criminals, was there in the mid-seventies for our prestige years, and was there for the subsequent demise into a rather confused, misguided, polarized group of young men who courted defeat as an unwanted companion. Good times, bad times. Days of surprises and sorrows. I lived it all.

I hope you enjoy, as I did, reliving some of these memories that made up my decade with the Bengals, the important games, the embarrassing incidents, my whatever-happened-to? teammates.

If by chance I have missed some of your favorite Bengal memories and players, just give me a call on my WCKY radio show. I'll be glad to give you an inside look.

See you at the stadium....

Bob Trumpy
July 1, 1979

TEN YEARS WITH THE BENGALS
TRUMP

BEGINNINGS:
Getting There

That a professional football team selected me in the 1968 college draft ranks right up there in unliklihoods with the probability that the OPEC nations will begin marketing electric automobiles.

Who else can you name in the history of the game that was drafted from the roster of the Beneficial Finance Corporation? Only Robert T. Trumpy, Jr.—I'll lay odds on it.

Most NFL players come to the pros fresh from the gridirons of football factories like Ohio State, Michigan, USC and Notre Dame. Not me. I came from a high-rise office building at 607 Hill Street in the concrete heart of downtown Los Angeles. At the time the Bengals selected me, I was a bill collector grossing $83.50 a week.

But from this inauspicious beginning I managed to go on to become a four-time All-Pro tight end and one of the highest paid players in the history of the Cincinnati Bengal franchise.

Let me tell you: it wasn't easy.

From the time I left high school in 1963 until the time I joined the Cincinnati Bengals as a 12th-round draft choice in 1968, I had somehow managed to attend three colleges (one in the Midwest, one in the near-west and one in the far-west); hold five jobs (security guard at a home for delinquent boys, clothing salesman, sod farmer, bill collector and travel-trailer assembler); spend nine weeks confined to a hospital bed; do a short hitch for Uncle Sam in the Navy, and, for variety, get married. In all that time I played in exactly sixteen college football games. Hardly your outstanding credentials for a budding professional football player.

If all this sounds a little convoluted, it is. And I guess the logical place to begin is with my high school graduation.

I graduated from Springfield (Illinois) High School in 1963. I was a good athlete there, what sportswriters like to refer to as "all-around." In track, I set the school and city records in the broad jump (also winning the state title) and in the long jump. In football, as a wide receiver (I also was a starting linebacker), I led the team in pass receiving and helped to win three consecutive city titles, never having lost a city game. I was named to the Illinois All-State football team in my junior and senior years.

1

My true forte, however, was basketball. As a center-forward, I led the team in scoring, averaging somewhere around twenty points a game. As in football, we won three consecutive city championships. Not only was I named to the Illinois All-State basketball team in my junior and senior years, but I also earned the prize plum—as a senior I was named a high school All-American in basketball.

The college scholarship offers were many. UCLA, Illinois, Kentucky, Davidson—all the basketball powers from across the nation—made me attractive offers; I received several dozen for football, too. I guess in all I had more than a hundred full rides to choose from.

Trouble was: most of the scholarships were for only one sport, and that wasn't the way I wanted to do it. As a young idealistic "all-around" athlete, I long had designs on playing *two* collegiate sports, basketball and football.

I found out, though, that this desire was about as popular with coaches as a head cheerleader with an infectious rash. First of all, there is great competition for the quality athlete even between coaches *at the same* school! The football coach is doing what he can to make his sport number one on campus; the basketball coach knows that it is really his sport that pays the freight. Each is clawing for additional scholarship allocations for his particular sport from the college administration or board of regents. Then too: there seems to be a pervading belief that a two-sport athlete cannot give full effort and concentration to both sports during the year. What if he gets hurt during the football season? That'd put him out of action for the basketball games. And so on.

Fortunately, there was one school that seemed at least curious enough in my football-basketball proposition to weigh the dual scholarship possibility judiciously. Oddly, it was the college that I really wanted to attend all along, the University of Illinois. There were several reasons why Illinois turned me on. First, it was located in Champaign-Urbana, just ninety miles east of my hometown. This meant that it wouldn't be a hardship for my folks to come see me play whenever they wanted. Secondly, I was already very familiar with the Illinois campus, physical layout and sports programs. As a high schooler, I had made several trips to the campus with the Springfield teams to participate in statewide track meets and football and basketball playoff games.

So it was with great expectations that I was matriculated at Illinois in 1963. As it turned out, I only played one sport, and that was football. It was the Illinois basketball coach himself—the very man who had spent countless dollars and manhours recruiting me for his program—who inspired the football-only decision.

It happened toward the end of my senior year at Springfield High. My parents and I were invited to East Lansing by Michigan State to be guests of the university during the NCAA regional basketball games being played there. It was a recruiting effort by the school to entice me—and five other high school All-American basketball players—to opt for their school.

We were wined and dined royally, met all the important people. Then, on our last night there, something occurred that would evermore make me a one-sport student at Illinois. My folks and I had boarded the elevator at the campus' Kellogg Center which would take us to our rooms. About three floors from our destination, the elevator stopped, the doors opened, and three guys stumbled aboard. It was obvious by the immediate gin-mill stench that filled the close confines that the three had been out on one helluva binge. The worst for wear was the guy in the middle. He was so crocked that each of the other two had hold of him to keep him from toppling over right there in the elevator. The guy's eyes were glazed and at half-mast. Blood was streaming down his face. He was cursing mercilessly.

My father and I recognized this crude drunk at precisely the same moment. We had met him on numerous occasions in the past months, during recruiting sessions. He was the head coach of the University of Illinois basketball team! He was on the Michigan State campus because he had taken his team there that weekend to participate in the NCAA regional playoffs.

Well, the elevator door hadn't been closed behind us three seconds when my father grabbed me by the elbow and said, "There's no way in this world that I'm going to allow a son of mine to go to Illinois to play basketball for *that* bum." All I could do was nod at him. Experience had long taught me that the lamentations of Jeremiah couldn't change my dad's mind once it's made up.

So, OK, it wasn't really so bad, I told myself. So I don't play two sports. The chances of that happening anyway were looking slimmer and slimmer. On the good side: at least I'd still be able to go to Illinois, the school I wanted all along, to play one sport—football. And I'd still be doing it on a full ride. Yep, I admitted, things could have worked out worse.

They could have. And did.

No one had bothered to inform me that freshman football at the University of Illinois didn't exist. Practically, anyway. Freshmen footballers do nothing but practice and practice and practice some more. No scheduled games, no competition, aside from scrimmages, no nothing. Just practice.

Frankly, I hated it. And I was disappointed as hell, but I decided to stick it out. It turned out to be a wise decision because the next year, 1964, I found myself to be, as a sophomore, the starting split end for the varsity. This was no small feat. There was a lot of talent on that Illinois team; it had just come off a Rose Bowl victory the year before and it still boasted a roster that included such future pro players as Dick Butkis and Jim Grabowski.

Although I wasn't a better-known player on the Illinois squad,

I nevertheless led the team in pass receiving and I played a key part in several early-season victories.

My luck as a receiver lasted only six games. In the seventh game, I got my hand stepped on in a pile-up; the injury not only sidelined me for the game, but when infection set in, it put me in the hospital for nine weeks and left my hand partially paralyzed for two years. I didn't know it at the time, of course, but I would never again don the navy and orange of the "Big U" football uniform.

It was my own fault, really, I guess I was a little naive. Because, despite the nine-week stay in the hospital, I insisted on taking my semester final examinations. I failed two of them and they flunked me out of school. I found out later that the university would have given me a medical exemption from the exams and I could have made them up at a later date. But I guess the hospitalization had me so depressed that I said, what the hell, I might as well take them now.

After I received my flunk notice I headed home to Springfield to seek employment. Seek I did. And find. Three jobs in the next twelve months, each a little worse than the other.

The first was as a security guard (we were called "cottage parents") at the DuPage State Boys' School. A friend of mine, Ron Leonard, and I got the jobs through the state employment office. The boys' school was located in Warrenville, Illinois, a sleepy town which has as its only claim to fame the reputation of having been the summer home of Scarface Al Capone. Some distinction, right?

Listen, our boys' home had a clientele of about two hundred juvenile delinquents, several of whom made Scarface Al look like a choir boy. We had one hoodlum who was in on his third charge of rape. He was thirteen years old. We had another named Eddie who scared the hell out of me my first night on the job. I heard this commotion from one of the rooms and ran in to find Eddie, fast asleep in his bed, frantically waving his head from side to side. Immediately I took off for the warden's office to find out what the story was on this guy. The warden told me that Eddie's father was an alcoholic who used to come home after a night on the town and waylay the daylights out of the boy. After a while, Eddie for protection took to sleeping in a locker so his father wouldn't find him. He would beat his head against the wall to knock himself out—Eddie knew he could never fall asleep standing up. So ingrained had this routine become, that when he did sleep in a bed he'd simulate knocking himself out in the locker, screaming from the pain of the constant headbanging.

I got $400 a month for this job, plus room and board. It wasn't nearly enough. First of all, I could see no future in riding herd over a group of teenage delinquents who basically had no desire whatsoever to be kept under house guard. Secondly, I came to realize that the fifteen-foot wall that surrounded the security barracks was incarcerating *me* as well as the delinquents. And *my* only offense was that

I had flunked out of the University of Illinois.

It was in May of 1965 that I finally resigned this endeavor and, after some searching, landed a second job. I became a sod farmer. I managed to get the job through an employment bureau. I even talked my friend Ron Leonard into working along side of me. The sod farm was located in West Aurora, Illinois, near Ron's home-town, so I was invited to live with him and his folks. Ron's dad, an ironworker, and mom already had six offspring to provide for, and I made number seven. The Leonards lived in a one-bedroom home. The parents slept in the bedroom downstairs and all the kids, including me, slept in a hollowed-out room in the attic which they had converted into a makeshift dormer. Can you imagine—already having six kids to care for and then extending a welcoming hand to a seventh? Yet, despite the fact that they lived under these hardscrabble conditions, I've never met a finer family and happier bunch of people in my life.

I wish I could have found such happiness in my job. No way. Sod farming is authentic ass-busting work, and from morning light to dusk Ron and I did nothing but dig, cut, roll and stack sod. Our boss, a retired insurance man, worked us to the bone.

Finally, after driving us in this godless toil for five months, he upped and fired us, on the spot. You can imagine how shocked Ron and I were. We had done everything he had asked of us without complaint. So why the sudden dismissal? Later we learned that he thought we were going to ask for a raise, which he didn't want to grant. At the time, he was paying us $2.50 an hour!

In September 1965, bidding farewell to the Leonards, I moved back to where it all began, my hometown of Springfield. There, I entered into my third profession. I became a clothing salesman for the Harvey Brothers Clothing Service. If by some chance you were in Harvey Brothers during the months of September 1965 to February 1966 to buy a shirt or suit, odds are pretty good that the tall, broad-shouldered lad who waited on you was me. I was the only floor salesman Harvey Brothers had. You might say it was a small, family-run operation, and the threat of it someday absorbing, say, Marshall Fields seemed quite remote. Needless to say, the work was dull and unchallenging, and I was to the point of quitting this job when my first big break came.

My father, then a securities salesman, had been talking to a friend of his, a Dr. James Hunter. Dr. Hunter had just been named dean of men at the University of Utah in Salt Lake City, and somehow dad was successful in convincing the good dean that what he needed his first year out there was to add verve to Utah's infam-ously lackluster football program. How could the dean do this? My father suggested he knew of an out-of-work, standout 6'6" split end with Big Ten experience who'd be willing to do what he could to straighten out the football program. And—what luck!—the lad was

5

right there in Springfield at the time.

Out of all this came a full ride football scholarship for me to Utah. And I must admit I was exhilarated at the prospects of playing college football once more. Frankly, I had had quite enough of selling sport coats, working small sod patches and keeping all-night vigils over a gang of midget criminals.

The first thing I did was go to the library and check an atlas. You see, I really wasn't too sure where Utah was. I mean I knew it was out around Nevada and Colorado somewhere, but I didn't know *exactly* where. In the back of my mind I had it that Utah's two renowned natural resources were salt and polygamous marriages, and, what the heck, one out of two ain't bad.

I located Utah in the atlas, it was being squeezed to death by its neighbors, Nevada, Idaho, Wyoming, Colorado, New Mexico and Arizona. And the only city name I recognized was Salt Lake City. Truthfully, the state looked a wee sparse to a guy from the Midwest who was used to the ever-crowded cities.

What the heck, I thought, beggars can't be choosers. I'm being presented here with a golden opportunity to get back into college and to play football again (it had been fifteen months since I had touched a football). Besides, if Brigham Young could make the trip from Illinois to Utah 120 years earlier, surely I could too. And Brigham couldn't run a post-pattern worth a damn!

Of course, I had to put a personal quirk into my trek West. Brigham Young made the 1,900 miles by wagon in more or less a straight line; I went to Utah by way of Southern California!

It seems that there was a slight hitch in my going to the University of Utah. The school was on the quarter system, I was informed, and Illinois had been on the semester system. In order for any of my passing Illinois grades to transfer as credits, I would have to take a few summer courses towards entrance requirements.

So, in late February 1966, I packed up my now-worn suitcase again, once more said good-bye to my friends and folks and for the umpteenth time was on the move. This time west, specifically, toward Glendale, California, home of Glendale Junior College. Dean Hunter had personally suggested this school, and for a good reason: its total football coaching staff had just been hired to coach at Utah the next year. I could spend a few months going to school and at the same time show my future coaches what I could do on the receiving end of a football.

Only a few things of note occurred during my three-month stay in California. The first was that I actually began to work out again; a little running, a little weightlifting, a little catching of football. It had been a long time.

The second, and alas, by far the most important event to take place in California was my meeting a shy, comely girl by the name of Patricia Lynn Feith. She was a secretary at Merle Norman Cosmetics at the time, and I met her at one of the nightly beach parties. Neither of us knew it at the time, of course, but four months after that first meeting I would be flying back from Utah to California to make her Mrs. Robert T. Trumpy, Jr.

At Utah, we had a lousy football team and a lousy coach. You sure get a different perspective of college football in the Western Athletic Conference. In the Big Ten, football is played as a religious experience; out west, football's but an entertaining interlude between cutting classes and parties. The fans were about as enthusiastic as eunuchs at a love-in. I wasn't too disappointed, though. We finished with, I think, a 3-7 record that year, and I led the team in pass receiving, averaging over 17 yards a catch.

You'd think that after three colleges in five years I'd be ready to earn a degree. Well, I was—*ready*, that is. It never came to pass. Before going from Springfield to Glendale Junior College, whim encouraged me to sign up for the Navy Reserve. Whim told me the draft was plucking out guys right and left for Vietnam, and I didn't want to be one of them. Whim told me that if I joined a Naval Reserve unit, I could at least have some say in my own destiny. What whim didn't tell me was that my reserve unit would be called up in June of 1967 before I could earn my degree at Utah.

Being a newlywed, I didn't like it, of course. But that mattered little to Uncle Sam, so, once again, I found myself with packed bags in hand, kissing my new bride good-bye, and heading off for Treasure Island in San Francisco to begin what I knew would be a several-year hitch in the Navy. I was pretty depressed about the whole thing.

Fortunately, my depression was short-lived because, thanks to a military screw-up, I earned a discharge from the Navy my second day on base (more on that later). It took ninety days to process my papers, during which time I remember perhaps only a dozen days or so. The rest of the time you could have found me in the officers' club celebrating; chances are you'd have found me drunk as, well, a sailor.

So three months after my induction into the military I found myself scot-free and living in the Los Angeles suburb of Reseda. Pat had moved there when I went into the service so she could be close to her parents, who lived in nearby Tarzana. Pat's folks, Marge and Larry, were great to us. We were poor as pickaninnies in those days and lived from month to month on the "Care" packages they would send to us.

And things looked bleak on the employment horizon: I had no college degree, no experience in a practical job, no strings to pull. Finding gainful employment was not the easiest thing in the world. In the back of my mind I had it that I would one day return to college; but until that time Pat and I needed money to live on. So, when I saw an ad in the *Los Angeles Times* classifieds offering a "career-oriented" position as a "management-trainee," I applied. It sounded pretty good to me, really; the word "management" evoked a mental picture of guys sporting grey pin-striped suits and long, dark cheroots. As it turned out, the job was with Beneficial Finance Corporation. They were willing to pay me $400 a month to be a bill collector.

It didn't take me long to find out how much I hated my job. I suppose some corporate lackey has to go around prying the loose change out of poor people's pockets, but not me. I'm just not cut out for that type of thing. Since I was low man on Beneficial's corporate totem pole, I was assigned a bill collecting territory no one else would touch with a pair of tongs. It was bordered by the Harbor Freeway on the west, 51st Street on the north and 118th Street on the south. For those unfamiliar with the typography of Los Angeles, I'll tell you that they call this particular section of L.A.: Watts.

It was a little known niche in the world until the late sixties, when its name became emblazoned on front-pages from coast to coast; it became the shibboleth of civil rights riots and Black freedom struggles.

Want to know what tough is? Tough is being a young honkie from the Midwest out hustling around alleyways in Watts, trying to squeeze a dime here, a dollar there, out of born-poor Black people. *That's* tough! And you might say my being blond-haired, blue-eyed and light-skinned didn't go too far in allowing me to work incognito. At 6'6" I stuck out like a flamingo in a crow's nest.

I knew I'd had enough when a big Black gal pulled out a .38 revolver and aimed it directly at my head, possessed with intentions of blowing my brains out. This narrow escape went a long way in encouraging me to seek a more viable occupation; and I was sitting in my office scanning the classifieds when I got a phone call. It was my wife Pat; and it turned out to be the singular most important phone call in my life.

Pat informed me that I had just been drafted in the 12th round by Cincinnati's new franchise in the American Football League. I was flabbergasted. Me drafted? By a professional football team? Impossible! No one has even heard of Bob Trumpy, let alone the pro leagues. I mean, six college games in 1964 and ten more in 1966 doth not a pro prospect make—right?

"Jeez, Pat," I mumbled into the mouthpiece, "you don't think they made a mistake do you? I haven't touched a football in a year and a half."

Pat assured me that there was no mistake, that she had the telegram—"from some guy named Paul E. Brown"—and that she was holding it tightly in her hand that very moment.

The earpiece of my telephone hadn't even had a chance to cool before I was in my boss' office at Beneficial Finance. "I've just been drafted by a professional football team . . ." I began, and then went on

8

to suggest—in terms not lacking explicity—what he could do with my job. I believe I kept indicating that he could locate it on his body in a place where the sun never shines.

Shortly after receiving the telegram, I signed a contract with the Bengals for $15,000. I know it doesn't sound like much compared with the immoderate salaries players are getting today, but to Pat and me it was an unheard-of fortune. We had never even allowed ourselves the luxury of dreaming about so much money. I received something else, too: a brochure from Paul Brown describing ten techniques of physical fitness, and a personal note suggesting that draftees were expected to report to summer training camp in top condition. Well, a glance at my long inactive muscles told me they were, physical condition-wise, quite far from the top indeed; and a peek at the calendar told me I had exactly fourteen weeks to pummel them into some sort of workable shape. Yep, Moses had his ten commandments from the Lord; I had my ten physical conditioning dictates from Paul Brown. The latter was what I was going to live by daily.

So that Pat (who was now with child—our first) and I would have at least some source of income, I obtained, through my brother-in-law, part-time work as an assembler with the Shasta Trailer Company. But most of my hours were spent at San Fernando State College where I concentrated on getting into shape. Fortunately, several veteran NFL players worked out there, too, and they willingly welcomed me into their ranks.

The player who helped me the most that summer was Zeke Bratkowski, quarterback of the champion Green Bay Packers. Hour after hour Zeke worked with me on grass drills and pass patterns used by the Packers. He also provided me with some insight into the inner workings of the pro fraternity through his invaluable advice. One day after I had hauled in a few pretty good catches, he signaled me over and said, "Bob, I don't know in what round you were drafted (I had been too embarrassed to mention it) but I'd say you have an excellent shot at playing pro ball. You possess a natural talent." He also told me things like: "Confidence is the name of the game. If you believe in yourself and in your own abilities, some team, somewhere, can use you." And: "You're tall, Bob, and that's good: but there are a lot of tall and big guys in pro football. In the NFL there is a premium on speed and quickness; develop these to your fullest. Let them work to your advantage and you can't miss."

All through the summer I worked at getting into shape, practicing what Zeke had been preaching about speed and quickness. And when, in July 1968, I kissed my eight-month pregnant wife good-bye in a tearful departure, I told her: "I'm not coming back here as anything other than a professional football player. You can bet on it."

I meant it, too. And it was on the plane to Cincinnati that I formulated a plan of action that I would follow throughout my career. Taking Zeke's advice, I was never going to allow the confidence I had in

9

my innate talents to wane, and I would, from the outstart, approach the "game" in the most businesslike of manners. After all, pro football is big business, and if I understood that and treated it as such going in, it was logical to assume my chances of survival were at least breakeven.

The initial test of confidence came almost immediately. The first day I stepped out on the practice field at Wilmington College I learned there were close to two hundred other players aspiring to make the roster; worse, some thirty of them were listed as receivers. *Easy Trumpy*, I told myself. *Remember: you are blessed with innate talent. Have confidence! And be businesslike!*

You know how it worked out. This lowly 12th-round draft choice went on to become the Bengals starting tight end in 1968. Not only that, I led the team in receiving. There would be other good years to follow, and further accomplishments. Perhaps the easiest way to sum up my career, modesty notwithstanding, is to quote directly from the Bengals' 1975 Press Guide:

Bob Trumpy: *Big, talented veteran tight end entering his eighth season with the Bengals, all as a starter...Cincinnati's all-time top pass receiver with 231...all-time Bengal leader in TD pass receptions with 26...and in yards gained with 3760...Caught 21 passes during the 1974 season including two good TDs...Played in Pro Bowl in 1970 and 1973 and in AFL All-Star games in 1968 and 1969....Named to All-AFC team in 1973 by Associated Press and United Press International.... Outstanding speed for a tight end.... Big man and can make the big play.... Good hands, goes deep.... Drafted by Bengals in 12th round in 1968.... Played at Illinois and finished (sic) college work at Utah.... High School All-American in football (sic) and basketball.... Assistant buyer for Pogue's department store in Cincinnati in off-season.... Bob and his wife, Pat, have two sons, Matthew, 6, and Jason, 2.... Born March 6, 1946.... Hometown is Springfield, Ill.*

If, back in 1967 when I was a bill collector for Beneficial Finance, you would have told me that I would accomplish what I did in professional football, I would have thought you bereft of mental faculties. Hard to believe that I am already an NFL veteran—ten memorable years tucked deep under my belt. In all those years, there would be fun times, hard times and sad times; the highs were very high, and the lows were very low.

It is my intent to incorporate the most noteworthy of the highs and lows in the body of this book. Unfortunately, we'll have to start at one of the annual low points of any season.

That would have been summer training camp....

GOOD-BYE, AGAIN

...and the good-bye makes the journey harder still....
—Cat Stevens in "Oh Very Young"

I think I said good-bye more times than Cyrus Vance.

To my wife, Pat, my saying good-bye meant, "July is here again. If you need me during the next quarter of a year, I'll be forty miles up the road, in Wilmington. Take care of the bills, see to the kids, try to work an agreeable balance in the checkbook, and handle, by yourself, all those hundred-thousand things you've been used to having me do when I'm home. Oh, yes: if I'm not maimed or killed over the course of the upcoming season, I'll see you in January."

Perhaps this seems a little extreme, but it makes my point. There are *always* good-byes to family and friends, during the summer camp season as well as during the regular season. Even when I was at home during the regular season I wasn't *really* there. Normally I was beat, tired as all get-out from practices and games, physically banged-up with sufficient bumps and welts to make a sadist froth, and my mind was a million miles away—each week there was a new game on which to concentrate, a new team to study, a new player you had to somehow figure out how to beat across the middle on a pass pattern. That alone occupied all your mental energies.

Not that I'm complaining, really. It was the dues I paid for being a professional football player. And I can think of few other professions that return so much on the initial investment of time, body and mind. What other profession can you name that takes a boy in his twenties and, if he is willing to work a little and sacrifice a lot, allows him to make a very large amount of money, have instant community recognition, earn select-group prestige and have doors opened to hand-picked second careers after the first is over?

Professional football provided me with a very comfortable home fifteen miles north of Cincinnati and four cars (including a vintage 1937 Packard and a 1929 LaSalle coupe). Football enabled me to play in celebrity golf tournaments from the West Coast to

11

Puerto Rico, to be seen on national television in United Appeal ads, to make brief appearances on NBC's "Today" and "Tonight" shows, to read Ogden Nash verse before the Cincinnati Symphony Orchestra, and to appear on virtually every local variety talk show, just to name a few. Aside from payment over and above my lucrative Bengal salary, I also received free gifts and services including such things as fifty-dollar dinners, four-track stereo tape decks, radios, cameras, expensive suits, sweaters, sport coats and too many more to mention here. And it set up my post playing days as host on my own WCKY radio call-in show and as a color commentator on NBC Sunday football games.

You can see that by putting up with a few unpleasantries— summer camps, for instance— you could make for yourself a life that was extremely liveable.

So psyching myself up with these thoughts of the good benefits of professional football, I kissed Pat and the two boys good-bye for the thousandth time, climbed into the car with my training camp roommate, center Bob Johnson, and headed up Interstate-71 for Wilmington College. It was Sunday, July 13, 1975.

We watched the flat Midwest farmland roll by for a few minutes. Finally I asked, "You ready for camp, Johnson?"

The big guy turned, rolled his eyes back in his head and let out with a harrowing moan.

We knew our summer was over.

During the annual weigh-in that year I tipped the scales at 228, which made me pretty happy. True, it was light compared to the other tight ends around the league—normally tight ends weigh around 235 or 245—but at that weight I possessed superior speed and quickness. This, for a big man, kept me in the pros for ten years, and it was what separated me from many of my tight end peers.

When I was first drafted by the Bengals in 1968 I weighed a paltry 207, a shocking weight for *any* pro football player, let alone a tight end. And I realized right off that I'd have to do something about it. This became even more evident when I rolled into camp as a lowly 12th round draft choice and discovered there were twenty-seven outside receivers and eight tight ends listed on the roster. To make matters worse, most of the guys were either fresh from college campuses or already had NFL experience. (These latter players were selected by the Bengals in a special allocation draft held in 1967; in that draft the Bengals were permitted to select players from the other NFL teams around the league. The Bengals were allowed to choose from a list of players who were not "frozen" to a team; of course, teams froze all their good players.) On the other hand, I hadn't touched a football in a year and a half.

My task was clearcut: I somehow had to convince Paul Brown

that one of the receiver "keepers" should be Bob Trumpy. I tried to analyze the situation in a businesslike approach, from management's point of view. I asked myself, of all those receivers in camp, whom would they keep? Well, for outside receivers they'd keep the speed merchants, the super-fast guys who probably ran a little track in college and who would be able to fly down the field to catch up with a long bomb. I had pretty good speed—at 6'6" my strides were long—but I surely didn't possess sprinters' speed. Yet, I was way taller than most outside receivers, and that was a plus.

What about tight end? My height was good, right in keeping with tight ends who played for the other NFL clubs. My speed for this position was tremendous, considering most lumbering tight ends didn't move too fast. My weight was the one glaring disadvantage. At 207 I lacked the bulk needed to block the behemoth defensive linemen in the league; and blocking is about sixty percent of the tight end's game.

Thus, there were good and bad points for each position, and it was presenting me with quite a dilemma: which position should I go for? Suddenly it hit me: *don't go for one or the other, Trumpy. Why not go for both positions? This will double your worth to the team.* I liked my reasoning—the new Bengal franchise would be getting somebody who could play two positions for the price of one salary. I knew this would appeal to the business instincts of Paul Brown, if for nothing else than for the economics of it.

I also knew if I got on those scales at 207 pounds and told him I wanted to play tight end, he'd laugh me all the way back to the west coast.

The idea came as I was watching a few guys lift weights while waiting to get weighed in by the coaches. I was in line myself, stripped down to my jockstrap, trying to at least "think heavy." That's when my mind clicked, and suddenly I found myself reaching out and scooping up a ten-pound weight from a nearby barbell. Quickly I slipped it under the towel I was carrying in my hand.

It worked like a charm. I tipped the scales at 217 pounds. The coaches knew this was still light for a tight end, but they simply couldn't believe that a guy who stood 6'6" and (now) weighed 217 could run as fast as I could.

From that weigh-in on, they worked me at both positions, tight end and wide receiver. And of course I went on to make the team as a starter. In fact, during the years I would play three—not two— receiving positions for the Bengals: wide receiver, flanker and tight end, depending on where the team needed me at the time. Some guys would have gotten perturbed at having to learn all those different pass patterns and blocking assignments. Not me. I was just happy to be playing. I mean it beat the hell out of collecting bills in Watts.

Summer camp tradition was the Paul Brown welcoming address. Toward the end of my career I used these meaningful encounters with management to get a little shut-eye, but not that first one, in 1968.

I'll never forget the excitement of that one. Here we were, about two hundred of us, crowded into a hot, July room at Wilmington College, going to see for the first time this legendary man-deity who had in his hands the absolute power to control our destinies.

At precisely nine o'clock it happened. The door opened and in walked this smallish, lean wisp of a man dressed in a tee-shirt and black cap like baseball players wear. There wasn't a sound as we watched his meaningful gait, his serious, knowledgeable countenance demanding our immediate respect. All I could think of was what an amazing man he was. Lombardi carved himself a legend because he was flamboyant and he was a winner. But nobody could touch Paul Brown. The guy *was* Mr. Football. The Great Innovator they called him. The game of football, good or bad, is what Paul Brown made it.

What made him do it? What drove him out of his self-imposed retirement to lead an untried expansion team on the football field of battle? Maybe it was just the game itself—the adrenaline-pump of competition, the taking of forty disparate men and honing them into a singular, winning unit. Or maybe it was the personal satisfaction of being, at sixty years old, the ranking officer of pro football. Or maybe it was strictly financial, although he had already made millions in the sport. I didn't know, or care. All I knew was that the man standing up there looking like what every grandfather in the world should look like had saved me from a life of chasing down alleyways in Watts. So when Paul Brown spoke, I listened. Every word. About the challenges facing us as a young team, the opportunities to prove ourselves as men, the need for togetherness and brotherhood and teamwork and, of course, the unquestioned necessity of strictly adhering to each and every club rule.

I actually got chills. During the second year's, too, as I recall. I guess it wasn't until about the third year's address that the inspiration began to wear thin, and by the fifth year I was more often than not two nods from unconsciousness.

Come to think of it, the welcoming address did perk up for a period of time in the mid-seventies when certain "unsavory" societal elements were making intrusions into the pristine world of pro football. In those years it wasn't unusual for Paul to go into lengthy dissertations about these elements, warning us about the "predators" and "eavesdroppers," referring to the sportwriters who, he said, were in the business of digging up and spreading around whatever dirt they could about professional football, the implication being that you never knew who was out there attempting to undermine America's best-loved sport. He also warned us that he would have no "political aspirers" or "revolutionists" on his team, assuring us that President Nixon could manage the Vietnam War while he could take care of the Cincinnati Bengals, thank you.

Then he would vow that he was not going to put up with long-haired, unshaven "druggies," as he called them. Here he was referring to former teammates like defensive lineman Bob Maddox, a big country boy from Maryland who was busted by federal agents in Cincinnati in 1975. For his drug rap, Maddox received a sentence of five years' probation, and, as I understood it, the NFL league office requested that Paul give Maddox a second chance with the club. Paul agreed, but with the proviso that Maddox—whom we affectionately called "Mad Dog"—be given a urine test at any time to see whether or not his body was functioning with a little aid from illegal drugs.

Actually, Maddox lasted for a season or two with the Bengals before being traded to Kansas City. That certainly made him more fortunate than several other Bengals who had stepped out of line.

For instance, Mike Ernst, a reserve quarterback, was arrested on a drug charge and booted off the team overnight—even before the court had tried him to see whether or not he was actually *guilty* of the charge! Fletcher Smith, a defensive back, was once nabbed on a drunken or wreckless driving rap and was immediately cashiered by the Bengals. Fletcher was *acquitted* of the charge three weeks later. And, back in 1968, we had a rookie named Ted Washington who had managed to get slightly snookered before our long plane ride to San Diego for an exhibition game. He was really zonked out in the plane when Paul Brown entered and walked right past him. Suddenly, realizing the atmosphere was afoul with whiskey-breath, Paul did a comedic double-take that would have made Jackie Gleason proud and approached the sleeping player. His face was red in anger and he shook a threatening finger toward the rookie. "You, Washington," he shouted, "this is disgraceful. Get off of my plane this minute." And that was the last we ever saw of Ted Washington.

A final note on Paul's annual welcoming addresses: I sat through ten of them, and all ten ended the same way. He said that he hoped he hadn't bored anyone with his comments, and that the veterans who had found them repetitive should consider the career of a former player with the Cleveland Browns, Lou Groza. "Louey," proudly reported Paul, "sat through my annual address a total of twenty-one times!"

I've reached a conclusion: Lou Groza was 1) stone deaf, 2) had the ability to sleep with his eyes open or 3) had a very short memory.

Summer camp of '75 presented an odd phenomenon. Was there evidence before us that the Old Coach was mellowing?

For the first time in my Bengal career, Paul Brown actually invited us to use the Wilmington College swimming pool! "We've had a very long week of two-a-day drills," Paul said one day, "you are hitting hard and learning fast, and you deserve a reward. I've obtained permission for you to use the campus pool tonight."

You could've knocked us over with a flick of a chinstrap. The rookies didn't know any different, of course, but we veterans could do nothing more than sit dumbfoundedly and exchange blank stares with one another. For years we'd heard over and over again about the lurking evils of swimmings pools—how they softened ligaments and loosened muscles. And now this!

There weren't many protests, though, I can tell you that. And as far as I know there was really only one guy who later regretted Coach Brown's magnanimous offer.

That was Ron Carpenter, our big defensive tackle.

Ron, a southern boy from North Carolina who, off the playing field, was one of the most unobtrusive, even-tempered individuals you'd ever like to meet, was a favorite target for practical jokes and horseplay.

I don't think there was any player on the team who more anticipated the night's dip in the pool than Ron.

Poor Ron. From the moment he set foot into that pool until the time he left an hour later he was jostled, pulled, dunked, shoved and grappled with by a whole slew of players, including Kenny Anderson and reserve quarterback John Reaves.

Finally, Ron had had enough. Over rabid protestations from the others, he just upped and left, seeking the protection of his small room in Picket Hall. I couldn't believe it when he passed me in the hallway. He was beet red, sweat cascading out of every pore in his body. When he saw me he just shook his head and said, "Man, Trump, ahm beat. Our practices are easy as pie compared with that mess out there." With that he dragged his limp body down the hall, looking as though each step would be his last.

Seeing him wander off, I was reminded of a real effective summer camp practical joke. It was, naturally, played at the expense of Ron's easy-going southern manner and his shy personality.

He had only been in training camp about two weeks his rookie season when Steve Chomyszak and a guy named Bill Peterson got to him. Chomyszak was nothing more that a big kid, really, and the strongest guy we ever had on the team. When he joined the team in 1970 he was bench pressing just a few pounds under what the world's record was. Aside from his size and awesome strength, the most noticeable trait of Chomy was his laugh. It sounded like a semi tractor-trailer trying to turn over on a cold morning, a sort of long, monotone *Heh-aheh-aheh-aheh*. And, when he was laughing at your expense, it seemed to carry for miles.

On this occasion he had instructed Peterson, a tight end-turned-linebacker out of San Jose State, to go up to the third floor of the dormitory and call down to the pay phone on the second. Peterson obeyed, and when the second floor phone rang a few minutes later,

16

Chomyszak was sure he was close by so he could get to it first.

"Hello," he said as he answered, "yes, this is the Bengals' training camp. Ron Carpenter? Hold on a moment, I'll see if he's in." With that, Chomy turns and yells into Ron's room, "Hey, Carp, some guy's on the phone for you. Says he's a writer from New York or something."

In his own way, Ron Carpenter finally made it out the door and over to the telephone, smiling diffidently as he took the receiver from Chomyszak as if he were embarrassed that a writer would actually call *him* for a story.

"Hey-low," said Ron.

"Hello, Mr. Carpenter?" said the voice on the other end. "My name is C.W. DeWitt, and I'm with UPI in New York."

"U-h-u-h," said Carpenter. "Wh-ut kin ah do foe you'awl?"

"We'd like to do a story on you for our syndicate. Sort of an inside look at training camp, you know, from a second-round draft choice's point of view." Somehow Bill Peterson was being successful at not breaking up over the phone, but you just knew that he was upstairs holding his belly. "Could you be so kind as to hold the line for a moment? I want to get a pencil and piece of paper so I can get every word down."

"W-h-y, sh-ore," Carpenter said. And with that Peterson put down the third floor phone receiver and headed down the stairs to the second floor. When he turned the corner to go into Chomyszak's room, he passed Ron, who was standing there hunched over the telephone, staring at the floor, sort of patiently whistling under his breath. Peterson walks in front of him and says, cool as you please, "Oh, hi, Ron."

Carpenter looks up and nods innocently. "H-ey, there, Pete," he answers, and watches him disappear into Chomyszak's room.

Well, twenty minutes pass and Ron Carpenter is still out in the hallway waiting for his nonexistent New York hack to get back on the telephone for the interview. It never occurred to him that someone was playing a joke on him. And for that entire twenty-minute period all you could hear on our floor was that incredible monotone *Heh-aheh-aheh-aheh* of Chomyszak's resounding through the hallways.

Finally, it dawned on Ron what was going down, and he merely hung his head with embarrassment, replaced the phone on the hook and sheepishly ambled back into his own room. A lot of guys would have gotten steamed at being the butt of such a joke, but not Ron. He was just too nice.

That's one reason what later happened to him seemed so unfair. Ron hurt his back in '76 during a game, had a disc operation and spent the entire next season unable to play. Even after months and months of rehabilitation, Ron was in a great deal of pain just trying to stand up. It was then that a doctor recommended to Paul Brown that Ron never again don a football helmet unless he wanted to take the risk of some paralysis for the rest of his life. It was an odd situation. Paul paid for the entire operation and rehabilitation for Ron, but then waived him without explanation to the media. To a player that hurts. It's one thing to be waived because of back surgery, but it's quite another to be waived without an explanation, the implication being that you were simply unneeded and over-the-hill. There is a difference. Fortunately, it worked out well for Ron in that he moved to North Carolina to run a beer distributorship with his father-in-law. And although he is doing very well and quite content, there must linger the thought that he was just another one of pro football's casualties, having sustained an injury which will hobble him for the rest of his life. And he'll remember the hurt of being waived the way he was by the Cincinnati Bengals.

It happened every year, like clockwork.

By the second week of camp, the two-a-day practices, the increasing classroom studies and the searing weather would take their toll.

Not surprising, the first to go would be a linebacker. In 1975 it was our outside linebacker Ron Pritchard.

Pritchard was a walking time bomb anyway, a total contradiction. Off the field he preached Christian brotherhood and the philosophies of Jesus Christ; on the field he was a holy terror. Any little agitation lit his fuse.

This one occurred during an afternoon practice. All players not immediately involved in the scrimmage stood in an umbrella-shaped line behind the offensive halfbacks. Throughout the practice this umbrella unconsciously moved closer and closer to the half-backs, to the point where it must have appeared to the defense that the whole Bengal team was playing in the backfield.

A screen pass was called in the huddle by our coach Bill "Tiger" Johnson. On a screen pass the quarterback needs plenty of room so he can drop back deep before dumping off the ball to a halfback. Tiger, a rawboned Texan, saw that the umbrella line of onlookers was way too close to permit Kenny Anderson a proper drop. So he turned and yelled, "All right, all you guys, back the hell up. Give us a little breathing room up here, will you?"

Almost in choreographed unison, the whole team took three gigantic steps backward—all, of course, except Ron Pritchard. He refused to budge; he just stood there alone and glowered at Tiger. Tiger was not unfamiliar with Pritchard's testiness, however, so he scowled right back and hollered, "Now don't give me that insolent look of yours, Pritchard. Just get your ass behind the line, right now."

Belligerently, Pritchard took a step backward and said, loud enough for everyone to hear, "You're not my father; you can't tell me what to do."

Don't ask me what that meant. I agree, it made no sense at all. But I can remember thinking to myself, uh-oh, I believe I hear the unpleasant sound of a bomb going tick-tick-tick. Sure enough, the very next play Pritchard put himself in at linebacker. (I note this and graciously tell Bruce Coslet, my back-up, that he can run this play because I need a blow; I could see what was developing out there and I didn't want any part of it—I was a family man with a pension to worry about.)

I stood way back and observed. Bob Johnson snapped the ball to Kenny Anderson, who handed it off to Stan Fritts (then a rookie halfback trying to make the squad) and Fritts started off around left end. Suddenly, the time bomb exploded—KER-BAM!—Pritchard blitzed, meeting the poor rook, helmet first, with the full force of anger and momentum behind him. Fritts sailed eight feet in the air and landed with a thud fifteen feet behind the umbrella line of players.

It was a bush move by Pritchard and the veterans climbed all over him: "Oh, real good, Pritchard," said one; "Hey, a real tough guy," said another. Pritchard ignored the comments and looked around in puzzlement, as if wondering what all the hullabaloo was about.

After practice Pritchard came up to my room. He stood there for a moment looking in the worse way like he needed a friend. Finally, he said, "Hey, what's the matter, Trump?"

I glanced at him and came up on one elbow, and said, "You really pissed me off."

"Why? Because I hit that rookie?

"Yea, because you hit that rookie. It was ridiculous, man. You were like a wound-up rubberband out there, ready to snap apart at the least little thing. You've snapped so many times in practice that people are really getting tired of it."

He didn't say anything for a moment. Then he muttered, softly, "Well, I apologized—"

"Crap, Ron," I cut him off, "you've apologized to everyone on this team three or four times and it doesn't mean a thing any more."

He nodded. "I know, Trump. I'm trying, though, I really am. I know I'm not perfect, nobody is." With that, he turned and walked out of the room.

I'll tell you, a psychology student could have had a field day with him.

Want to know another one of Pritchard's hang-ups? Bologna sandwiches. Bologna and cheese, to be precise. What can you say about a guy who had the greatest food in the world—steaks, potatoes, salads, deserts—as much as he wanted, at his beck and call, and he eschewed it all in favor of bologna and cheese sandwiches, light

on the mayo? Man, I just don't know. Ron Pritchard—you figure
him out.

Bedchecks were always a part of Paul Brown's master plan, in
summer camp as well as during the regular season. The rules stipulated that players had to be in their rooms by 10:30 p.m., with lights
out at 11:00 p.m. This rule was strictly enforced and anyone caught
in the hallways after 11:00 p.m. was socked with an automatic
fifty-dollar fine.

The coaches took turns doing the bedchecks, and they handled
it pretty much alike—throwing open the door, flicking on the light,
checking to see whether there are two warm bodies and moving on
down the hall.

Howard Brinker was just not cut from the same cloth. Our
defensive coordinator, he was very shy and quiet, almost meek-
acting. He never yelled at a player in front of others; rather, he took
the malefactor aside for a personal conversation. He spoke low,
controlled and with a mild-mannered tone. When Howard did the
bedchecks, he walked up to the door in the quietest of steps and
always—but always—gave a polite little knock on the door. Rap-
rap-rap. Then, courteously, he paused a few moments before darting
his head quickly in then out again. We theorized he was afraid of
what he might see. If he didn't see anything, he had nothing to
report to Paul Brown, right?

As far as I know we never had anyone actually get caught
sneaking in or out after hours. That's not to say none of our guys
hadn't done it. I assure you we had our share. The one who immediately comes to mind was Jess Phillips. Jess, a fullback, was recruited by PB out of the Michigan State Prison back in the late sixties,
where he was doing time on some sort of fraudulent check rap.

Anyway, Jess had one problem; he was an incurable insomniac.
Frequently about two or three in the morning he would sneak out of
the dorm, climb into his car and drive the forty miles to Cincinnati.
I'm not sure exactly what he did once he got there, but whatever it
was he made sure he was back in camp for breakfast.

It always provided us with a certain amount of mirth to walk
past the line of Bengals' cars on the way to breakfast. Most of them
would be cool as cucumbers; but there'd be one so hot you couldn't
touch the hood without sustaining a first-degree burn. It'd be Jess
Phillips' car, and we'd all look around at one another to say. "Poor
Jess, he just couldn't get to sleep again last night."

Bedcheck stories were legion around the league. You always
heard the one about the Packers' camp, the one where the veterans
selected a pretty cocky rookie and ordered him to go pick up a pizza
for them about midnight. As the rookie left the dorm the players
called the coaches and reported that they thought they just saw

someone sneaking out of camp. Of course, when the rookie returned with the piping hot pizza in his hands he was at once met by a very upset, fifty-dollar fine-wielding coach. The poor rook can do nothing but stand there and accept chastisement.

My all-time favorite involved Johnny Robinson and Sherrill Headrick (who, in 1968, became a Bengal) when they played for the Kansas City Chiefs in the mid-60's. They were roommates, veterans of Super Bowl teams, and I guess they wanted to properly initiate a zealous rookie coach into the pro football fraternity. When they heard the coach coming down the hallway, the players climbed into the same bed together and pulled the covers up over them.

You can imagine what the coach witnessed when he opened the door. There they were—these two vaunted football players, Super Bowl heroes—going through all the hectic motions and noises of a full-course sex act; the story goes that the coach had thrown open the door to day "OK, boys, this is a bedchec—" but about then his eyes adjusted to the dark and he observed the tiny bed rocking all over the room. They say the coach's eyes got about as big as pigskins, and it was all he could do to wheeze out an "Oh my G-A-W-D" before departing the room in a sudden leap. The gruesome sight just scared the bejesus right out of him, and he never once uttered a word about what he had witnessed to anyone, especially not his own head coach.

I guess he just felt that some things were better left unsaid.

One of the major topics around summer camp in '75 was the sudden retirement of our All-Pro defensive tackle Mike Reid.

I say sudden, but it really wasn't. Mike had thought about it seriously on a number of occasions over the past years, especially on those days he was despondent. And they were many.

Because of his apparent moodiness, a lot of people thought Mike was pretty weird; I prefer to say that he was *intricate*. He had as many moods and ups and downs as a centipede has legs. And I guess, finally, in the winter of '74 while playing piano with a group called the Apple Butter Band in a Colorado ski resort, he made his decision to quit. When he returned to Cincinnati in mid-May, he called Paul Brown and told him the news.

His retirement naturally made headlines. After all, it wasn't every day that a two-time All-Pro defensive tackle retired at the ripe age of 26. But I understood Mike's reasoning. He always considered himself an accomplished pianist and composer (he was a music major at Penn State) and had written several songs and appeared with symphony orchestras across the country. He simply decided to form his own band and concentrate all his energies in that direction.

I must admit: I admire a guy who can look $50,000-$90,000 in the eye and turn it down because he'd rather do something else. It was giving up quite a bit in "quest for inner peace," as Mike put it.

He was one super athlete, and I firmly believe that if he had stuck it out his name would be in the record books as one of the great defensive tackles of all time. Mike wasn't big as defensive tackles go—only about 6'2", 245 pounds—but I'd never seen anybody quicker. He could shoot across the line and get to the quarterback as fast as anyone. His reactions were so honed that it would sometimes appear as if he and the football reached the quarterback at precisely the same time. I think some of the fans felt Mike didn't have a very good year in 1974, but that's not really true. They don't realize that about eighty percent of the teams we played double-teamed him on virtually every play—that shows you what type of respect *they* had for him.

There were other considerations in Mike's decision to retire. Injuries, for example. Mike had four knee operations, each one taking just that much longer to heal, stealing just that much more quickness away from his cat-like charge. And, I think, in the back of his mind lurked a nightmarish image of one of his hands being stepped on or somehow disfigured. It didn't take a genius to realize that a pianist with deformed hands is about as practical as a surgeon with a dull scalpel.

Nobody I knew actually enjoyed training camp, but I never met anyone who detested it more than Mike Reid did.

We had a nickname for him in summer camp—the Midnight Marauder.

You'd be in your room watching television when all of a sudden Mike Reid would appear, stark naked except for a worn pair of bedroom slippers, and he'd plop down in a chair right next to you without saying a single word. There he'd sit, from eight o'clock till bedcheck watching television or lost in his own world, but not saying a word to anyone. A few minutes before bedcheck, he'd lift his nude body out of the chair and shuffle back to his room, never so much as saying good-bye.

It was just his way. He was a great studier of people. I'd look over at him and notice that he'd be intently studying all the other people in the room—their personalities, the way they talked, what they said. He was always toting around these heavy books with long titles dealing with philosophy, psychology and far eastern religions, and I suspect he was just doing a bit of casework analysis on his teammates.

I don't want you to get the impression that Mike was always a taciturn, forlorn soul. He had his lighter side, too.

One of his favorite practical jokes was to sneak into our room while Bob Johnson and I were watching television. When Johnson watched TV he somehow put himself into a near mesmerized state. So Mike would quietly tip-toe up behind him, put his mouth close to Johnson's ear and yell, in a deep voice, "B-o-b." Well I mean to tell you Johnson would go through the ceiling. In four years Mike

Reid must have done that a hundred times, and each time Johnson would jump a mile; then he'd turn around and yell, "Dammit, Reid, cut that out!"

Reid and I had our own personal duel of nerves going, too. We called it a Scare-a-thon, and the object was to jump out and scare the other fellow senseless when he least expected it. It got so bad that Reid and I were walking paranoids halfway through summer camp. We'd routinely check our closets whenever we entered our rooms, and we bolted our doors tightly after the bedcheck. We were afraid to walk down the hallways alone, knowing that somewhere, perhaps at the next turn, one of us was ready to pounce out and scare the daylights out of the other. I had visions of being on the toilet in one of the stalls some night and suddenly seeing Reid's head appear under the stall door to say "Boo." I mean, that's an awful feeling. You're so vulnerable in that position.

I really got Mike Reid good his last year. I had it arranged with Bob Johnson. He was to tell Chuck Studley, the coach doing bed-checks that night, that I wasn't really missing from our room, but that I was hiding under Reid's bed. Studley went along with the gag, and I waited for about twenty minutes after he had looked in on Mike to do my stuff. Mike was writing a letter or something at the time. He was sitting on the edge of his bed, which he had pulled around to a desk that was bolted to the wall. He was really lost in thought, and his foot was pumping up and down on the floor a mile a minute, not six inches from my nose. Finally, sensing the time was right, I just reached out a slow hand and grabbed that ankle with a very firm grip.

Reid jumped fifty feet, straight up. In fact, he flinched so hard that his thigh smacked against the table top with sufficient impact to rip the table, bolts and all, clean out of the wall.

I was so excited about my perfect ruse that I could hardly get to sleep that night. I replayed the moment of stark fear time and again for Johnson, but he had long since lost the appreciation of my efforts and was dozing soundly.

Unfortunately, my reign as King of the Scare-a-thon lasted exactly twenty-four hours. Because the very next night, Reid return-ed the favor.

I had been laying in bed comfortably for about twenty-five minutes, and I was approaching that sort of befuddled twilight sleep when the mind is dull and lifeless. As I had done to him the preceding night, Reid waited for the proper moment and then reached up a heavy arm from beneath the bed and allowed it to fall, full-weight, convincingly across my chest. I let out a holler that's still ringing across Wilmington College's tiny campus. And over his shouts of glee I cussed him up one side and down the other. And Johnson, my *simpatico* roommate, didn't help matters much. He lay over there in his bed for hours clucking like a hen laying a size twelve egg.

During that second week of camp another minor skirmish was fought on the battlefield. Need I tell you that one of the combatants was a linebacker?

Paul Brown must have known it was coming, because before we went out for afternoon practice he called us together: "I know that it's quite warm out there," he said, understating the facts significantly since it was ninety-six with humidity to match, "but remember, you are all teammates and friends here. Keep your tempers under control and your hands in your pockets."

His words didn't help a heck of a lot. About halfway through scrimmage, my roomy, Bob Johnson, snapped the ball and cut down middle linebacker Jim LeClair pretty good. LeClair bounced to his feet and warned Johnson not to do it again. "I'll get you for that, Johnson," Jim said. "Listen," answered Bob, "I'll take care of myself, you try to take care of yourself."

Man, linebackers are a special breed; like elegant Tiffany lamps, they are extremely fragile. If you nudge them too hard in practice they go all to pieces. If you block them too hard, they'll charge you with malicious harrassment. Then the first chance they get they'll fire on you with all they have.

As usually is the case, it wasn't my roommate who felt the brunt of LeClair's wrath. It was Bruce Coslet, the guy who was supposed to block LeClair on the very next play. Coslet took a helluva shot from the middle linebacker, and he didn't appreciate it too much. So he called LeClair an unkind name and gave him a little shove. That's all it took. They grabbed one another's face mask with one hand and began flailing away with the other.

Soon they were lovelocked on the ground, rolling over and over in a blanket of dust. Finally, Coslet managed to get on top and pin LeClair down. "Cool it now, Jim," he kept yelling, "just cool down, will you?" This was a wise move on Coslet's part; he knew, as well as we all did, that Jim LeClair was one tough dude. It wasn't a real wise policy to go around challenging him; sooner or later you'd lose out.

"OK, OK," LeClair said, out of breath, "let go of my face mask."

Coslet complied, and was in the process of getting up when LeClair drew back his fist and let go with a vengeance. A loud THUNK resounded across the field as contact was made. Unfortunately for LeClair, his fist caught Coslet smack in the middle of the helmet.

With a holler he quickly withdrew his fist, and for the next few moments he could do no more that sit and watch it swell to about twice its normal size. For the sake of machismo, he stayed in another play or two, but then he took himself out of the scrimmage.

X-rays revealed a fracture, and LeClair spent the next several weeks in a cast.

The whole thing was LeClair's own fault, really. He should have known the old professional football axiom: "In every fight, the helmet always wins." Afterwards, in the locker room, Charlie Davis, Charlie Joiner, Boobie Clark and Ed Williams were all standing around shooting the bull. I approached this aggregate of black players and said, "Hey, guys, why is it that in all the fights during summer camp it's always the white guys who are involved? Why don't the brothers ever mix it up?"

Charlie Davis, our quick running back, spoke on behalf of the group. "Sheet, Trump," said Davis, grinning widely, "by the time I was twelve years old I was all fought out. I had to fight for my food, fight for my clothes, fight for my bed, fight for my women. That's why we brothers don't fight now: we're simply all fought out."

There were a lot of belly-laughs and "Right-on brothers," and, of course, the obligatory slapping of one another's hands.

Later, Bruce Coslet was talking about classic confrontations during summer camp. I think the hard-hitting, flared tempers and the sight of blood out on the practice field gets everyone's juices flowing.

He related the story of linebacker Bill Peterson when, a few years before, he hit a rookie offensive guard head-on. The impact was so great that the rookie's helmet simply exploded off his head. This was followed by a scream, sufficient to curl even Boris Karloff's blood, and he went down on one knee in excruciating pain. For days the rookie had trouble seeing and eating, and he finally got cut. In two weeks his weight had dropped thirty-five pounds, from 255 to 220.

"That was one of the hardest hits I've ever see," Coslet said, a glint in his eye. "When they collided it sounded like a gunshot—BAM! And Peterson's arm was black and blue from the fingers to the elbow for a month. Man, that was something!"

Too bad Ron Pritchard wasn't with the team then. He would have loved it.

Want to know how to strike fear into the heart of a rookie? Do what Chuch Studley did to Gary Burley.

Burley, a big, talented defensive end, reported to camp that year at 260 pounds. After a few days, however, his weight shot up to 265, then 270 and climbing.

Burley was going through the chow line one day when he was approached by Studley. "Hey, Burley," the coach said, "what did you tip the scales at today at the weigh-in?"

Burley stopped in his tracks and stared across at Studley's square jaw, knowing he was a real stickler for discipline.

"I think it was about 270, sir."

"TWO-SEVENTY! Do you know what your weight limit is?"

"Well, sir, I believe it's 260."

"That's right, Burley, 260." Studley scowled at him a moment and then began rubbing his sandpaper chin. "Burley," he began...

"Sir?"

"I'm going to give you exactly ten minutes to get down to 260!"

I mean to tell you, Gary Burley's jaw dropped to the floor, and his eyes grew to the size of platters. It became obvious that he was slipping into shock; all he could do was stare at Studley's serious face speechlessly. The coach managed to withhold a guffaw by averting his gaze to the hands of his wristwatch, as if he were already ticking off the seconds.

It's hard to tell how long Burley would have stood there rigid as a pillar, but I guess we'll never know. Because we veterans standing nearby began to roar. Soon, Studley could no longer contain himself either and he broke up. Finally, a still-unsure Gary Burley joined in, too.

It was a pretty funny scene, and yet—the point was made. Burley *was* overweight and the coaches had taken it upon themselves to assure swift remedial action. The word had been passed down that, henceforth, Burley was on a mandatory diet; a coach would usher him through chow line every meal until his 260 playing weight was reached and maintained.

It's not hard to see why rookies, perhaps not accustomed to all the available good food, could go a little berserk at camp. Think of it: sirloin steaks two inches thick, mounds of potatoes, salads, bread, and deserts—as much as you wanted, all for the asking.

The biggest eater to ever grace our training camp tables was Bob Maddox. Once he downed six steaks—with all the trimmings—at one sitting. Then, still tinged with hunger, he scooped up a whole turkey, tucked it under his arm and hauled it back to the dorm for a midnight snack. And I don't think there was any leftovers for sandwiches the next day, either.

During that week of camp, Vernon Holland pulled a muscle and he was absolutely grief-stricken. It was the first muscle pull of his career; until then he had never had any muscle to pull.

Suki, as we called him, was a mountain of a man, a 6'7", 270-pound offensive tackle. He was the Bengals' first-round draft choice in 1972 out of tiny Tennessee State. As soon as the Bengals drafted him, Suki was flown in to Cincinnati and given the royal treatment. One of the stops on his tour of Bengal-land was the team's regular season training complex, Spinney Field. There were about a half-dozen rookies working out in the weight room, most of them struggling at about the 275-pound mark in benchpresses, when the coach saw big Vernon walk in. His eyes lit up and he said, "Move over, boys, our number one draft choice is here; he'll show you how to benchpress that baby."

Suki looked at the tremendous weight on the bar and said, "Uh, coach, I'd rather not."

"Come on now, son," answered the coach, "don't be modest. Show us what you can do."

He was trapped and he knew it; he had to think fast. "I'm a little stiff right now, coach," he said, "how about if we take off a few of the weights? You know, til I get warmed up."

"Sure, kid, sure," the eager coach said, "how much weight you want to start with—200?"

Suki cleared his throat, and when he tried to speak only the slightest of squeaks came out.

"How much was that?" the coach asked.

"I said," offered Suki, "let's give it a whirl at 95 pounds."

An immediate hush settled over the training room. The coach's expression looked as though he had just been goosed with a cattle prod. Finally, he laughed. "Ho, ho, a draft choice with a sense of humor; I like that. Ho, ho, 95 pounds—that's a good one."

Suki stared down at the coach and shook his head from side to side. It was no joke, he wanted a shot at 95.

So, OK, the coach thought, I'll play along. He quickly stripped the barbell of a couple gigantic 50-pound weights and replaced them with a few puny weights on each side. Then he stepped back to watch the number one draft choice go to work. Suki, stripped to the waist, put everything he had into it, almost instantly a running lather worked itself up across his monolithic body. He grunted and groaned and strained, until every fiber was trembling under the weight of the barbell. It was no use; the best he could do was to get the barbell about halfway up.

The coach couldn't believe it, and like a shot he turned on his heels and bolted toward Paul Brown's office. So eager was he to impart the unbelievable news that the Bengals had wasted their first-round draft choice on a 270-pound weakling, that he left poor Suki lying there with the barbell dangling threateningly over his chest cavity. Fortunately, the other rookies stepped in and helped place the barbell back on its stand.

Things were in an uproar for a while, and it wasn't until Suki came to summer camp in July that the coaches found, to their collective relief, that they had drafted a very good football player after all. Don't think for a moment that Suki's inability to bench-press the 95 pounds meant he wasn't a good football player. Brother, this guy was as tough as they come. He got tremendous power on the field from a lightening-fast charge behind his weight and from a forearm shiver that would shake acorns from a tall oak. Suki called his forearm swing "bringin' death," and when he hit someone with it the sound carried all over the field. We all just looked at one another with a knowing smile and said, "Old Suki's out there bringin' death again."

It's true that he wasn't much to look at when he was struggling to lift weights or doing push-ups, but he was one beautiful sight to halfbacks who followed him through the gaping holes he created in defensive lines.

Actually, Suki had worked out on Nautilus equipment one winter, and he was about twice as strong as he was that first year. This was also the reason for his discontent, when he pulled a muscle. "Dammit, Marv," he complained to our trainer Marv Pollins, "I wish you guys would leave my fat alone. Three months on that danged Nautilus equipment and you got me pulling muscles." He winced a moment. "That weight training ain't no good for you, Marv, don't you know that? Hell, everybody's runnin' around here with a pulled this or pulled that. Me? I never use to have to worry about it—I mean you just can't pull *fat!*"

Suki was one beautiful human being.

I remember one day when several of us were congregating in a cool spot outside the locker room before practice. Suki, who had been mopping his forehead, turned to my roommate and said, "Hey, Johnson, did you take a nap after lunch today?

"Oh, yea," Bob answered, "I just shut my eyes a little."

"Shut your eyes?" said Suki, alarmed. "*She-it*, man, that's not sleepin'. If when you wake up you don't have slobber runnin' down your cheeks, have your eyes matted so shut you caint hardly open 'em and have deep wrinkles impressed all over your body from the sheets—if you don't have these things you ain't been sleepin'...you just been screwin' around."

Geez, can you imagine a mammoth black body like Vern Holland's with deep wrinkles all over it? He'd look like a whole mountainside of Moms Mableys.

During camp in '75, speculation about who would eventually replace PB as head coach, who would be the next Captain Absolute of the Bengals, provided much entertainment for players, fans and the press. Everyone seemed to have his own favorite to step into PB's venerable shoes, although none of us knew when that day would come. Repeatedly, Paul had stated that he would take himself out of the picture when the game no longer seemed fun to him, or the day he became too physically unfit to serve. My personal feeling was that he wanted to make his exit after the Bengals' first trip to the Super Bowl. Let's face it, PB was 66. If he could gracefully bow out that year—having taken a squad of rookies and castoffs and successfully molded it into a Super Bowl team in just eight years—I think he would've jumped at the opportunity to depose himself while the cheering was still ringing in his ears. That dream, as it turned out, was never realized, and his announcement to retire after the '75 season took us all by surprise. Then again, that's the Brown way of doing things.

But back in summer camp, who was the frontrunner in the race to the top? Some said Bill Walsh, but I never believed Paul was leaning that way. Others claimed that Paul's son, Mike, was the rightful heir apparent. Admittedly, at the time this had some logic behind it. PB was adoring of all his sons and by having Mike, who was our assistant GM, lead the team (and keep a protective watch over dad's $8 million investment) it would keep the power of the franchise "in the family" and would also preclude the ascension to power of any pretenders to the throne.

A problem was that Mike had little or no coaching experience. And going from no-coach to head coach is a jump more harrowing and impractical than the leap Evel Knievel attempted over the Snake River.

Another name bandied about back then was that of Ara Parseghian, the famed former coach of Notre Dame. Personally, I didn't see this as a possibility at all. I felt sure that, although Paul would give up the head coaching duties soon, he wouldn't relinquish the position of team general manager for quite some time. And it was my opinion that he would still call all the shots, not actually down on the field, but from on high, the air-conditioned glass-enclosed GM's office. I think my opinion since has been borne out. And from everything I had read about Ara Parseghian, it seemed that he was definitely his own man, and I doubted whether he would have accepted such a lackey posture in the Bengals' scheme of things.

My favorite-son candidate to replace PB was our offensive coach, Tiger Johnson, which is what happened. Here was a man who had proved himself to be a loyal member of the Bengal football family. (I know he had been offered several lucrative contracts from other teams, yet he stayed a Bengal—which led me to believe that something was in the wind regarding the future head coaching job and Tiger had picked up the scent.) Tiger knew the Paul Brown system and he understood the intricacies that motivated both management and players. And—for a few years at least—I thought Tiger would have been willing to put up with merely taking "advice" and directives from "Paul the GM" and passing them along to the players.

Tiger should have been a very good head coach. He was knowledgeable, fair, much respected by the players and could handle people with grace, mixing well-timed constructive criticism with a necessary touch of Texan humor.

I can remember one time when I really blew a block on the practice field, Tiger turned to the rest of the players with this bit of philosophy: "I've formed many opinions in my years, boys. But the one I feel most certain about is this: in pro football, a good-blocking tight end is an rare as a sweet-smellng asshole."

Once we had a rookie receiver who was getting downfield extremely slow and therefore missing his blocks on the defensive backs. When the rookie came back to the huddle after one particularly slow-moving display, Tiger said: "Son, you've got to get downfield quicker than that." To which the rookie replied, "Gosh, Coach, I was going as quick as I could." Tiger sighed and responded, "Well, son, sometimes you just have to run faster than you *can*." And he didn't bat an eyelash.

What later happened to Tiger shouldn't have happened to a dog. That in three years he would be ignominiously driven from the head coaching duties of the Bengals was one of the greatest football sins I ever witnessed.

It should not have happened. We were all to blame—the players, the fans, the press and Paul Brown.

The players absolutely loved Tiger, would've died for that man. Unlike PB, Tiger was a former player—he understood players' need for recognition, their ups and downs, their motivations.

Actually, his first year as head coach in 1976 was pretty much of a success, 10-4, with some bad breaks prohibiting us from getting to the playoffs. However, things began to deteriorate in '77, my last year, and we went a disappointing 8-6. Then, after the Bengals dropped the first five consecutive games in '78, Tiger had to pay the price. He was out and Homer Rice was in.

I have some opinions on what went wrong.

First, when Tiger was named head coach, Bill Walsh quickly sought greener pastures. He told me, "I don't want to be an assistant coach for *another* eight years." When Walsh departed for San Diego we lost the best offensive game man in the business. On top of that, when Tiger became head coach we also lost one of the best offensive line coaches in football, Tiger himself. He now was no longer a teacher but an administrator. Tiger and Walsh—two of the finest teachers in the business, and both were gone from their jobs overnight. There was no way to replace the quality and leadership of these two coaches. And the offensive development of the Bengals came to an abrupt halt right then and there, period.

Another reason contributing to Tiger's demise: his own physical impairments. Most fans didn't realize that Tiger was hard of hearing, wore hearing aids in both ears. It took a season or so before the players began to take advantage of this malady, but eventually they did. It started slowly, giggling and horseplay in the back of the room during team meetings. Then it built. Open gab sessions ensued and distracting conversation. As a result, concentration on what was being said was at a minimum. A whole screw-off attitude, a laziness, insidiously began to invade our quarters, and Tiger couldn't control it. With Paul Brown it was different. During his

30

meetings a mouse could walk across the carpet and forty-five players would have heard every step.

Then there was Coy Bacon, whom we got from the Chargers for Charlie Joiner. What a mistake that was. Someone in San Diego upon hearing the trade said, "We got a good pair of hands, the Bengals got a big mouth." How right he was. Coy was an expert on everything. He criticized players and coaching decisions, instructed teammates on how to play their positions, that type of thing. And for the first time in Bengal history a real black-white polarization began to materialize. Bill Johnson, wanting team unity in the worst way, put up with Bacon. But he failed to realize what a disruptive influence Bacon really was. When the other blacks saw what he could get away with, they soon too began pushing discretion to the limit. No longer were the Bengal parties where forty-five teammates came together with wives and girlfriends. Now there were black parties and white parties; parties for rookies and parties for veterans. Everyone was sloughing off, and the situation slipped out of Tiger's hands. I'll never forget that day I went to see Tiger right before he was fired (or, as the official team statement went, before he "resigned"). Tiger looked terrible—haggard, red in the eye where that cowboy sparkle used to be. When he spoke his voice had lost its he-man Texas resonance. "Bob," he said to me, looking at the ground, "it's a very bad situation, very bad. I have lost control. The team is no longer mine. Somewhere, somehow, it all went wrong."

It truly broke my heart seeing this fine, fine man in such a state. I suppose it was fortunate that his suffering lasted only two more weeks. That's when Paul put him out to pasture.

When that happened, I wondered whether Paul even realized that much of the blame for what happened was really his fault. The problem was that Paul never gave Tiger the freedom a head coach deserves to call the shots on his team. The Browns—Paul and Mike—made final decisions on draft choices, on who stayed and who went on the team, on hiring Tiger's own coaching staff. I was surprised Paul wasn't more sensitive to this situation. After all, it was the very thing that helped drive him out of Cleveland years before. Paul wanted total control as Browns' head coach and Art Modell wouldn't give it to him. Whether Paul realized it or not, he put Tiger in the exact same predicament.

An example: On final cut down day of the '78 season, two players were in competition for one job, a defensive backfield position. The choices were between Jerry Anderson and Ray Griffin. Tiger felt strongly about keeping Anderson and argued into the night with Paul over it. At the end, Tiger understood that he had won the battle and Anderson was to be retained, Griffin cut. But by the next morning when Tiger walked into the coaches' office, Anderson was gone. Paul had elected to keep Griffin.

Tiger was understandably upset about the turn of events and, as

I understand it, really went in and vented his spleen to PB. It would be his last confrontation with the Bengals' GM. The Bengals would go on to lose its first five games of the season (Kenny Anderson did not play in any of them because of a broken finger) and Tiger was issued his walking papers.

I was in a downtown bar when I heard the news. They interrupted television programming to make the bulletin announcement. And when they did, virtually every person in that place stood and clapped and howled and whistled with approval.

That really hurt. They didn't even know Tiger Johnson, they didn't understand what a sensitive, beloved coach he was, a real friend to his players. All they knew was that the Bengals were losing football games by the handful and that the press was being hard on the head coach. (Tiger never really learned how to handle the press well. He was such a competitor that when he lost it really got to him, got him down, and he conveyed this easily to the fourth estate.) And the fans never realized the many separate circumstances which somehow all came together at one time to conspire against a great, great football man, Tiger Johnson.

That day I really felt like crying.

In the end, it was our linebacker Bo Harris who put things in perspective. "The players," said Harris, "simply didn't play for Bill Johnson like we should have. If we had treated Tiger the same way he treated us, today we would be Super Bowl champions."

I couldn't have said it better myself.

That summer camp brought an out-of-the-past visitor to Wilmington, one who held a special meaning for me. His name was Tom Bass and he had just been named director of player personnel for the new Tampa team, which would join the NFL in 1976.

Bass was in Wilmington visiting his old boss—Paul Brown—to learn whatever he could about the entire operation of a pro football team, from the ground up. A former coach and scout for the Bengals, Bass knew that there was no more structurally sound franchise in the country, and he wanted to learn from the best.

"I don't pity you a bit, Tom," I said to him. "Now that you are with Tampa it means you will be going through your second expansion club in a decade. I wouldn't wish those kind of headaches on my worst enemy."

Bass smiled. "You may be right," he said. "But I tried selling real estate last year and my wife couldn't stand having me around all the time. She had gotten too used to me traveling when I was with the Bengals."

The first human contact Pat and I ever had with the Cincinnati Bengals was with Tom Bass. It occurred about three weeks after we received the telegram saying that I had been drafted in the 12th round.

Bass called in late afternoon and introduced himself as the defensive backfield coordinator for the Bengals.

"I'm in San Diego now," he said, "I'd like to drive up to L.A. this evening to meet with you. We can talk contract."

"Sure," I told him, and gave him directions to our apartment. Then I hung up and turned toward Pat, who was already scurrying around, dusting the apartment. Why, I asked her, was a *defensive backfield coach* coming to sign me? "I can't play defensive back," I protested, "I'm 6'6", for crissakes." Pat stopped cleaning long enough to shoot me a look that implied, *don't question why, Trumpy. Just sign the nice man's contract and don't make waves. This is our future you're toying with, so don't screw it up.* Pat has a way of being direct when she wants to.

While we waited, Pat and I didn't exchange thirty seconds of conversation. We were each lost in our individual dreams of professional football life and what it could bring. Our pipedreams came hurtling back to reality, however, with the sound of a tremendous thumping on our front door. We must have jumped two feet of the ground, and my first thought was that a bill collector from Beneficial Finance was outside. (At Beneficial, we were instructed to always knock obnoxiously loud—the contention being that it showed *authority*.) It wasn't, of course; it was Tom Bass. And if his door-splintering knocks seemed to have startled us a bit, it was little compared with what the actual sight of him did.

He was awesome looking, standing there with a monstrous 250-pound physique taking up the entire doorway. He was dressed in bad-guy black from the tip of his turtleneck to the toes of his shiny shoes. And on top of it all sat a great, white gleaming head, bereft of a single hair.

As he introduced himself and stalked in from the dark night, I observed that he walked with a noticeable limp. Immediately a mental flash of Long John Silver rushed through my mind, and it wouldn't have surprised me in the least if our visitor had suddenly squinted one eye and beckoned for his parrot. (Later I found out that Bass' limp was vestige of a bout with polio; and, belying his ominous presence, we found him to be one of the nicest people we've met in professional football.)

Pat busied herself making coffee while Bass and I engaged in obligatory small talk. I was polite enough, I thought, but all I could really concentrate on was *how* and *when* we were going to get to the good part—negotiating my worth. Finally, to my relief, Bass said in that powerful, well-deep voice of his: "Listen, Bob, let's get down to business."

As well as I can recall, our "negotiating" went something like this:

Bass: "I have a professional football contract here that Paul Brown has authorized me to offer you."

Me (Nervously): "OK, let's hear it."

Bass: "If you play for the Bengals, we will pay you $15,000."

Me (Stunned): *"$15,000?"*

Bass: "That's right. And we'll pay you an additional $1,500 in bonus money, right now, just for signing your contract."

Me (Aghast): "An additional $1,500? Payable tonight?"

Bass: "That is correct. And if you stick with the club through training camp and make the team, we'll pay you another $1,000."

Me (Weakly): "Another $1,000?"

Bass: "That's right, Bob. This is our package offer. I know the bonus money isn't as high as some offered around the league, and, frankly, neither is the salary. But 1968 will be the Bengals' first year. We think the salaries will go up in the succeeding years."

I sat back practically mindless, and allowed the figures to whirr around in my head. What had Bass said—small bonuses? Small salaries? Holy Crimine, I had never been so close to so much money in all my life. When you're used to pulling down $83.50 a week as a bill collector, $17,500 sounds like a veritable gold mine.

Throwing any thought of further negotiating to the wind, I literally yanked the ballpoint out of Bass' immense hand and signed all five copies of my contract. I didn't even pause to read one word, fully realizing that I should move with celerity, lest Bass discover he had made some dreadful mistake, perhaps confusing me with a higher draft choice.

Contract signed, I sat back and breathed deeply for the first time. "Tell you the truth, Mr. Bass," I said, "I would have signed for birdseed just to get a shot a playing professional football. All I really wanted was a ticket back to Cincinnati and a fair chance to prove myself."

Bass laughed, and we wasted little time bringing the night's business to a close. And I found that, by the end of the evening, I had already managed to get over my initial shock, and the old Trumpy cockiness was once again emerging. As he was leaving, I said: "Thank you for coming tonight, Mr. Bass. You've made my wife and me very happy." Then, for some reason I still don't understand, I added, very straightforward: "You can tell Paul Brown that he'll have to pay me even *more* money next year. Because I am going to make that team, and make it big."

Suddenly, there was a crashing sound emanating from the kitchen. Pat had dropped a coffee cup on the floor and it had splintered into a thousand pieces. She had obviously overheard my last words.

Fortunately, my comment didn't seem to bother Tom Bass at all. He just looked across at me and smiled. "We like a confident

34

attitude on the Bengals, Bob. And I'll be sure to pass along your thoughts to Paul Brown."

With that, he was out of the door and on his way back to San Diego. And me? I just stood there for a moment, blinking. I told myself that if it weren't for the check for $1,500 that I was squeezing in my right hand, I could easily have doubted whether all of this had just happened. Finally convinced, I turned and began sprinting for the kitchen, just as Pat was hustling out to see me (and the $1,500 check). With perfect timing, we met and clasped in a mid-air bear-hug the way you see them do it in television commercials. We both realized that that night was marking the beginning of a new life, and that Tom Bass would evermore have a special meaning for us. We were right on both counts.

By the way, that telegram from PB telling me I had been drafted was one of the great days of my life, despite a slight faux pas on my lovely wife's part. I was sitting behind my desk at Beneficial Finance in downtown L.A., when the phone rang. It was Pat, and I could tell she was excited about something.

"Wait a minute, Pat," I said, "slow down a bit. I can't understand a word you're saying."

There was momentary silence before she started bubbling again.

"I'm trying to tell you," she said, "that you've been drafted."

"Drafted?" Again? Man, that really knocked the wind out of me. "That's ridiculous, Pat," I said finally. "They *can't* draft me again. The Navy just gave me a medical discharge and I—"

"No, you big dummy," Pat replied. At times she shows very little patience with me. "Not by the military. You've been drafted by a professional football team! The Beagles."

"A football team?" I was absolutely flabbergasted. Why would anybody draft me? I was a total unknown. And for the past year (three months in the Navy and seven months at Beneficial Finance) I hadn't even donned a jock strap, let alone run a post pattern.

I figured my wife was putting me on. "C'mon, Pat," I said, "what's the big joke?"

"Dammit, Bob, I'm telling you the truth. We got a telegram a few minutes ago."

I was home 30 minutes after hanging up (I quit my job as soon as I said good-bye to Pat). It was then that I found out my wife had misread the telegram.

Pat met me at the door and, of course, was all smiles.

"Where's the telegram?" I asked, still a little leery that all this was as good as it seemed. She handed it to me and I read each word a half-dozen times, just to make sure it wasn't some sort of morbid mistake.

It was addressed to me, all right. It said:

*I am happy to inform you that you have been selected
by the Cincinnati Bengals. You will be contacted in*

the near future. I am looking forward to a pleasant relationship with you.

Sincerely

Paul E. Brown,
Head Coach and General Manager,
Cincinnati Bengals.

"Pat," I mentioned, "it says Bengals, not Beagles." My wife shrugged. "Beagles, Bengals, what's the difference?" I just shook my head, unable to think of a reply. I knew Pat wasn't all that detail-minded.

"Freddie Franchise" was our nickname for Kenny Anderson. We gave it to him because the press and the fans had convinced themselves—perhaps rightly so—that Kenny was the Bengals' franchise; as Kenny and his golden arm went, so went the Bengals.

Freddie was unbelievable, and a far cry from the cold, stoic almost mechanical man that he appeared to be on the field. Really, he was still a little boy, always skulking around the hallways with a devilish look in his eye, searching for whatever mischief he could get into. And it usually ended up that he got hurt.

This time in camp, Anderson started a talcum powder fight in the hallway with a few teammates. In his haste to get away, he unfortunately failed to negotiate an opened door and BAM! KER-PLOP! He went down in a heap, momentarily dazed. When he regained his senses he realized that blood was spurting from a deep, jagged scalp wound.

The first thing we did was to put in a call for Doc Casanova (Tommy Casanova, our defensive back who attended medical school in the off-season). Doc washed the wound carefully and somehow managed to put a stop to the bleeding without resorting to fancy stitchwork.

Everyone thought the incident was pretty funny—everyone except Anderson; he was scared stiff about how the Old Coach would explain to an inquiring reporter that his star quarterback sustained an open head wound in a dormitory talcum powder fight?

Freddie decided that he would not want to put himself in this embarrassing situation. So, the next day he was in the equipment room by 8:15 in the morning, a half-hour before anyone else. Carefully, he worked his helmet down over the wound...and he didn't remove it for three days. Admittedly, Freddie looked pretty stupid in our morning shorts drills and our afternoon 90 degree heat practices wearing a helmet, but at least the coaches didn't discover the injury.

Situations like that were exactly the reason we nominated Kenny Anderson as the Bengals' "Rookie of the Year" for the fourth consecutive year. He had no close competition.

Some of us veterans, Kenny's best friends, had another nickname for our QB. Faggot. I think there's always one guy in every group who becomes the butt of jokes. Kenny was that guy in our group, mainly because he was so darned nice, so innocent, so genuinely red-blooded and sincere. The thought of him, or any pro football player (Dave Kopay notwithstanding), being a real homosexual was outlandish.

Professional football is perhaps the singular occupation that magnifies the division of the sexes. You think of a professional football player and you visualize a he-man with a massive chest, thick neck and heavy five o'clock shadow. The dress code itself manifests the accents of male physique. Bulbous helmets create enlarged heads; shoulderpads exaggerate upper torsos; slim waists and thick legs are spooned into tight-fitting pants, displaying rippling muscles. Even crotches noticeably bulge with the curvatures of metal cups.

The symbolism is one of total masculinity. The very thought of a gay quarterback successfully throwing the bomb with a limp wrist is totally unacceptable.

That gave us all the more reason to dig Kenny Anderson about it. Until one night after practice I went home and told Pat what we were doing and she got very upset. "You really shouldn't tease Kenny about that," she said. "It's not funny at all."

When I asked for an explanation she told me that Anderson and his wife Bonnie had for some time been unsuccessful in trying to have a baby. "And," she added, "they are now running tests on Kenny to see whether there's something wrong with him."

Brother. I was so upset I couldn't sleep that entire night. I really felt like a heel. Here I had been getting on his case day in and day out about being a faggot and he wasn't being successful in getting his wife pregnant. Before the night was over I had managed to blame myself for the entire thing, assured that my constant jibes had, at least unconsciously, made Anderson doubt his own maleness.

I reported to practice early the next day; when Kenny came through the door I grabbed him by the shoulder and hustled him off to a private shower stall.

"Jesus, Kenny," I began, "I'm really sorry. Last night Pat told me about your trouble, that you and Bonnie aren't being too successful at making a baby." He looked a little surprised, but he nodded and allowed me to continue. "I want you to know that I was just kidding when I called you 'faggot.' Believe me, Partner, I'll never again call you queer or gay as long as I live."

Kenny just stood there a moment staring at me. Then he did something totally surprising. He began to laugh. Long and loud, resounding off the shower stalls.

"Jesus Christ, Rookie," I snapped. "What the hell is this? I try to be humane about this and apologize and you laugh in my face.

Thanks a lot."

Between outbursts, my teammate managed to inform me that Bonnie had gone to her gynecologist the day before and tests had shown she was, indeed, pregnant.

I stood there in disbelief, feeling the world like a fool. Here I had lost a night's sleep and spilled my guts to this sideburnless quarterback and he had the audacity to stand there in the shower stall laughing in my face.

I watched him for a few moments before shaking my head and walking away. I said, "I'll bet Bonnie was artificially inseminated, you faggot."

Saturday, August 4, the first day of the '75 pre-season, was a day you'd have to classify as a "downer."

With high hopes and rookie eagerness we opened in the annual Hall of Fame game played in Canton, Ohio.

That game had special meaning for Paul Brown. PB, who was already enshrined in the Hall with a bronze bust, had begun his coaching career just a few miles down the road from Canton, at Massillon High School. And before this game he was to partake in the induction ceremonies, presenting the famed Cleveland Brown receiver Dante Lavelli for football immortality.

Paul had often said that Lavelli was the best receiver he ever coached. "Lavelli had one of the strongest pair of hands I've ever seen," Paul said in his ceremonial pre-game speech at the Hall of Fame. "When he went up for a pass with a defender you could count on him coming down with the ball. No one could take it away."

It should have been quite a day for our Old Coach, surrounded by the press, friends and associates from near and far, basking in the limelight right along with the Hall of Fame inductees. Unfortunately, his own team managed to wipe away a little luster from his Hall of Fame bronze bust. We lost to the Redskins 17-9, and Paul told us later that we spoiled the day for him.

We looked very bad. Oh, sure, we were playing in sweltering 105 degree temperatures, but so were the Redskins; and they are a team whose youngest player would make Georgie Jessel appear adolescent. The oddsmakers had favored us in the game on the age factor alone, figuring the heat and the early season competition would soon take their toll on the "Over-the-Hill Gang."

The oddsmakers were wrong, although at the outset we looked like we were going to blow Washington out of the park. In our first series of downs Kenny Anderson, sore scalp and all, marched us 60 yards in only 11 plays—completing six of seven passes, the last one being a touchdown strike to Isaac Curtis. That was the last touchdown we were to score all day. Anderson suddenly went sour and completed only three more passes in sixteen attempts the rest of the way. Once I was all alone and heading for the end zone, stopping only to wildly wave at Kenny. He never saw me. Another time I was wide open and he overthrew me by a mile.

Kenny's backup, John Reaves, played the second half. Twice I was in the end zone and twice John threw it to me. On one Ken Houston just got a piece of it and deflected it out of my hands. On the second, Brig Owens got no more than a fingernail on the ball, but it was enough to make me drop it. I could have and probably should have had both balls, I know. I guess it just wasn't our day all the way around.

The only thing I could think of after those two missed passes were the words Paul Brown had said earlier in the day about his boy, Dante Lavelli. "When he went up for a pass with a defender you could count on him coming down with the ball. . . ." So, OK, I was no Dante Lavelli. According to PB, nobody is. . .or ever will be.

Poor Paul, he was fit to be tied. He charged that we had embarrassed him (the implication was that we had done it *purposefully*) in front of his friends and fans. He didn't mention it—he didn't have to—but ABC had carried the game on national television.

It was hard for me to believe that Paul got so upset over it. After all, it was only our first exhibition game. One of my gripes about the exhibition season was the way the coaches geared—or didn't gear— us for them beforehand. Everything was calm and cool in the locker room; no speeches or threats or team rallying or anything. Then, gradually, quarter by quarter, the tension on the sidelines built and the coaches, including Paul, began hollering at each other and at the players like we were in the middle of the Super Bowl or something. My contention is that if you're going to treat exhibition games so seriously, let the players know about it going in—and then do something to help get their psyches up.

Before the Washington game, for instance, Paul was walking around in a convivial mood because of the festivities. He kept telling us that this was our chance to become the "darlings of Ohio." His meaning, of course, was that a strong performance could have gone a long way in swaying Ohioan loyalties away from the Cleveland Browns, our arch-rivals who were expected to have a bad team that year. Well, I think our performance fell a great deal short of being "darling." And the only thing we could do was forget the game and work for the next week's meeting with Miami.

Actually, the Canton trip was, in one way, fruitful for me personally; I learned someting I never knew—my name was inscribed on a plaque which hangs nicely against a clean white wall in pro football's Hall of Fame. Each year, it seems, the Hall selects its own all-star team for enshrinement. I was surprised when I looked at one all-star team plaque and saw that they had selected none other that Bob Trumpy as the best tight end in football for 1969.

Imagine that. Bob Trumpy in the Hall of Fame. Know what?

This lowly 12th-round draft choice got his name in the Hall of Fame *six years before* Paul Brown's pride and joy, Dante Lavelli! "The best pair of hands I've ever seen"—Ha!

If Paul was pissed at us for our showing against the Redskins, his sphincter must have been tight as a button after the Miami game. The Dolphins only gave us one field goal all night and we lost 7-3.

Our main problem was, once again, Kenny Anderson. Just like in the Washington game, Kenny had a very hard time hitting his receivers. He completed only eight of seventeen passes, and the whole offensive unit gained a mere seventy-two yards.

The worst part of the game was what was going on *on the sidelines!* I have never seen such disorganization in my life. We had coaches, who were feeling pressure to produce, yelling at players, and even at one another.

With about ten seconds left in the first half we had a fourth down and short situation near midfield. Against the advice of Bill Walsh, the offensive coordinator, Paul Brown elected to try to pick up the first down and at the same time run out the clock. As it turned out, we didn't make it, and Miami took over possession with time for one more play. They threw the bomb, as everyone in the stadium knew they would, and our rookie defensive back Marvin Cobb blew his coverage assignment. The only thing that saved seven points for us was that the Dolphin receiver, standing all alone in the end zone, let the perfectly thrown pass slip right through his hands.

When Walsh saw how close Miami had come to scoring on that play he turned to PB and yelled, "See there, see what I told you! You can't gamble at fourth and short at midfield. If you don't make it the other team still has a shot at scoring—which Miami came damn close to doing just now. You've *got to* punt in that situation."

PB didn't say a thing—then. He waited until we were altogether in the clubhouse at halftime before he vented his anger. He began by chewing us out for our sloppy performance and ended by saying, "I want you all to know that I will handle the situation out on that field, and I mean that I am the *only* one who will." He turned in the direction of Bill Walsh and added: "And that goes for you coaches, too."

I think Paul made his point, and Bill Walsh lost a few as far as future head coaching possibilities were concerned.

In the second half PB and I exchanged some heated words. It was really the result of a block I missed the week before in the Washington game. We had had another key fourth and one situation then, and the decision was made from the bench to go for it. The play was a "56-solid," a handoff to the fullback off the right side. My assignment was to fire out and hit the linebacker, who was sitting outside my right shoulder. Just as the ball was snapped my man did a stutter step and shot inside; Bob Johnson's man did the same stutter and shot to the outside. The end result was that both defenders found themselves in the hole where our back big Ed Williams was running and stopped him for no gain.

When I ran off the field, several coaches, including PB, came up to me to ask what had happened. "They put on a stutter," I said, "and my man and Johnson's shot into the hole. It was my man who got Ed, though, not Johnson's." I took a breath and added. "I can promise you that it won't happen again."

After the game PB was ticking off the endless list of faults we displayed in the loss when suddenly he cast a glance over in my corner of the room and said, "Can you imagine the gall of some players—we actually have one guy who *apologized* for missing a block tonight!"

Man, that really burned me. And after his talk I rushed up to him and said, "Listen, Paul, I did not apologize to you for what happened out there. You wanted to know what happened out there. All I said was that it wouldn't happen again, and it won't. If you take that as an apology, you are dead wrong. I don't have to apologize for anything; I'll take my blocking percentage during the past seven years over any tight end's in football, and you know it."

PB, not saying anything, just turned and walked away.

I missed another block in the Miami game. The play was a "39-Under." I was playing the left side that time (the first missed block was on the right side) and I was supposed to hit the defensive end. When we lined up, I saw that my man was Bill Stanfill, an All-Pro selection and one tough customer. He was playing way inside of me, near where the play was about to be run by our halfback Lenvil Elliott. I decided that the best course of action, since I had a good angle on him, was to drive Stanfill even farther inside, past the hole. Well, when the ball was snapped I hit him, all right. Right into Lenvil Elliott.

Paul Brown was waiting for me when I came off the field.

"That was your man, wasn't it?" he asked.

I just looked at him and said, "I've got nothing to say to you."

"The hell you don't; you're going to stand right here and tell me what happened."

"No I'm not. I'm going over to talk with Bill Johnson; he understands the play and the defensive alignment."

Man, Paul got mad. His veins stood out like the yard lines on a football field. "I'm telling you," he glared, "you're going to stand here and talk to me."

I simply said, "No." Fortunately for me Tiger Johnson had overheard our conversation and rushed up to us. When he arrived he stood on the other side of PB, so when I began telling him that Miami had pulled a stunt line with a gap charge, I looked straight over Paul Brown's head and into Tiger's eyes. Throughout our conversation I noticed Paul Brown's eyebrows. He was so mad they were forming a wiggling vee up on his forehead.

After the game, Paul became calmer. And whenever he passed me on the plane back to Cincinnati he nodded to me with civility. I doubted whether he even recalled our run-in. Things are so emotional down on the sidelines and so many things are happening every minute, that you tend to say things you don't mean. You just have to forget about these outbursts and look ahead to the next play. It's a game of forgive and forget, really. I for one hoped Paul Brown always remembered that...

Sometimes coaches don't, you know.

Several years ago we had a rookie named Ruby Jackson, a 6'5", 270-pound defensive tackle. Ruby, a black guy, was the strongest guy the Bengals have ever had, next to Steve Chomyzsak. One time he was working out with a rope-pulley contraption we had at Spinney Field to tone muscles, and as he was doing this Vince Costello, a former linebacker coach with the club, walked in; he was giving a guest of his a tour around the facilities. Vince and the visitor stopped where Ruby was working out; he was doing a tough exercise where you put your arms straight out and pull down on a bar attached to the rope and pulleys. Ruby did a few dozen of these, and Vince remarked loudly to his guest: "You see, this boy Ruby Jackson here is doing it all wrong. He's loafing. His arms should be straight as a board when he pulls down that bar, not bent." (If Vince had been paying attention he would've noticed that Ruby Jackson was so muscle-bound that it was physically impossible for him to straighten out his arms!)

Naturally, Jackson was a little perturbed at Costello's comment. So he turned and said over his shoulder, in front of the visitor, "Fuck you, Coach." Then he turned back around and calmly headed toward the showers.

Costello's jaw dropped about three feet. He couldn't think what to do about this blatant insubordination of Ruby's, and he was reduced to weakly calling out after him, "Uh, Ruby. Uh, Ruby, come back here. Uh, Ruby, you can't talk to me that way; I'm a coach...."

We all thought Ruby Jackson's move was the greatest thing since artificial turf. Apparently Costello didn't. Ruby was cut forthwith.

If my pride didn't suffer in the Miami game, my back did. Spasms. Happened every year. The muscles in the mid and lower back region tightened up harder than a rock. It had all the docs a little stumped, but they kept jabbing me with needles and prescribing special heat treatments. I knew from experience that only rest would make it go away.

I suppose that if I had one regret in my career, it is that I was not more durable. Each year one injury after another, many just the nagging variety, hampered me. I doubt whether there's an NFL player alive who has gone through an entire season injury-free (a little hurt is as much a part of the game as posing for the team picture) but I sure would have been willing to have given it a try.

My injury list—although it didn't contain any major broken bones—would have made a Blue Cross agent shudder: a separated shoulder, a dislocated shoulder, two broken noses, strained knee ligaments, dozens of dislocated fingers, pinched nerves, a jammed neck, a chronic sore elbow (from blocking) and probably fifty or sixty stitches.

By far the most frustrating injury I had—and the one that made me begin to look upon physicians somewhat skeptically—was an ankle injury incurred in 1969. It was at Christmas time following the season, and I was in Springfield to play in a special alumni basketball game. I went up for a rebound and came down off balance. My right foot hit the floor at an odd angle, and I twisted the hell out of it.

The injury, diagnosed by a Springfield doctor as a "severe sprain," put me on crutches. This was particularly frustrating because I was scheduled to leave for Houston in three weeks to play in the AFL All-Star game. As it turned out, I did make the trip, and I did try to practice. I lasted from Monday until Thursday before I was back on crutches again, unable to walk.

I had X-rays taken and was told the ankle was broken. Wonderful. Within hours I was back in Cincinnati and in our team doctor's office. "Your ankle isn't broken," he told me, "you have a sprain fracture. With rest, it should heal itself in no time."

"No time" never came. Throughout the remainder of the winter and into the summer I limped around in pain. And since I couldn't run or work out, I reported to Bengal summer camp in July 1970, very much out of shape. The team docs looked at the ankle and determined that the best course of treatment was a lot of work. "You've got to run these things out," I was told.

I tried throughout the season to "run it out," but the ankle just didn't respond. My weekly schedule for nearly the entire season went like this: Monday (following the Sunday game)—on crutches; Tuesday—off crutches but barely able to walk; Wednesday—walk but not run; Thursday, Friday and Saturday—light practice; Sunday—played game, and Monday—back on crutches (and the whole process started all over again).

Finally, twelve games into the season, I went to Mike Brown. "Mike," I said, "the team has got to do something. This ankle of mine is worse than ever."

Mike thought a moment. "Tell you what we can do. After our game in Cleveland Sunday, why don't you stay over and go to the Cleveland Orthopedic Clinic. Let them have a look at it."

That's exactly what I did, and after a few tests a doctor told me I probably had some calcium deposits in my ankle. He also stated that some dried blood from that basketball injury (almost a year before) had settled in the sheath that houses an ankle tendon, making the tendon stiff as a board. He asked me what pattern of treatment I had been following for the injury. "Well," I shrugged, "for the past twelve weeks the team doctors have been giving me weekly shots of novocaine and cortisone in the tendon area."

"Jesus Christ," the doc screamed, "you're lucky they didn't ruin you permanently. Just one more shot could have ruptured that tendon but good." He went on to explain that the shots were taking all the elasticity out of the tendon, and that the only "cure" was rest. He put me in a leg cast.

I was only in it for three weeks...but it took a full two years before I could once again walk without a visible limp.

It sure makes you wonder about doctors, doesn't it? I get the feeling that if Quasimodo would have gone to the same doctors I did, they'd have inspected his hunchback and told him not to worry about it. They'd probably say, "You just have to ring these things out."

Being injured was bad enough, but not practicing was hell. Because agonizing as summer camp was, if you didn't practice the boredom weighed on you like the Steeler front line.

There wasn't a lot to do in Wilmington.

To show you how bad it could get there, several of us would go over to the fairgrounds to see what was happening at the Clinton County Fair. Now that's being hard up! We watched tractor pulling contests, pig-judging finals and trotter horse races. One year, four of us put in $20 each to see whether Ron Pritchard would paint a number on his back and run from one end of the grandstand to the other, like a sulky horse. Pritch actually contemplated the offer for ten minutes before finally declining.

I can remember one rookie back in 1968 who had a real unusual way of passing summer camp. For reasons that will become obvious, I won't mention the rookie's full name, but his nickname was "Bulldog," and he was an unbelievable kid.

Bulldog was only a kicker, but definitely not your run of the mill variety. This guy absolutely craved contact; he thrived on it. If Bulldog had had his way he would have enjoyed playing every other day without equipment, at both fullback and linebacker, against the Super Bowl champions.

One time he walked into our taping room and said he needed a quick tape job. One of the allocation draft veterans, a big guy, looked over at him sardonically and said, "Bulldog, what the hell do *you* need tape for? You ain't nothin' but a lousy kicker." Without saying a word, Bulldog quietly closed the taping room door and proceeded to clean this veteran's clock, but good. Like I say, Bulldog loved contact.

Anyway, I had been in training camp only for a few weeks when I saw a young kid responsible for cleaning up all the players' dormitory rooms approach trainer Marv Pollins. His face was red and flustered. When he talked, it looked like he was about ready to cry. "Mr. Pollins," he said, "I just ain't goin' to clean Bulldog's room anymore. I've had it. You can get somebody else to do that crummy job." Marv looked at the youth incredulously and asked him to explain himself. "Bulldog keeps painting murals on the walls," the kid said, and he took Marv to show him what he meant.

What was happening was this—it seems that during those hot edgy nights of summer camp, Bulldog was releasing the day's stored-up tensions by lying in bed and jerking his meat. And he was doing it without using any aids to catch the fruits of his work. He simply let it splash against the wall next to his bed (and, I suppose, even on the ceiling, on those nights of extreme tension). Worse, he allowed it to hang there, unabated, in a rather macabre free-form masterpiece. Personally, I think it was quite understandable that the youth didn't want to touch Bulldog's unique mural design. After all, you wouldn't take a pallette knife to a Goya, would you?

Then there was Sam Wyche. Sam was a summer camp insomniac. So, being a quarterback, he specifically requested that the coaches provide him with a blackboard and chalk for his room. Unable to sleep, Sam got up, turned on the light and passed the pre-dawn hours by drawing x's and o's on the board.

I've never seen anyone who could get by on as little sleep as he did. You could get up any time of night and see Sam wandering about the dorm hallways as if he were in search of something. Or you'd see him in the shower, or in his room—anywhere. He was like a shark who has to keep moving all the time so there is continuous water flowing across his gills, lest he sink to the bottom of the sea.

One time in training camp my rookie year I got up about 2:00 in the morning to take a leak. I staggered down the hallway toward the john when I passed Sam's room. On the other side of the door comes the sound of someone playing guitar and singing rather woefully. So I duck my head in and say, "Hey, Sam, what in the world are you *doing*? It's 2:00 in the morning!"

"I couldn't sleep," he said, and continued to randomly pluck at his guitar. "I got lots of things on my mind."

I shrugged and began to leave. Then I heard him say, "Jeez, I bet I'd feel a lot better if I'd smash this guitar to bits."

Then I began to back out of the room, slowly. I didn't want to make any sudden moves. It occurred to me that I'd only been in training camp a few days and I really didn't know this guy Sam Wyche very well.

As I turned to go, I heard this loud splintering crash, and I wheeled around in time to see Sam sitting there, smiling. In his hand is about three inches of guitar stem and a mass of dangling strings. A thousand wood chips cover the floor beneath him.

I tried to think of something to say, but nothing appropriate came to mind. Suddenly Sam sighed and said, "Well, I was right. I *do* feel a lot better now." With that, he reached over, switched off the light and went sound to sleep. Sam Wyche was different, to say the least. And the thought of him ever taking up piano chills to the bone.

Over the years, Bob Johnson and I passed the time with an improvised game we called Human Billiards. In Human Billiards the object is to have one guy stand in a fixed spot in our room, take a rubber ball and—playing planned-out ricochets and caroms— attempt to hit the other guy, who's all scrunched up somewhere attempting to be the smallest target possible. The more walls struck by the ball before hitting the target, the more points awarded to the thrower.

We literally spent hundreds and hundreds of training camp hours in this competitive endeavor, most of them after the mandatory "lights-out" period.

One time we were caught red-handed. Just as I had let go with a great three-wall bouncer, Chuck Studley walked into our room. Johnson didn't see him, of course, because he was standing on his bed with his face pressed against the wall, head awkwardly pushed under one arm, shoulders all humped over and a leg tucked up under his torso.

You can imagine Studley's reaction. "What in the hell are you guys doing?" he asked. It was a logical enough question, and we were momentarily stumped for an answer. So, simply, I stated, "Playing Human Billiards."

"Playing WHAT?"

"Human Billiards, Coach," I repeated, and went on to explain the specifics of the game.

Now Studley is a real disciplinarian, and both Johnson and I expected the worse. To our surprise, he was absolutely taken with the simplicity of the game we had invented. (I demonstrated a few shots for him, pulling off a nifty four-wall job—very, very difficult maneuver) and he stood there in the middle of our room nodding his head in appreciation. Then, for the next half-hour, Chuck Studley proceeded to give us tips and hints, from an experienced coach's point of view, on how we might better refine the game and our performance. I swear it—for thirty full minutes Johnson and I stood there accepting Studley's critique of the game; we couldn't believe what was happening. We could, however, tell by the competitive glint in Chuck Studley's eye that he wanted in the worse way for us to invite him to join in the game.

We never did, and after a while he turned and walked out of the room. To our amazement, not once did he ever mention that we were breaking training camp hours with that silly game of ours.

Bob Johnson, by the way, is quite a story. As most Bengal fans know, his uniform number 54 was retired on the final day of his last game in 1978. I don't believe another Bengals' jersey will be retired in my lifetime. Bob was unique. Now a successful marketing vice president in Cincinnati, he was the first-ever draft choice of the Bengals in 1968, and he snapped the ball on virtually every play for ten years (excluding the games he was forced to sit out with a broken ankle in 1974). To tell you what the management thought of Bob Johnson, they didn't even carry a back-up center on the roster— until his last season in 1978, when they recruited Blair Bush. Now that was pretty fair job security!

Johnson was a statewide hero in Tennessee. He was an All-State center there as well as a consensus All-American at the University of Tennessee. He was so popular that one of the large dairy concerns signed Johnson to a promotion contract and within weeks he had his face plastered on billboards all over the state endorsing milk. And he kept in the public eye by working for one of the candidates for governor of the state. Fan mail from his home state poured in each of his eleven years in the league. One in particular I got a charge out of, from an inmate of the Tennessee State Prison. In the letter, the prisoner asked Bob to use his influence in Tennessee to get him pardoned from his life sentence.

"I've been in the slammer about six months now," the inmate wrote, "and it really's beginning to get to me." He was in for murder. He had stabbed a guy two dozen times with a chisel.

Johnson read the letter and shook his head, and said, "I think he overestimates my pull in that state." On the good side, though, Johnson did send him a 5″ x 7″ glossy and an autograph.

Most of the time Johnson and I got along well, despite the fact that we were two separately structured individuals. He was a number one draft choice; I was a lowly 12th-round selection. He arrived his rookie year with All-American status and a briefcase full of press clippings; I was a complete unknown. He was born in the South and went to a southern university; I was raised a midwesterner and went to college everywhere *but* the South. He is a deeply religious indi-vidual, a deacon in his church and a member of the Fellowship of Christian Athletes; I haven't seen the inside of a church in twenty-five years. He was anti-smoking; I was an inveterate chain smoker. On and on the differences went. Still, we primarily got along.

And if it's not bad enough that we lived practically as husband and wife for a decade of summer camps, we also still live within 500 yards of each other in Cincinnati, our houses situated catercorner to each other, connected by a small pathway. As a result, we saw each other virtually every day of the year. If our wives found fault with this year-round proximity, it was that it led us to be too competitive. We found ourselves with overlapped lives, competing for neighborhood friends, community prestige and so on. Several times during the off-season we found ourselves in a few serious push-come-to-shove situations in backyard basketball games, and occasionally we walked away really pissed off at each other. But not often.

Actually, as a roommate Johnson was a saving grace for me. He added a dimension of security that never existed before. Believe it or not, my rookie year I had six different roommates, some of them only as long as one day. Six times there were knocks on the door, telling a player "Paul Brown wants to see you." Those were dreaded words around summer camp—they meant you were just cut. Each time one of those knocks came, a jolt zipped through me. Was I the one this time? Fortunately, a seventh knock never came.

All those night-visitors to our room my rookie year could have driven me to sleepless paranoia had I not taken matters into my own hands. After two weeks of these knocks on the door, I decided to put a stop to them—by confronting Paul Brown face-to-face for the first time.

A few of us draftees were sitting around one evening, each nervously discussing the likelihood of making the team. We were all too aware that several of the guys who used to participate in these nightly speculations were already gone, having been cut earlier. It made the rest of us feel a little insecure, at best.

I don't know why, but when my turn came to evaluate my chances of sticking with the club I just stood up and said, "Well, I'm through playing guessing games. I'm going to ask Paul Brown whether I've made the team or not."

You can imagine the reaction I got from that statement. To a man they thought I was (a) full of crap, (b) totally insane, (c) masochistic or (d) suicidal. Whichever, none of them believed I would go through with it. As I left the room, the last thing I heard one of the guys crack was, "Say goodbye to crazy Trumpy, boys. That's the last we'll ever see of him."

I must admit, when I finally found myself in front of PB's door, second thoughts crept into my mind.

I'm approaching this thing in a strictly businesslike manner, I kept reminding myself, but somehow it sounded less and less convincing. Only the thought of returning upstairs empty-handed to face the sneers and jeers of my teammates for the way I shot off my mouth encouraged me to see it through.

So by the time I entered the Coach's room I had my psyche back up.

I knocked softly.

"Come in," a voice said. I recognized it as Coach Brown's. He was sitting at his desk, wearing the ever-present black Bengal hat and going over some papers.

"Coach," I said, "can you spare a few minutes?"

"Sure," he answered, "sit down."

I complied, but it was quite a while before I could say anything. "Coach," I finally began, "my wife, Pat, is eight-and-a-half months pregnant with our first child. She's in L.A. right now and the doctor tells her that in another week she won't be able to fly."

Coach Brown nodded patiently, but said nothing. I took a deep breath and continued: "If you tell me I'm going to make this ball club, I'll call Pat tonight and our baby will be born in Cincinnati. If you say I'm going to get cut, I'll leave camp tomorrow morning so I can be by her side when she delivers in L.A. If it's at all possible, I'd like to know one way or the other about my status with the team."

For a moment I thought perhaps the Old Coach hadn't heard me. He just sat there without moving, and when he didn't answer I began to shift about nervously. "I don't want to back you into a corner or anything," I offered, filling in the silence, "but I'd just like to know so I can plan my future—"

Suddenly I realized that he *had* said something; I asked him to repeat it.

"I said," he whispered, "why don't you bring your wife Pat to Cincinnati to have her baby."

I sat dumbfounded, unable to think of anything appropriate to say. I know my first inclination was to grab Paul Brown by the collar and place the biggest kiss he ever had right on the top of his bald head, but I somehow managed to suppress this urge. Actually, I don't recall what I *did* say in those few minutes, but I'm sure it was something like, "You won't be sorry, Coach. I'll be the best damn receiver this club'll ever have," or "I'll give you a 110% out on that field, Coach, you can count on that,"—or words along these lines. At any rate, I remember backing toward the door as quickly as possible—I wanted to get out of there before he had a chance to think it over—and I was just about to bolt from the room when another thought struck me. "Uh, Coach," I said, hesitatingly, "when Tom Bass signed me up, he said I would get $1,000 if I made the team. Well, I sure could use that money right now. As things are, I don't even have enough to buy a plane ticket back here for Pat."

I was afraid that I might be pushing my luck a little too far. But PB just looked up and grinned. "I'll have my son, Mike, draw up a check for that amount right away."

That was all there was to it. For six weeks the rest of the guys continued the nightly discussions about who was and wasn't going to get cut. Not me. No sir; when I left Paul Brown's room that night in 1968 I knew two things—I was a member of the Cincinnati Bengals and I was $1,000 richer. And I never lost another night's sleep because of knocks on the door.

Speaking of roommates, it might be appropriate to point out one of the oddest pairs of roommates we ever had: Pat Matson and Ron Lamb. They roomed together during training camp in 1968 and were about as similar in personality as John Wayne and Abbie Hoffman.

Matson was a "clean" freak, fastidious to a fault. He'd dust down the room every day if he thought it would help exterminate even the smallest particle of bacteria. If you coughed within thirty feet of him, he turned, pointed an admonishing finger your way and yelled, "Get the hell out of my room. And take your germs with you."

Aside from a neatness fetish (his belongings were always systematically stacked in their proper place) Pat was also an absolute fitness nut. The guy lived for body building. He lifted weights or worked out on Nautilus equipment constantly (in fact, he now owns commercial Nautilus health clubs in Cincinnati); he'd think nothing of getting up at 6:00 in the morning and standing on his head in the corner of a room for half an hour, naked. So misproportioned were his narrow hips to his massive chest and shoulders, it boggled the mind to see him walk without toppling over. Our nickname for him was "Hercules," or simply "Herky."

For polarity, we had Ron Lamb. The Bengals traded to Denver for Ron, a fullback, in 1968. And, if Herky was Mr. Clean, Ron Lamb was Peter Falk's raincoat. Let's just say that Ronny didn't get too uptight if there was a little dirt and grime about the premises. And he, unlike Matson, was a real summer camp extrovert. His idea of passing time was a boisterous, smoke-filled evening of poker with the guys and a couple of six packs of beer.

I remember one night, about halfway through the first training camp, Ron really tied one on. Somehow he managed to find his way back to his room and successfully locate the pillow with his head. He was fully clothed, of course, when he crashed. I'm sure this drunk swaggering through the dark room must have galled Matson, but not half as much as what would occur a few hours later.

About 2:00 in the morning, Herky was awakened by a commotion; this time it was the sound of drawers being rifled in the vicinity of Lamb's corner of the room. Herky flipped on the light and, through the shadows, saw his roommate standing there, fumbling wildly through his chest of drawers, yanking out all his socks and underwear and scattering them over his shoulder.

"What the hell are you doing, Lamb," Pat inquired, a bit short. To which, Ron merely put two fingers to his lips and replied in a beery voice. "Sh-sh-sh, Pat. Go back to schleep. There's somethin' I got to take care of."

With that, Ron ripped the drawer clean out of its housing, inspected it a final time and, apparently satisfied, leaned it up against the wall. Casually, he cranked down his pants zipper and proceeded to urinate in the drawer for a good thirty seconds. Once completed, he turned, calmly aimed himself back to his bed and passed out on the mattress, cold.

I really don't know exactly what Herky said to his roommate in the morning, but I bet it wasn't something you'd hear on a Billy Graham crusade.

Neither Johnson nor I was ever accused of inordinate fastidiousness. Our room was about as neat as an apartment building in 1945 Hiroshima. We made a habit of hanging all of our possessions on the floor—much the way the old-time cowboys used to do—so that when we needed something, we knew exactly where to find it.

Toward the end of our careers, we upgraded the surroundings substantially. We put in a refrigerator and an air-conditioner. The refrigerator, kept in the closet, was always stocked with pop and beer. The air-conditioner was a real God-send in that blessed heat. But more than that, for me it was a real status symbol, an indication of how far I had come in pro football.

There were no air-conditioners my rookie year, only electric fans. And I didn't even have one of those. Back then, you could determine how a player was drafted just by looking in his room. Players taken in the allocation draft (those with a year or two of paychecks under their belts) and the high draft choices (those who received large bonuses for signing) all had fans, having taken their money up to the local hardware store to purchase them. The rest of us—the low draft choices with no money—suffered.

Needless to say, my room didn't have a fan. Neither I nor my first six roommates had the money to buy one. So to combat the heat I took a shower before bedtime and, without bothering to towel off, jumped right into bed soaking wet. My prayer each night was, "Lord, grant me sleep before I dry off."

Fortunately, those days are behind me. And bad as it may have been, our little room at Wilmington had been a second home to Johnson and me for nine years, our personal screening room for witnessing world happenings. Among the history-making events we saw together in nine years were the Vietnam war, Man's first walk on the moon, the 1972 and 1976 Olympics, the resignation of a president and a U.S.-Soviet meeting in space.

We always had other plans, too. We had hoped to one year be watching film clips of a Super Bowl, starring, of course, the Cincinnati Bengals.

Apparently not all dreams are realized.

FLEAS ON MY DOG

Early in summer camp, we began playing the Bengal version of "musical coaches."

Chuck Weber, our defensive coordinator, went into the hospital for a serious gall bladder operation. In his absence, Jack Donaldson, the offensive backfield coach, was switched to defensive coordinator. Filling Jack's shoes as offensive backfield coach was—guess who?—a guy who has never coached in his life. By name, Mike Brown.

Sad but true. Mike Brown took his first practice jump over the Snake River, leaping from front-office paper-pusher to professional football backfield coach in one fell swoop. I think he got the job because of somebody he knew in the organization.

There was no love lost between Mike Brown and me. The mutual bitterness stemmed from a salary negotiation battle we waged against one another in 1971. Actually, whole thing wasn't entirely Mike's fault. Our confrontation merely culminated a number of unpleasant salary disputes I had with Bengal management beginning in 1970. (In 1968 I signed immediately the total $17,500 contract offered to me in my home by Tom Bass; in 1969 I negotiated with Paul Brown, and it went something like this—Paul: "This is what I have on my mind. We'll increase your salary from $17,500 to $19,000." Me: "No, I'd rather have $20,000, just because it's out of the teens." Paul: "OK, you got it." And that was all there was to it.)

But in 1970 it was a different story. I had a great year in '69, named to the AFL All-Star team, and I worked in the off-season as an account executive for WLWT television in Cincinnati. The station and the Bengals' offices were located in the same building, the Carew Tower, downtown. So one day, having nothing better to do, I decided to drop in on the Bengals' staff. As I was going in, PB was just leaving. He greeted me with, "I'm in the process of sending out your contract. You're going to thank me when you see it."

"Well," I said, "you don't mind if I wait to thank you until *after* I see it, do you?" He replied that he didn't, and walked out.

I began a conversation with Paul's secretary, a wonderful lady named Betty, with whom I had struck up a pretty good friendship during my tenure with the team. As we talked, I looked down and noticed that my contract, the one Paul referred to, was sitting in her out-basket.

"Betty," I said, reaching for it, "I'll save the club the price of a stamp. I'll take this with me now."

I made it as far as the elevator before the urge to look at my contract overtook me. I slid it out of my pocket, unfolded it, read the figures, blinked once, re-read the figures, folded it back up again, turned, and went back into the Bengals' office. "Tell Paul Brown," I said, handing the contract back to Betty, "that this is totally unacceptable and I refuse to play for this kind of money." The contract called for $22,000, a raise of only *$2,000*—and I was coming off an exceptionally good year! On the way back to my office, I passed WLWT sportscaster Phil Samp, the "voice of the Bengals." So I told Phil what I told Betty.

Well, you'd never guess what Phil Samp's headline story was that night on his 6:00 and 11:00 news shows. That's right—"Cincinnati Bengal tight end Bob Trumpy today returned his contract to head coach and general manager Paul Brown calling the contract—quote—'totally unacceptable' and that he, Trumpy, refuses to—quote—'play for that type of money.' "

Pat answered the phone at 8:00 the next morning. "That was Betty," she said. "Paul Brown wants you in his office at 9:15."

You can bet I was decently prompt.

"Why," Paul asked, "did you bring our negotiations before the public?"

"Sir?"

"This is not a public matter, Bob. Why did you do it?"

Calmly, I tried to explain the situation, that as a WLWT account executive I felt an obligation to the station to let them in on a sports item of interest.

Paul looked at me with a very sad-eyed expression. "We frown on that type of thing," he finally said. "We frown on that very, very much."

I didn't exactly know how to respond to this, but I had the feeling that PB was on the verge of giving walking papers to his starting tight end. Surprisingly, he suddenly sat back in his chair, folded his hands and said, "Now here's what we're going to do, Bob. The Bengals are going to pay you $26,000 next year, plus a $9,000 bonus for signing. That's a total of $35,000. Take it or leave it."

Without hesitation, I said, "I'll take it." I didn't know whether they were paying me my true worth, but I realized that in 18 hours my value had jumped from $22,000 to $35,000, and I wasn't in a right frame of mind to quibble about it.

This minor vendetta only set the stage for the big showdown a year later, in 1971, with Mike Brown. Mike had taken over all negotiations for his dad then, and he offered me a contract for

$32,000, but no bonus.

For months and months we exchanged very heated conversation on the subject. The real bone of contention was whether I was getting a salary cut or an increase.

Mike's position was that I was getting a $6,000 increase over 1970's base salary of $26,000. My version was that the club had paid me $35,000 in 1970—$26,000 base and $9,000 bonus—and that no matter how you sliced it, the current offer of $32,000 was $3,000 less than what I made the year before.

I was the first to admit that I did not have a good year in 1970, a lingering ankle injury kept me on crutches most of the time between games, but a $3,000 cut was a real slap in the face. I argued on the principle of the thing, really.

We disputed my salary endlessly, neither side budged an inch. Many of our negotiating sessions got down to some real name calling and, finally, negotiations broke down altogether.

As a result, I went to training camp in 1971 without having signed a contract. I was determined to play out my option and sell my services to the team with the highest bid for 1972. All the way through summer camp and the exhibition season I went unsigned, up until just a few days before the regular season was to begin. At that point Mike called me into his office in the Wilmington College training complex and we sat down once more.

He pulled out a contract and asked me to sign it. I looked it over and saw it was for the same $32,000 he had offered me six months before. Quickly, I handed it back to him. "I told you, Mike," I said, "I am not going to sign for this amount of money. I think it's ridiculous that you are trying to pay a starting player and a four-year veteran this kind of money—and at a $3,000 cut in pay!" I paused to clear my throat. "Mike," I continued, "I am going to play out my option unless you come up with a better offer than that. I mean it."

That did it. Mike got red in the face and his eyes got narrow and glazed. All of a sudden he exploded and called me about every name in the book. He ended by saying, "My personal opinion is 'screw-you, Mr. Trumpy!' You can go your own goddam way anytime you want. In fact, as far as I'm concerned you don't have to wait around until you play out your option. You can leave this team right now."

"Fine," I said, and got up to leave. I walked out of Mike's room and headed straight for PB's office. Mike could see exactly where I was headed, and he suddenly became very uneasy. "Hey, where are you going, Trumpy?" he called after me.

"To see your dad. I think it's only fair to apprise him of what has transpired here and exactly where our negotiations stand. Your dad knows my worth to the team and what I have contributed, and frankly, Mike, I don't think you do. If I'm leaving the team, I figure I at least owe him a good-bye."

Quite rapidly, Mike Brown's mood changed. He bustled out of

his tiny room and grabbed my arm. "Listen, listen, Bob," he pleaded, "I'm really sorry for the way I shot off my mouth. That's the worst thing you can do in negotiations. Why don't you come back in my office and we'll see if we can work out some of the details."

"OK, Mike," I agreed, "but I don't want to go through this crap with you every year. So when we talk this time, we better be talking in terms of a multi-year contract, not just a once a year job."

He agreed, and I came out of the session with a contract calling for a $34,000 salary in 1971 (still $1,000 a year under what I received the previous year) and a $38,000 salary in 1972.

I was pretty contented with it, I must admit. I mean, for a draftee from Beneficial Finance Corporation, it wasn't too shabby at all.

None of the following years were ever as bad with Mike Brown as 1971. Still, negotiating your personal worth was never easy: it was really about the hardest part of playing pro football.

There would be a few more minor squabbles along the way, but that one year with Mike Brown was as close as I ever have been to a one-man mutiny. From the $38,000 I climbed slowly and steadily to $45,000 in 1972 and $47,000 in 1973.

I'd really not like to get into the specifics of my following contracts, but I will tell you that because of a ludicrously enormous sum offered to me by a WFL team, the Bengals were forced to offer me a multi-year contract with certain fringe benefits over and above the salary. Frankly, my final contract virtually eliminated financial worries for me the rest of my life.

Listen, at age 30, that was a pretty good feeling.

A funny incident occurred during our first exhibition season victory against Buffalo, which we won 38-28 behind Ken Anderson's now on-target passing and Boobie Clark's crunching running. A rookie quarterback, Gary Scheide, replacing Kenny, unloaded a 44-yard touchdown bomb to John McDaniel. Naturally, he was excited as hell about it and as soon as he ran off the field he began to plan what he would do on the next series of downs to duplicate the feat. When he got back in there, one of Paul Brown's messenger guards brought in a halfback running play to the left side. The team lined up and suddenly Gary called an audible at the line, a pass to the fight flat. The ball was snapped, Sheide faded back and let go. He threw a perfect strike—right to Buffalo cornerback Dwight Harrison who returned that ball 24 yards for a touchdown.

I had seen it happen a million times before. A rookie does great on one play and thinks, "Hell, the NFL ain't so tough. I can make it here easy." The next thing they know they find themselves on their butt, or, worse, with packed bags in hand, waiting for the bus.

Maybe I should have consulted with Gary about the Sad Saga of Solomon—Solomon Brannon, that is.

A defensive back taken in the allocation draft by the Bengals in 1968, Solomon apparently figured he had the team made. And you'd have said he did have an upper hand: after all, unlike most of us that first year, he had four years' NFL experience behind him. He seemingly knew all those little tricks of the trade that raw rookies spend months trying to absorb. And his status on the roster appeared to have been even more enhanced in our first exhibition game ever, against Kansas City. Before the hometown folks, he picked off an errant Chief's pass and scampered across the field and into the end zone for a touchdown. Thus, Solomon Brannan carved his niche in Bengal history: it would evermore be written that he was the first player to score a touchdown while wearing a Cincinnati Bengal uniform. Nobody else would ever be able to stake that claim.

With all of this, I guess Solomon saw stars—and dollar signs— in his football future. After the Saturday night exhibition game with the Chiefs, he went out on the town to celebrate and to spend some of the sweet salary he was sure to get from the Bengals. Apparently he looked around until his eyes landed on a gigantic, gleaming white Electra-225. Needless to say, when he glided into our Wilmington training complex Sunday night, quite a crowd gathered. There was a lot of kidding and whistling going on, and I, like the other rookies, was a little over-awed by the whole thing. I noticed, however, that some of the allocation veterans on the club just shook their heads and wandered back into the dormitory.

Maybe they knew something we rookies didn't. Because the next day, Monday, Solomon Brannan was cut from the squad.

It was just a matter of him not fitting into Paul Brown's plans for the future.

They say a little good can be found in almost all bad. Look at it this way: when Solomon came to training camp he had nothing but a weather-beaten suitcase. But when he left, Solomon Brannan went in style—in a classy new $6,000 car. Sadder but wiser, to be sure.

Another oddity in the Buffalo game was that our strapping Texan 6'5" Howard Fest, jammed his neck and had to sit out practice the next week. This was a near cataclysmic revelation: silent Howard hadn't missed a single practice (or game) since he joined the team in 1968!

He was incredible. I don't think Howard even knew the location of our taping room, and if he passed our trainer in the hallway someone would have to introduce them to each other. He wouldn't let team physicians get near him either, rejecting them the way a hermit eschews a Tupperware party.

Marv Pollins said that, in seven years, he never heard Howard speak and he was beginning to wonder whether the Bengals had a mute playing offensive guard. "One time," Marv said, "in 1968, I thought I was going to catch Howard Fest saying something. John Murdough (the Bengals' business manager) was taking orders from the players for the complimentary tickets for the upcoming game. When he approached Howard to ask him how many tickets he wanted, I rushed over to where they stood. I figured I would get first-hand proof that Howard Fest could say even a single word. You know what Howard did? He thought a moment about how many tickets he wanted, then he looked right up at Murdough and *raised two fingers in the air*! I was crestfallen."

By the way, whatever you do, around Howard Fest you don't talk about the administrative football genius of Paul Brown. Fest wouldn't believe you. You see, the coaches got cute and tried to "sneak" Howard Fest's name on the list of veterans the Bengals were willing to give up to the expansion teams in '76. For some cock-n-bull reasons, Paul thought no one would notice Howard's name on the list and the Bengals would get to keep him. Someone noticed. Tampa. Howard, who loved playing in Cincinnati, was in absolute shock, unable to talk for days afterwards. Poor Howard. He went to Tampa and was part of a team that lost twenty-four consecutive football games. Then he hurt his ankle, was placed on injured reserve, went back to Texas to fulfill a life-long dream of becoming a short order cook, got a call from Detroit before the '78 season, had a try-out, hurt his knee but didn't tell anyone, cut, had another try-out with Detroit, cut, had surgery and went back to Texas where he is now driving a dump truck hauling soil. You can't help feeling that if Paul hadn't blundered in trying to "sneak" him by the rest of the league, things would have turned out a whole lot better for Howard Fest.

During the final month of summer camp we won three of four exhibition games, and it appeared that we were really beginning to gel as a team. For one thing, Kenny Anderson began to find his receivers, like in our 27-10 victory over the Packers. The Rookie played only the first half but went fifteen for twenty-one for 148 yards and three TDs, one being to number 84, me. It was my first touchdown of the season. The play was an "86-slot-corner," a pass to me in the right (the "slot") corner of the end zone. I put a pretty good move on Packer cornerback Ken Ellis, and when I got to where I was supposed to have been, Freddie Franchise's perfectly thrown ball was waiting for me. All I had to do was reach out and pluck it out of the air. Six points.

Funny, I almost didn't even have a chance to make that TD catch, not because of the Packer defense, but because of a man in blue who worked for the City of Cincinnati. He wanted me behind bars. Why? Well, it went this way:

For seven years Johnson and I had been parking in a special section beneath Riverfront Stadium, near the players' locker room; for seven years we had been doing this without a parking pass (we would give our parking passes to our wives so that when they came to the game they didn't have to park in a city lot seven or eight blocks from the stadium).

But on this occasion, before the Packer game, when we pulled up to the special parking entrance one of Cincinnati's finest—a young recruit-looking cop with close-cropped hair and a pencil mustache—waved us to a halt. "Where do you think you're going, mister?" he asked me.

"Right there," I answered, pointing to an empty row of parking spaces some 30 feet ahead.

The policeman looked over to where I was pointing and then shook his head. "Not without a parking pass you're not. Nobody gets in there without a pass, those are the rules."

"Look, officer," I said with irritation, "my name is Bob Trumpy and this is Bob Johnson. We play for the Cincinnati Bengals and we've been parking here for seven years."

"I don't care if you're Edgar Bergen and Charlie McCarthy," he said, "you are not getting in here without a pass."

I turned to Johnson and shrugged. "Any ideas?"

"Yea," he said, "let's turn around and park in a city lot. This guy looks like he means business."

"You are going to pay the three bucks for us to park?"

"No," he said.

I nodded. "OK, then. I suggest you hold on. I've had enough of this clown and I'm going through."

I began to apply the gas, but the cop had anticipated my move. He took a step in front of the car and, in the same motion, unsnapped his holster with a quick flick of his wrist. "Stay right where you are, mister." His eyes became the same luster as his shiny badge. He stood there bent slightly, his finger wrapped around the trigger. When Johnson saw this his mouth fell open about two feet and he threw his hands into the air and let out a loud, "W-H-O-O-A." Then he jumped out of the car and started for the locker room in a series of rapid back-pedaling strides. "Stay here, Trumpy," he said, none too charitably. "I'm going to the locker room to get John Murdough. He'll handle this."

Wonderful. Johnson was safely inside and I was out here all alone, figuring out some way to humor Machine Gun Kelly. As my loyal roommate disappeared, the cop approached me once more. "That was a stupid move, buddy," he said. "Now I'm going to tell you this one time: turn this car around and head out. Right now."

I sat, unmoved. "No," I said.

"What was that?"

I repeated my answer. "I'm not moving this car an inch, officer."

By this time there were a half-dozen cars queueing up behind me and the officer's face was turning the most frightening shade of purple. "If you don't move this instant," he said, "I'm going to run you in."

"Fine," I responded, "you'll go down in history as the only policeman to have locked up a Bengal starting tight end an hour before game time."

"OK, buddy," he snapped out, "that does it. Let me see your license. You're getting a ticket for creating a disturbance here."

My alternatives were few. I could run the striped-arm barricade and park in my old spot, but I would be risking a gunshot wound in the back from the law-and-order freak. I could just sit there, backing up traffic, until he carted me off to the slammer. Or, I could turn my car around and park seven blocks away, paying $3 for the privilege.

After some thought I opted for the last contingency. Game time was drawing closer and I had had enough of dickering with Cincinnati's police force. So, not waiting for the irate officer to finish writing out the ticket, I wheeled my car around and hit the gas pedal. In the rear view mirror I saw him waving madly, standing there in the fumes of burnt rubber.

Inside the locker room I complained to John Murdough. "This idiot policeman's going to give me a ticket," I said, "he's still got my driver's license." Murdough just laughed. "Don't worry about it, Bob. Nothing will come of it."

Sure, right. About this time Johnson came hustling in. "I just talked to the captain who heads up the stadium police force," he reported, "and you know what he told me? He said that the guy who stopped you is new to the force, and he called him 'an absolute maniac.' "

"Fine," I said, "probably a former linebacker."

I'll tell you: Sometimes the glitter of being a professional football player was somewhat tarnished by the actions of a few dumbasses. I remember reading somewhere what Walt Disney said when asked what it was like being such a celebrity. "It's nice," he said, "but it doesn't do a bit to keep the fleas off my dog."

Now I know what Walt meant.

Our other two pre-season victories were against Detroit, 22-14 and New Orleans, 20-0.

Playing against the Lions was like being in a street brawl with a tribe of Cossacks. If league rules were to have suddenly changed to permit the use of brass knuckles, garrotes and chains, the Lions would have felt right at home. In all, their turbulent style of play against us cost them twelve penalties and one hundred yards. And, ultimately, the game.

After the game the Lion's head coach, Rich Forzano, told reporters that he was very disappointed in his team's bare-fisted tactics. He should have been. The Lions were then 1-4 on the year, and their season looked as if it were going to be a very long one indeed.

Forzano was a coach with the Bengals in our first year, and the one thing I remember about him is how hung up he was on us players always having our chinstraps fastened. "I once had a player," he told us during a practice, "who was running for a touchdown when all of a sudden he realized that his chinstrap was loose. So he slowed down to snap it up. A defensive man caught him from behind and we lost the game by that one touchdown."

From then on, we always made sure that our chinstraps were in good working order.

Yes, sir, that night we may have pounded the peanuts out of the Lions, but I'm willing to bet that, to a man, their chinstraps were snapped on tighter than a pair of newly washed jeans. Which goes to show you that there's no substitute for solid coaching.

Speaking of coaching, our P.B. pulled off quite a surprise. In the final month of pre-season, he picked up two real veterans to add to our squad. First he rescued from San Diego a 6'6", 285-pound mountain of a man named Bob Brown. Next he grabbed Maulty Moore, a weathered veteran from the Miami Dolphins. These two acquisitions gave us much-needed depth and experience—between the two of them Brown and Moore had played in four Super Bowls!

When Bob Brown introduced himself to us, he mentioned that he was a gourmet cook in his spare time and that he enjoyed eating his own concoctions. "Not long ago I was around 325 pounds," said Bob, as if to attest to his culinary prowess. "But now I'm down to a scrawny 285." He then turned to Ken Johnson, our defensive end, himself no slouch when it comes to size—we call him "Big-Un"— and asked about our workout routine.

Big-Un said, "Twice a week we are scheduled to work out on the Nautilus equipment for an hour or so."

"Nautilus," asked Bob Brown, "what's that?"

"Uh, well," said Big-Un, "it's sort of like weights and barbell equipment for strengthening muscles."

"Oh," replied Bob Brown, "I never lift weights."

We all just stopped and stared at him. He's bigger and stronger-looking that any *two* players we've ever had on the team...and he doesn't lift weights. Collectively, we gulped.

All except Suki Holland. He just smiled and said, "Right on, brother."

I think Jack Novak, our rookie tight end, could have testified to Bob Brown's abilities. As luck would have it, during a pass-rush drill we did, a drill that pitted an offensive player against a defensive player, Novak drew Bob Brown. He was absolutely mauled by the brute, bounced up and down on the AstroTurf like a beach ball. And after the drill he came limping off the field with raw, red knuckles and a bloodied nose. His helmet was perched atop his head in a strange, obtuse angle. "Hell," Jack said of Brown, "he ain't so tough." I think Jack was being facetious.

A few days later, our weightlifting specialist, Kim Wood, was telling us that defensive tackle Bill Kollar, a second-year man, could do 25 plates on the special bench press machine we had. That's about 400 pounds. Kim was explaining to us that no one else on the club could do as many plates as Bill Kollar when all of a sudden Maulty Moore walked in. Lackidaisically, he slapped *28* plates on the machine and did a half-dozen bench presses. Then he got up and walked away, hardly sweating.

We just looked at Kim Wood and whistled.

It was hard to predict just how much these two new additions would actually mean to our club that year. To tell you the truth, I was surprised we picked them up on waivers at all. Never before had Paul Brown picked up such high-salaried veterans who were fairly well up in years—Bob Brown, 35; Maulty, 29. And acquiring them so late in the exhibition season, too. PB was always a stickler for developing young talent from *within* the organization. Well, it definitely indicated a new direction for the Old Coach, and I had to think that he knew exactly what he was doing. Personally, I felt Brown and Moore were going to make a tremendous contribution to our drive toward the Super Bowl. I mean, I had to feel good about having new teammates that weren't measured with tape measures but with altimeters.

There were other positive signs late in that pre-season, too. Like fullback Boobie Clark, receiver Isaac Curtis, runningback Essex Johnson and even me (I had my best exhibition season with four TD receptions).

Clark seemed ready to play, down to where he should have been at 242. I could tell he was getting into mid-season form because the first three times he carried the ball against Buffalo three defenders had to be helped off the field. He always had had the potential, like in 1973 when he gained just under a thousand yards and was named the league's Rookie of the Year. But in '74 he reported to camp twenty pounds overweight, and because of the lengthy players strike that year, ended up being out of shape and broke his arm early in the season. But in '75 he seemed to be making a serious comeback, which was great because it was beautiful to watch him run. He moved extremely fast for a big man, with exceptional power and balance. There was a problem, though—Clark never learned to use his blockers. He just got the ball, buried his head and tried to bull his way through the opposition's defensive line all by himself. Alot of the time he just plowed right into the middle of the back of one of his own offensive lineman, which didn't endear Boobie to these people. He should have treated them more kindly. He never did realize that in his thousand yard season of 1973, Boobie made only five hundred of those yards himself while the offensive line made the other five hundred for him.

As far as Isaac Curtis was concerned, he finally showed why he was pro football's most gifted receiver this side of Paul Warfield. The last few pre-season games he really came on strong, pulling balls off his shoetops, easily out-distancing befuddled defensive backs. There wasn't a player alive who could keep up with Ike's blazing sprinter's speed. And he had those beautifully soft hands for catching a ball, hands so artistic they'd make a sculptor cry.

Ike had me worried, though. For the first six weeks of camp he was doggin' it bad and making noises like he didn't want to play ball anymore. Then he said his toe hurt and began sitting out practices in his shorts while the rest of us busted our fully-clad tails against blocking sleds. We began referring to any questionable injury as "Ike's Terminal Toe." I warned Ike to be careful. One of PB's main vexations was faked injuries—I was convinced Paul could sniff out malingerers during a plague. Superstar or not, you just didn't cross the Old Coach without suffering dire consequences. Bill Bergey crossed Paul once. Now he's in Philadelphia.

In the Packer game, the highlight of the night was the return to action of Essex Johnson, Ess, injured the previous year, only ran the ball four times, but it was enough to tell that his knee was completely healed. His first carry went for five yards, the second for fourteen, the third for ten (and a touchdown which was called back because of a holding penalty), and the fourth for fifteen yards and a touchdown (which wasn't called back). This final run was a beautiful piece of footwork, the kind of run we had been used to seeing the Express pull off. He caught a little flat pass from Kenny Anderson on the fifteen and, legs churning, body bent in that patented low-to-the-ground style, he twisted, turned, bobbed and weaved into the end zone, breaking three tackles en route.

To show you how much Essex meant to the team, all the Bengals on the field and on the sidelines stopped in their tracks and openly applauded Essex' performance. When the little halfback ran off the field after the last touchdown he had tears in his eyes. Why? It went back to an incident that happened on the second day of camp.

Believe it or not, Essex Johnson, one of the truly electrifying runners in the NFL, was cut from our squad! He was eating lunch and discussing the upcoming season with his good friend Isaac Curtis when the next thing he knew he was called into Paul Brown's office and—whoosh!—the big ax fell, loping off his livelihood.

Bob Johnson and I had been talking to a reporter when we heard the news. Bruce Coslet, my backup at tight end, came busting into the room with his face the color of alabaster. Out of breath, he said, "Did you hear about Essex?"

Johnson and I looked at each other blankly. "Essex? No, what happened?"

"He's been waived," Bruce said.

"*Waived?*" We literally leapt off our beds. At first we thought Coslet was pulling our legs, but one look at his nervous expression told us differently.

Man, it was hard to accept. Hey! Essex was a member of the elite fraternity, one of the six original Bengals remaining from 1968. (The others were Bob Johnson, Pat Matson, Al Beauchamp, Howard Fest and, of course, myself.) If they could cut Essex—probably the best player on the team—what could they do to us? I'll tell you, it was one uncomfortable feeling, and suddenly Johnson and I were a little uneasy about the high salaries we were making. Was a conspiracy afoot to purge the Old Guard—the ones pulling in heavy paychecks—from the team? Maybe economics alone would dictate who would stay and who would go that year.

It just didn't make sense.

Essex, an easy-going, likeable guy, had been *the* premiere runner in the history of the Bengal franchise. We called him the "Essex Express" or simply "E," and he was one of the fastest halfbacks I'd ever seen. In 1973 Essex gained 997 yards for us, teaming up with then-rookie Boobie Clark in the backfield for one of the best one-two punches around. ("E" had actually gone over the coveted one thousand-yard mark that year, but he was thrown for a loss on his last carry of the season.) Countless times I had watched in awe as the Express weaved through gargantuan defensive lines in that low-to-the-ground style of his and broke away for fifty-, sixty-, and seventy-yard touchdowns.

The odd thing was that only the day before he was waived Essex had been playing some aggressive tennis with a few of the coaches, and word quickly had spread around camp that his injured right knee, which sidelined him most of the previous year, was once again a hundred percent.

Obviously, Paul Brown had thought otherwise.

I'll tell you: afternoon practice that day was the quietest one in the history of our club. Nobody said a word. It was amazing, too, that all those muscle pulls which had been incurred during the forty-yard dashes were then strangely healed. And for the first time in memory the whirlpools stood alone and abandoned.

I didn't know how we were going to fill the void created by Essex' departure. At that point there was only one thing I was sure of—and that was that the famed Essex Express had made its last run in Cincinnati.

Shows you how much I knew, right?

I should have learned. After ten years in pro football under Paul Brown I now realize that when I was absolutely sure of something, I was usually wrong.

Guess who was in full uniform that next afternoon. That's right, the Essex Express.

It seemed that Essex, unbelievable as it sounds, managed to pass all twenty-five clubs on waivers and had renegotiated his contract with the Bengals. The money was the same, I understand, but there was a new clause. It stipulated that Essex would not seek legal action or disability claims against the club should he permanently damage his knee.

No one ever accused Paul Brown of not being shrewd. You've got to know that that special addendum to Essex' contract was what Paul was after all along. Beautiful, wasn't it? Man, pro football was becoming a game for corporate lawyers and fine print specialists. Paul Brown was just covering all bases, doing what any other corporate magnate would do to quash potential future litigation against the firm.

I'll say one thing, it was great to have the Essex Express back with us. And what kept me awake nights was trying to decide whether I wanted to spend my next Super Bowl check on a rectangular or liver-shaped pool in my backyard...

If the final month of the exhibition season had its positive moments, it also had its fair share of negatives. For example, there was the 30-20 loss to the Philadelphia Eagles.

Man, PB was really steamed.

It was a rare occasion that he singled out players for criticism. But during The Movies following the Eagles' game he went overboard to mention names of those who made mistakes. Normally Paul's personal comments were fairly general in nature, allowing the individual coaches to scold their particular players about mistakes—that's what they were paid for.

But not that time. PB really blasted some people. Fortunately, I wasn't one of them. That time.

I know what got to Paul. Simply, it was that the Philadelphia game was damn near like a scrimmage. They had on their roster almost as many Bengal players as we did. There was Bill Bergey, Horst Muhlmann, Wayne Clark, Stan Walters and Mike Boryla. Paul wanted to show them he hadn't made any mistakes in trading them.

Bergey, of course, was the most controversial trade. In 1974 he signed a contract to play in the WFL beginning in 1976. This didn't sit too well with Paul Brown, so the Old Coach traded Bergey to the Eagles. As it turned out, Bergey's WFL deal fell through and he signed a very nice contract with Philadelphia. This all worked out fine for everybody—except the Bengals. We were left without a middle linebacker; one that was pretty good, too. I said *pretty good* because that was all he was, and is. In 1974 he was named the best middle linebacker in the NFL, but that rating was somewhat overstated. I could name five or six middle linebackers in the league that were better than Bergey, but they lacked his nose for hyped-up, media-attracting antics and his flare for showmanship.

When I think of Bill Bergey the first image that comes to mind is that of Ebenezer Scrooge. I'll tell you, Bergey was one of the classic skinflints of all time. His pockets were so tight that the pieces of lint in them stood straight as pickup-stix. We used to kid him about how, each weekend before we left for an away game, he'd have the telephone company disconnect his phone so he wouldn't incur any excess charges. A favorite trick was to borrow a dime from a teammate each time he wanted to use the pay phone in Wilmington to call home. Only thing, Bergey wouldn't borrow just one dime, but five or six, from different players. He'd make his 10¢ call home and cache away the profits. Honestly, you would've thought the guy was poor as a coot.

Then there was Horst, or Herr Muhlmann, as we called him. Man, he was something else. You looked around the league and saw quality athletes busting ass to make a career of pro football and you respected their time, dedication and sacrifices they put into the game. Then you looked at Horst, and the only thing you could think was: "Is the whole thing a joke?"

Horst came to the Bengals from Germany where he was supposedly heralded as a national soccer hero. I always thought that contact was a great deal of the game of soccer, too, but you'd never know it to see how Horst handled himself on a football field. One of the funniest sights in professional football was Horst Muhlmann kicking off, then beating a hasty retreat for the sidelines so some player on the receiving team couldn't find him to throw a block. Some of the teams finally got wise to Horst's disappearance act and appointed one player to do nothing but chase him around the whole game. They knew that, if they could rattle him in the early going, it would probably pay of if the score was close at the end of the game. One time I saw a player chase Horst fifty or sixty yards in an attempt to get a block on him. It looked like a Barnum & Bailey circus act, where one clown chases another all over the place with what appears to be a bucket of water in his hands.

Horst used to report to summer camp weighing about 200 pounds, but because kickers don't have to attend our players' meetings he would spend all his off hours in a Wilmington bowling alley drinking beer (he call the "weisers") and eating cheese-and-bacon burgers. In three weeks he'd weigh 230.

I don't know if it was the language barrier or what, but Horst never did seem to catch on to American summer camp humor. One time after he had first joined the team, we decided to lock him in his room. When he realized he couldn't get out, he began pleading with us, saying that he had to go to the john. "Sorry, Horst," we said, "the door's stuck and we can't seem to get it open." After a few minutes we heard the sound of water splattering on the other side of the door. "What are you doing, Horst?" we asked. "I told you I had to go tinkle," he answered in a German accent. We opened the door and saw that he had urinated on the floor in the center of his room. Then he went off and told Paul Brown exactly what had happened, saying that he had had to "tinkle," and couldn't get out of his room.

There once was a great quote by Horst in *Sports Illustrated*. He was asked why he wasn't sure U.S. pro football would ever catch on in Europe. Said Horst: "It's hard to understand what is going on."

That's exactly how he played the game.

If the loss to the Eagles wasn't enough to get Paul's dander up, there was our activities with the players' union.

That's when it really hit the fan. Paul Brown flew into a rage over a players-only meeting we conducted, called by Pat Matson, our acting player rep. Herky had wanted to apprise us of recent action taken by the Minnesota Vikings, who voted to discharge Ed Garvey as head of the players' union. "We have to decide as a team," said Herky, "whether or not we want to take similar action."

You wouldn't have believed our meeting. Confusion was rampant: some players supported Garvey, some opposed him, and some didn't care one way or the other (and some just wanted to go out and get a beer). And the rookies—they never did understand what the hell was going on.

Finally, after a half-hour of uncontrolled "discussion," Herky put up his hands and said, "OK, OK, guys. It's obvious that we need more information on this issue." There was a general nodding of heads. "There's a players' association meeting Monday in Chicago. If there are no objections, I'll attend this meeting as acting player rep and get the details." There was no objection, except for someone who suggested that Bob Johnson go along, too, since he was the team captain. This was agreed upon unanimously. All of this was the easy part; the fur didn't start to fly until Matson and Johnson went to see Paul Brown. "We had a players' meeting tonight," Johnson said uneasily. "And we couldn't come to a decision as to whether or not to vote Ed Garvey out of office." "Yea," chipped in Herky, "and the team wants to send us to the players' association meeting in Chicago Monday so we can find out more about it."

There was a momentary silence. Then, according to reports, PB began to turn a scarlet hue, his lips began to tremble, and his eyebrows commenced to dance a jig on his forehead. When he could no longer contain himself, he burst out with, "Yea, you guys can go to Chicago; and for all I care you could keep on going and not come back here at all." He started to wheel them out of his room, then added, "And tonight's meeting was the last one you'll have on my premises. You'll have to go out and rent a hall for the next one."

With that the door slammed, and Matson and Johnson just stood there looking at one another.

There were several reasons why Paul was so upset. First, he hated Ed Garvey with a passion, which was not that surprising; all the club owners hated Ed Garvey. The fact that we, as a team, hadn't immediately voted Garvey out of office infuriated PB, who, in some sordid way, took our non-action as meaning there was at least an undercurrent of support for Garvey on the team. Secondly, our voting to send two players to the Chicago meeting was, to Paul, an indication that we were going to, once again, become active members in the affairs of the players' association. PB was a man accustomed to running his own show, with each little thing under his personal control; and he knew that no management would completely control players who acted in concert with association directives.

I kind of felt sorry for Paul Brown. Football used to be such a nice, simple, fun-loving game for him. Now there was more action in the courtrooms during the week than there was in the stadiums on Sundays.

The guy I *really* felt sorry for, though, was Pat Matson. He was gone in my mind, his fate sealed with an airline ticket to Chicago.

I wasn't wrong.

It happened during the Monday Movies. We were into the second quarter of the Detroit game when Mike Brown came into the room. Immediately the players suspected what he wanted and we all stared knives at him. As they say, "none love the messenger who brings bad news." We watched in silence as Mike approached Pat Matson, tapped him on the shoulder, and whispered something. Pat turned, looked up into Mike's square face and nodded. Then he got up and quietly followed Mike out of the room. When he left his face was white as a sheet.

It was going to seem strange, not playing football on Sundays with Pat Matson. Herky was a teammate for seven years. That would have been our eighth together had not Paul Brown traded him to the Green Bay Packers for "an undisclosed draft choice."

Herky was the last vestige of the Old Guard. He was one of the forty or so pro football veterans who came to the team in the special January 1968 expansion draft. Now none of those original forty remain. The only remnants of that first Bengal team were the five of us who were taken in the college draft held in the spring of '68. Each year our fraternity of original players became more elite.

In a way, Herky was a victim of his own bullheadedness. We constantly urged him to tell Paul Brown that, as our player rep, he was only acting as a front man for the rest of the players, that his actions were merely reflective of the team as a whole, and that he was

68

nothing more than an emissary attempting to keep team management abreast of the players' current thinking. But for some unknown reason, Herky always insisted on shouldering the entire players' union operation alone, openly accepting the consequences.

In 75' it caught up with him.

No doubt about it, his absence would be felt. Even now when I think of dedicated football players, I think first of Pat Matson. He was the only guy on the team who would get to practice an hour early just to lift weights and jog. And he would still be there long after everyone else had gone, lifting and jogging.

Herky had a higher threshold of pain than anyone else I've known. I remember a game in 1968 in which he broke his leg in the first quarter and continued to play on it the entire game—and as running messenger guard, too! X-rays were to later reveal a massive bone chip at the point where the shin bone meets the knee joint. You read how the old timers were so much rougher and tougher than today's player because they "played in pain"—broken fingers, sprained ankles, etc.—but I'll wager that there was not one of them who played three quarters of a game on a leg as badly broken as Pat Matson's was that day.

Lifting weights was Herky's religion, and his answer to any injury. If he had a dislocated finger, a hurt wrist or a twisted ankle, he'd go into the weight room, pile a ton of plates on a barbell, and do a lifting exercise that put direct pressure on the injury. Almost always the pain would disappear and he'd be ready to play again.

The only thing that irritated me about Herky was a tendency he had to play the bully. He was frequently giving a teammate a hard jab in the shoulder or a surprise slap in the stomach. It was always in a practical jokester-way, but with his strength it hurt like hell. A few years ago he caught me a good one in the gut and knocked the wind out of me. When I recovered I pointed a finger at him and said, "Damn it, Matson, the next time you do that I'm going to grab the closest thing in my reach—be it an end table, a chair, a shovel, whatever—and I'm going to bring it down across the top of your head with every ounce of strength I have." He was thoroughly amused, but he never bothered me after that.

It was odd how the absence of Pat Matson was first felt, not so much on the playing field but in the locker room before the New Orleans game. If there was one thing we could rely on it was having Herky be the first and loudest to speak when it came time to say the Lord's Prayer. "OUR FATHER," Herky would bellow out and the rest of us would fall in behind. Before the Saints' game, though, there was a general silence when PB said, "Let's bow our heads." Everyone was waiting for Pat Matson to begin but, of course, he never did. We just couldn't seem to get our timing down without him. I could see we were going to have to work on this part of our game. You never knew when we were going to need a real good

Lord's Prayer. Right before a Super Bowl game, perhaps?

I'll tell you: players threatening to strike, union negotiating, demands about this and that. It gave me an ill feeling, not that I felt sorry for management—no way. But you know who really suffers with all of that type of thing. The football fan, the very person whose hard-earned money ultimately built palatial stadiums, outfitted teams, and paid players' salaries. And so far the fan has had about as much to say in pro football matters as Telly Savalas has hair.

Football better watch out. I always felt civilians tended to view football players as immature, overpaid, subintelligent hedonists anyway. Most of the time players have been idly tolerated as over-grown peripheral members of the human race, lost somewhere between the ages of acne and spreading backsides, who do nothing more than get rich by playing a boys' game on Sundays. So when players begin to make demands for even more money, improved benefits, and better retirement plans, they should hardly be sur-prised if someday the fan determines this to be blatant greediness and suddenly draws the line at spending his money supporting football. Hell, who knows—maybe someday he'll boycott them!

After all, what football players must remember is that their livelihoods are really nothing more that selling entertainment to the public in the form of escapism. I don't want to downplay that aspect, because it's a lot more important than it sounds. For years pro football has been providing people a brief chance to forget—even if for a few hours—the compounding pressures of work (or lack of work), financial difficulties, family squabbles, crime in the streets, political coverups, wars and, yes, even presidential assassinations.

Even in times of economic hardships, attendance at many professional sporting events has continued to keep pace, most likely because people, if they have to, will do without almost anything except their fun. The public demands to be entertained and, until recently, professional football had met that demand quite adequately.

When you think about it, football affords the fan the unusual opportunity to channel unused energies, release pent-up aggres-sions, feel in a world impersonally large and complex a sense of identity with a team or certain player. In short, the fan has been willing to subsidize the players in return for a 22-man show featuring brutality, immediacy, excitement, and something that is happening *now*.

I doubt whether professional football will ever be successful in getting two belligerent nations to sign a peace agreement, and I doubt whether we will manage to feed starving people around the world, but I do feel that we are just one societal element that ultimately serves a public need, in its own small way.

My real fear is that once football doesn't provide that escapism, once it begins to merely mirror the daily bickering, the strikes, the aggressions, the greed and the dozens of other distasteful things that the fan experiences every day in his hum-drum world—it will have ceased to serve its purpose, it will cease to be entertaining. And that's when the fan is going to say, "The hell with it all, who needs this. If I want to get involved with the problems and politics of big labor dealings I'll go out and search a river for Jimmy Hoffa's body. But I sure as hell ain't going to pay $12.50 a ticket for the privilege to do it!" Yep, maybe it will be like Harry Nilsson says in his song, "...and the Rainmaker passed his hat to the people, but the people all turned away."

You know, if it ever came to that, pro football would have only itself to blame.

But back to when Herky was cut:

When Mike Brown interrupted the Movies to summon Pat, he whispered only three words. But they were three words that could bring a grown man to his knees: "Bring your playbook." It meant that you'd been cut from the team, or, as Paul Brown euphemistically put it, "You were being given the opportunity to go out and get started in your life's work."

The phrase could have come at any time—after breakfast or late at night. There'd be a knock on the door, and a coach would say, "Paul Brown wants to see you. Bring your playbook." Some players refused to answer the door when they heard that knock, others tried to hide in closets or shower stalls. It didn't matter. The "Turk," as we called him—the ominous sword-swinging specter of instant unemployment—inevitably got his man.

Aside from Herky, the Turk snarfed up another good friend— Steve Chomyszak, the practical joker with the infectious laugh.

I hated to see him go; Chomy was a real lift for the team. It was just a matter of Chomy, who first joined the Bengals in '68, having the years catch up with him. He was still strong as a bull, but he had lost a step or two in quickness. Our rookies—like Gary Burley— were younger and faster. And commanded lower salaries.

For me, the saddest thing about seeing Chomy go was that I was losing another good friend. That was the unsavory part of pro football. You quickly formed close friendships and just a quickly they were forcibly broken. I guess it was like anything else—the Old Guard must step aside to make way for the new.

I used to have a recurring nightmare of walking out on the practice field one day and seeing a bunch of strange, new players in our Bengal uniforms. Not one was recognizable, and they were all the same in appearance—young, lithe, eager-eyed. And they looked at me with hungry, grinning faces as if to say, "Your time has come, Trumpy, step down. We're taking your job away from you."

I talked to Wayne Walker about his retirement from the Detroit

Lions. Said Wayne, an All-Pro linebacker and a sports announcer for CBS: "I decided to retire the day I realized I didn't have a single old friend left on the team. I felt I still had some good years in me, but I just didn't belong any more. I still wanted to go out nights and have a few beers with the boys, but all the younger players just wanted to sit around and smoke dope. It was depressing as hell."

One thing for sure, I'm glad as hell I got out when I did, after the '78 season. For the most part, I haven't missed it a bit.

One player cut didn't bother Bob Johnson at all. Bob was in real pain. He could hardly walk because his testicles hurt so much. "That damn Gary Sheide," he said referring to our rookie backup quarterback, "he was going to ruin my love life." It seemed that every time Sheide went to take a snap, he put his hands way under Johnson, resting the top of his left hand against the center's scrotum. As he barked out the signals, he brought his hands up hard each time there was a "hut," as if to emphasize the word. The final "hut" would be the worst, because he rammed his hands up quick and hard against Johnson to receive the ball. At best, it destroyed Johnson's concentration on his blocking assignment.

"With Kenny Anderson it was different," Johnson said. "He placed his hands higher up on my butt and he worked them in concert with me, in a smooth manner." My roommate said he was thinking about complaining to the coaches and refusing to take any more snaps from Sheide. "Hell," he said, "I wouldn't have needed that vasectomy had I known what type of quarterback Gary Sheide was."

Because of all the cuts, some of our borderline rookies were beginning to wear that hollow-eyed look. Somehow they knew: they were marked men. The thought scared the hell out of them. Think of it—one day they were sipping the Elysian nectar of professional football, then next they'd be selling insurance in Posaic. It had to be a helpless, sinking feeling, being so very close to big money and prominence at an age when most guys were struggling to get by, then—*swish*—the sound of the Turk's lethal sword started to hiss about their heads.

What was sad was most of those rookies had been groomed for a life in professional football since high school days. For the past eight years they had been hand-fed and coddled for that glorious day when they would present themselves to the waiting world of the NFL. And then it'd be over for them.

A pro scout will tell you he knows everything there is to know about a player. Like a farmer carefully breeding special beef cows, scouts will observe a football prospect from calfhood to maturity. He knows how the player has matured physically and emotionally from high school through college. He has memorized how the player reacts in certain situations, how he spends his off time, who his friends are and, if pressed, with which hand he wipes his butt.

Hardly ever did an unknown make it in the NFL. Of course, there were exceptions, the most notable one—me.

I was an oddball, a freak, a glove with six fingers. I was a guy out of football for two years who was working a nine-to-five job who, through a weird set of circumstances, somehow found himself in the NFL. I simply didn't fit the mold for the stardom in this game, and that I ever came to be drafted defies even the most lenient laws of probability. The Trumpy road to the Bengals was paved with five years of such happenstance that it would boggle the mind of a science fiction writer. To wit:

In the spring of 1964, when I was a freshman at the University of Illinois, four fraternity brothers and I jumped into a car and aimed for Daytona Beach, Florida—as red-blooded collegians were often wont to do around Easter time. At daybreak we were driving down the main highway looking for a place to stay when my eyes landed on a small motel called the Safari. In the parking lot there was a guy operating a tractor, scooping up a five-foot mound of beer cans from the previous night's festivities. Right then I applied the brakes and said, "Hold it, guys. *That's* the place we want to stay."

After registering (claiming only one occupant, of course) and downing a few beers, we headed for the beach to toss the football. In a few minutes a nice-looking guy approached and introduced himself as a quarterback for some semi-pro team, the Orlando Panthers or something. Then he asked me if I would run some pass patterns for him. "There's a pro scout staying up at that motel," he said, pointing to the Safari, "and I want to impress him."

For a half-hour my new acquaintance threw passes and I ran under them. Eventually satisfied that he had sufficiently impressed whomever it was he was supposed to be impressing, the quarterback thanked me and walked away. For my part, I headed for the coolness of the motel pool, where my friends were waiting. One look and I could tell they were all abuzz about something.

"There were two guys up here watching you play catch," said one of my friends.

"Watching me?" I asked, puzzled. "They were supposed to be watching that quarterback."

"Didn't seem too interested in him," offered another fraternity brother. "They just asked us your name. And we told them who you were."

"Yea," a third piped in, "and one of the guys wore a gigantic pro football championship ring on his finger."

Years later I found out that the guy wearing the "gigantic pro football championship ring" was Sid Gillmam, then head coach of the San Diego Chargers. The man with him on that day was named Al LoCasale, a Charger scout. (Remember the name Al LoCasale—it will pop up again later.) It turned out that Gillman and LoCasale were conducting a football clinic in Daytona Beach that very week;

they stayed at the Safari because it was owned by Bud Asher, also a San Diego scout.

Now, shooting ahead two years—past my six college games at Illinois, past my hand injury and hospitalization, past my flunk notice, past my three jobs and past my stay in California:

It was now a Saturday night late in 1966 and we were at the Astrodome in Houston. The University of Utah was playing its last game of the season against the University of Houston. As always, Utah looked pathetic, except for one player—Bob Trumpy. He scored three touchdowns and personally accounted for all of his team's TDs.

In the stands at that game was Al LoCasale and he turned to a guy and said, "If I'm not mistaken, that Trumpy boy played at Illinois a few years ago."

Al was still with the Chargers then. He had accompanied the pro team to Houston because the Chargers and Oilers were scheduled to play a game in Rice Stadium the very next day, Sunday. On a lark, he had decided to take in the Saturday night college game for some relaxation.

Another year passed—it was now 1967—and the college draft was being held by the pro football teams. It was down to the lowly 12th round and Cincinnati Bengals' head coach Paul Brown was trying to decide whom to select. He said he wished he could get another receiver on his expansion club roster. The man next to him was a new man of PB's staff, and he had a suggestion. "I don't even know the whereabouts of this boy or even if he's still in the United States, but one time in Florida and a few years later in Houston I had a chance to see him catch a football. His name is Bob Trumpy and I think he could be a pro prospect." The man offering advice to Paul Brown was none other than Al LoCasale; he had recently left the San Diego team to join the Bengals as director of player personnel.

And so, because of a single out-of-the-blue suggestion by one man, my name was submitted by the Bengals in the college draft. The rest, you know, is history.

Hard to believe? It was pretty scary, really, and I still find myself playing the "What-If" game. Like—What if I hadn't gone to Florida with my fraternity brothers? What if we hadn't decided to stay at the Safari Motel? What if the semi-pro quarterback hadn't asked me to play catch? What if Sid Gillman and Al LoCasale hadn't been holding a football clinic in Daytona Beach at the time? What if they hadn't also stayed at the Safari? What if I hadn't ended up at the University of Utah? What if Al LoCasale hadn't attended the Utah-Houston college game that Saturday night in Rice Stadium? What if I had had a bad game? What if Al LoCasale hadn't later joined the fledgling Cincinnati franchise? What if he hadn't remembered my name and suggested it to Paul Brown in the 12th round of the 1967 draft?

What if, what if—

I'll tell you, the doubts could drive you crazy. I do know that, if all of these ten events hadn't occurred exactly as they did, in their very particular time sequence, I'd probably still have been running around the alleyways of Watts trying to collect past due bills.

The thought struck fear.

The busiest season for the Turk was our first year, 1968. Back then, we had about two hundred guys trying out for forty-seven roster spots; so there were one hundred sixty players who had to be eventually weeded out. We had some guys who would fly in from New York or California, run the 40-yard dash for time, then head right back to the airport to fly home again. It created a real uncomfortable atmosphere because you didn't know who to forge close friendships with because chances were that he'd be gone the next day. We used to lay in our beds at night and listen to the dozens of knocks on the dormitory doors and the whispering voices which said, "Bring your playbook."

There were so many knocks that first year you'd have thought Wilmington College was hosting a training seminar for Fuller Brush salesmen. Knock, knock, knock, up and down the hall, door after door. And on those days that the coaching staff made wholesale cuts—jeez, it sounded damn near like thunder in the hallways. I figured the coaches had to be carrying around tweezers and bandages in those days, their knuckles had to be full of splinters and swollen the size of turnips.

As far as I know, the first guy ever to get cut from the Bengals was a defensive back from Arizona named Wally Scott. My luck: Wally Scott was my first roommate.

I had gotten in at midnight, about nine hours before training camp was to officially open in 1968.

The lights were off in the room trainer Marv Pollins had directed me to, but through the shadows I was able to make out a lump in one of the two beds. My roommate had already called it a night, I realized, probably wanting to get a full rest before camp began that next day. The first I ever saw Wally Scott was the next morning. He was putting on a tee-shirt when I rolled over. "Hi'ya," I said. "My name's Bob Trumpy, a receiver from L.A."

He came over and extended his hand. "Wally Scott," he said, "defensive back, University of Arizona in Tucson. I was just leaving to go over for breakfast. Like to come along?" I suggested that I'd take a quick shower and meet him over at the cafeteria.

On the way over, following my shower, I saw coming toward me my new roommate. I watched the squat, square frame approach in easy strides. Outside in the sunlight he looked a lot smaller than he did in the room.

"Hey, roomie," I said as he pulled up even to me. "You finished breakfast already?"

"Yea," he answered, and I noticed a perceptible gleam shift into his eyes. "Man, do they ever feed you here. I've never seen so much food in my life. Mounds of it, all for the asking."

"Hey, listen, Wally," I offered, taking a step toward the cafeteria, "I'm going to catch a quick bite. Afterwards, I'll come back to the room and we can have a chance to get acquainted before the meeting."

"Fine," he nodded. "I'll be waiting for you."

I'll be waiting for you—that's exactly what he said.

Jeez, how wrong can a guy be?

Of course I didn't realize it then, but Wally Scott's parting statement has to rank right up there with "Honestly, Sir, I'm convinced the Edsel can't miss; the nation will eat it up."

By the time I had wolfed down a half dozen eggs and enough rolls and milk to feed a village of Korean orphans for a month, Wally Scott had upped and packed and was on his way home!

I mean the dude had cleared out. Gone. Vanished. Without a trace.

Naturally I had expected to find him roaming around our room, preparing for our first team meeting. But when I opened the door, I was greeted by nothing more than four blank walls, barer than a pornographic filmstar's bottom.

Feebly, I grabbed my bed for support. What had happened? I mean, summer camp hadn't even begun yet! The meeting to officially kick off the season was still fifteen minutes away!

Accounting for the three-hour time difference I knew existed between Arizona and Ohio, I realized that Wally Scott, who left his home only hours before and traveled 2,000 miles to make his mark on professional football, would be back home *before the people he just said good-bye to were even out of bed for their morning coffee.*

It was a grim awakening.

If they could cut Wally Scott *just on the way he ate breakfast,* what could they do to me—let me go because I brushed my teeth in up and down strokes?

Oddly, one thought kept reoccurring. And that was: all else aside, I had to admit that Wally Scott was one of the world's great packers. He had managed to pack up shirts, pants, razor blades—everything—and be out the door and on his way back to Tucson before I had a chance to finish my breakfast. It could have well gone down as one of the fastest getaways in professional football. In the years that followed, during the "remember-who" trivia games we played to wile away the sterile nights of summer camp, I would dust off my Wally Scott story and lay it on the newcomers to our group. It never failed to raise eyebrows of disbelief or elicit whistles of appreciation. None of the other veterans on our club had even met

Wally since he was only with us for an eight-hour catnap and a bite to eat. And I had to continually fetch our trainer Marv Pollins to corroborate my story.

And so, like so many before it, another pre-season came to an end, not vastly different from the others—the hard work, the sore muscles and bruises, the bull sessions at night, the horseplay, the fights, the wide-eyed rookies and season-wise veterans who came and went. And the homesickness for family and friends.

At the end of it all, Paul Brown called us together for a little talk. "We have a good team here," Paul said, then he paused to amend his statement. "We have a *very, very* good team here. I really believe that if you cut down on your mental mistakes and if you play together the way I know you can, I think we are going to make a very sincere run at the Big Brass Ring."

PB's reference was of course to the Super Bowl. In all my years of exhibition seasons, I had never before heard Paul be so open, so positive and so optimistic about his feeling for that team and the chances that year of winning it all.

When we broke camp, we were really geared up to open the regular season against our rivals, the Cleveland Browns, at Riverfront Stadium.

It was what we had been working toward for the previous ten weeks.

HEADING FOR BATTLE

Seems the Turk was never finished. Surprisingly, right before the opener with Cleveland, Bob Maddox, the farmboy from Maryland, was cut.

I guess the end was foreseeable the day we acquired on waivers the two veteran tackles, Bob Brown and Maulty Moore. After Maddox' drug-selling problems PB said he would give him a second chance with the club, and he did, but, apparently, Mad Dog just couldn't produce when it counted.

Mad Dog got his nickname because of his ferocious style of play. Unfortunately, it was not always during a Sunday game that he played with such animal abandon—sometimes it was on the practice field during the week. I called this style of player a "Thursday Hero."

Thursday Heros were nothing more than misplaced zealots, really, players whose timing was either sadly out of kilter or who were innocent victims of faulty bio-rhythms or something. Whatever it was, these guys inexplicably played their football games on *Thursdays* rather than on Sundays like the rest of us.

Generally, Thursdays were pretty slow. The hard physical preparation had wound down and the mental preparation was just beginning. On Thursdays, the offense spent most of the day running the Sunday opponent's plays for the defense. Everyone went about three-quarters speed so no one got injured for the upcoming game. Everyone, except the Thursday Hero. On that day of the week he really came loaded for bear, ready to go full tilt every step of the way. It was like he had a large, cumbersome burr in his jockstrap or something. Psyched up, taped up, padded up—and sometimes even pilled up—the Thursday Hero waged relentless war against the unseen enemy, namely, his own teammates. He'd hit you with sadistic zeal, curse you, expectorate on you, intimidate you, and pick a fight with you. He'd yell, scream, rant, shout and exhort on his own unit with the same fervor Teddy Roosevelt surely must have deployed in his charge up San Juan Hill. In the proper time frame, this style of aggressive play could set a head coach to drooling all over the sideline markers. Trouble was, on Thursdays it was woefully out of time. Depending on your viewpoint, it was either four days too late (for the previous Sunday's game) or three days too soon (for the upcoming game).

The first of the Bengals' Thursday children was a guy we had in 1968 named Bill Kendricks.

We dubbed him "Captain Mean" because of his felonious brand of football. Captain Mean was a 6'4", 285-pound sixth-round draft choice out of Alabama A & M. To see him operate on a Thursday you'd of thought he was the most awesome defensive tackle ever to play the game. Even now the recollection of Captain Mean's Thursday Special—the quick forearm shiver to the throat— sends chills racing through me. Exactly why this seemingly All-Pro candidate played like this on Thursdays and not on Sundays is beyond me, but I do know that it really made Bob Johnson mad as hell. While everyone else on the squad looked forward to Thursday's three-quarters pace, Bob had to go all out, just to defend himself from this half-crazed freak of warped timing across from him. Every play Captain Mean would be there, trying to take Bob's head off, and my roomie's body usually looked far worse after a Thursday practice than it did after even the most physical of Sunday games.

Bob Maddox brought the problem of dealing with a Thursday child closer to home. He nearly sidelined *me* right before our most important game of the 1973 season.

We were driving for the divisional championship that year. Only the tough Cleveland Browns stood in our way. The whole season had really built to this one game. Even if the divisional title hadn't been on the line, it would have been a big football game—*all* the Bengal-Browns games are big.

On the Thursday before the Cleveland game, we, the offense, were running the Browns' favorite plays for the defense. We were going about three-quarters speed, as usual. Late in practice, I was releasing downfield on a pass pattern, and as I passed by Mad Dog Maddox, he gave me a merciless elbow shot right in the back of the neck. It landed directly on the soft spot just beneath where the helmet ends. In an instant I was down on my knees. The pain was unbelievable. Shock waves shot up my spine and radiated through both shoulders and out my arms to the fingertips. My hands went totally numb. I thought I was paralyzed, but, gradually, my head cleared and I was helped onto my feet and into the clubhouse.

For the next two days I couldn't even move my neck despite countless hours of whirlpool baths and diathermy treatments. But I knew I couldn't miss Sunday's game, so I talked Marv Pollins into fixing me up with a special neck brace, which he did. It was uncomfortable as hell, but as it turned out I played a pretty good game and made a few receptions. Best of all, we won, 34-17, but no thanks to Mad Dog Maddox. Later I asked him why he had done it, and he just shrugged and said he was "playin' hard."

Funny thing about Thursday Heros: they never seemed to be around too long. It was pretty easy to be a standout during practice when everyone was going three-quarters speed and you were going all out. But several coaches weren't half as dumb as they appeared. They had learned to be result-oriented, to grade performance on only one day—Sunday. They realized that it really didn't matter what you looked like in practice on Thursday. The proof of the pudding was what you did on that field during a game.

As I recall, Captain Mean lasted a season or so before moving on. And Mad Dog left in 1975, on a Monday. If management had had any feel for the ironic, they would have waited until Thursday to release him.

Once the final cuts had been made, Johnson and I sat down to take a hard look at our entire roster. We both came to the same conclusion: barring injuries, we were going to be one heck of a team to reckon with. We were strong at virtually every position and we had a well-set blend of rookies and veterans, of passing and ground attack, of quick-strike and grind-it-out offense, and of stubborn, bend-but-not-break defense.

I didn't see how we could miss getting into the playoffs. The one possible stumbling block was that the Pittsburgh Steelers, the top-rated team in our Central Division and the reigning Super Bowl champions, had a schedule easy as a fast-talking streetwalker. Their only tough games were the two against us and one against the Rams, on the last day of regular season play. We may have had to get into the playoffs as the Wild Card team and then meet Pittsburgh (for the third time that season) for a shot at the AFL championship and the Super Bowl—but if that is what it would have taken to get there, that's what we were determined to do.

Of the nine rookies to make the squad that year, the most heartening to me was little Brad Cousino. You really had to admire him—all of his life people told him he was just too small to play football. Yet there he was, a Cincinnati Bengal. In the pro draft, teams passed by the 5′10½″, 210-pound Cousino with the haughtiness of a dowager passing a beggar in the street. Just too small to play in "the bigs," scouts said. Disappointed he wasn't selected, Brad called fellow Miami alumnae Paul Brown and asked for a look-see as a free agent with the Bengals. Fortunately for Brad, PB agreed. Brad soon became the leading "headhunter" on our special teams. His nickname was Kami-Cousie.

To be frank, Brad made me feel slightly guilty. His whole life had been a continuously dedicated, uphill battle, one arduous attempt to refute the charges that he couldn't do this or that.

It was never like that for me. Quite the opposite, as a matter of fact. My large frame and innate athletic talents carried me along without me having to apply a lot of hard work and dedication. Things almost came too easily for me, really. I experienced a tremendous amount of success yet somehow averted the grueling and obligatory sacrifices that were supposed to go along with it.

Take, for example, my senior year in high school. I was a track man, a hurdler and a high-jumper. During one of our big meets, our number one long-jumper, Dave Marko, was warming up for his event when suddenly he pulled a leg muscle. Our coach, Artie Cochran, was beside himself—he had counted on Marko's ability to win us some competition points. Worse, if nobody else from our team could compete in the event—and there apparently was no one else who could—our team would lose valuable entry points, and perhaps the track meet because of it. I was warming up for my high-jump competition when Artie approached me. "You gotta help out, Bob," he said. "Dave Marko has pulled a muscle. I need someone to take his place right now and enter the long-jump competition. Do you think you could handle it, as well as the hurdles and the high-jump?"

Sure, I told him, but added that I knew nothing about the event.

"Just run up to where the board is in the ground," Artie advised me, "then jump as far as you can. Just try to relax."

Obligingly I agreed to participate, and I did a few deep knee bends, took off my sweatsuit and took off running for that board. I hit it with my body relaxed, as Artie suggested, and flew through the air 22'7" before once again touching down. I set a city record.

Two weeks later at a state track finals I jumped 23'4¾" and became the new Illinois state long-jump champion.

Amazing, I know. And it was something that I couldn't really explain. It seemed most of my achievements in life had been that way. Things by force of circumstance just seemed to happen to me without my consciously willing them or working very hard for them. Believe me, I was not complaining about it. It just seemed so unfair to a guy like Brad Cousino.

Before the Browns' game, we spent the night in a downtown hotel, as was custom. Paul Brown was the first pro coach to implement the concept of gathering all the players in a downtown hotel the night before a game for dinner and a movie. I found it a little degrading. Here I was a 30-year-old husband and father of two and I found myself forcibly separated from my family who was at home, alone, just ten miles due north—and what was I doing? I was going to the movies with forty-three hairy brutes who, with the possible exception of Tommy Casanova, were far less attractive than my wife. The intent of this gathering of us players downtown was to assure that we didn't somehow get hurt around home the night before a game, and so that we kept our minds relaxed and full of comradeship. Actually, it kept our minds full of horniness. (Although Paul's never said as much, I suspected that he kept us down there because he frowned upon us having sex with our wives, or anyone

82

else for that matter, the night before a game. After all, an orgasm could sap our strength for the next day's combat, could it not?)

What that Saturday night ritual was really supposed to do was establish a pattern, a discipline, a feeling of familiarity of living and cooperating with one another on all levels, so that, when we got out on the field, we would know *exactly* what the guy next to us was thinking and how he was going to react in a given situation. Football is a *team* sport.

Still, I found it demeaning. Especially since PB only allowed us to see "G" rated flicks, and those were few and far between. I was the only father on my block who saw all the new Walt Disney movies before his two sons.

I bet if Paul had had his druthers, he'd have druthered that we not only spent Saturday nights downtown in a hotel together, but all the other nights of the week, too. My guess was that PB was afraid that, left alone, we players were going to do something stupid that would eventually hurt the team. Well, that would happen from time to time, sure. In any business. But, in the main, pro football players went out of their way to keep from getting in trouble.

Paul always particularly stressed that we players do absolutely nothing on Fridays before a game. At all costs, we were to avoid situations in which we could sustain a Friday injury which would jeopardize our availability to play on Sunday. No speeding around in fast cars, no playful wrestling with wife and kids, no mowing the lawn in the fall (he'd actually had guys cut off toes on Saturdays before Sunday games).

I wish I would have listened to Paul back in 1969. On the Friday before the big Oakland game, Chip Myers and I went out to a rural area north of Cincinnati to ride trail bikes with Howard Fest and Eric Crabtree.

About dusk we were tooling down a tree-strewn hill and as I worked my way through some tall grass I suddenly hit something that nearly split my leg apart. It was one of those triangular iron fence posts that had been embedded in the ground. My left leg hit the side of that iron post that had jagged teeth protruding from it. I was going about fifty miles an hour when we collided, and the initial impact was so forceful, so ripping, that the pain was only instantaneous. After that, my leg went totally numb.

The incident cost me thirty painful stitches.

And by the next morning my ankle had swollen to three times its normal size; it was grossly discolored, too, in a spectrum of yellows and purples. Man, I was scared to death. I knew that if Paul Brown were to find out how I came to injure myself he would have me hung from the nearest goalpost.

Saturday morning as I hobbled into our training room, I buttonholed our trainer and said, "Marv, put down whatever you're doing. I'm going to need your undivided attention from now until game time tomorrow."

"What do you mean?" Marv inquired.

"Just this." I unwrapped the bandages so he could get a close look. When he saw my ankle his face turned ashen.

"Oh, Jesus," he said. "How the hell did you do *that*?"

"Uh," I said.

"What was that?"

"Uh," I repeated, trying desperately to force words past the swelling in my throat. "Uh, you see, Marv, I was, uh, hiking in some foothills last evening when my foot slipped and I fell down this cliff. I caught my ankle on some jagged rocks."

Man, I hated like hell to lie to him. But what else was I going to do? One word about riding motorcycle at fifty miles an hour through grassy foothills at dusk and my career with the Bengals was over.

"I'm going to have to tell Paul about this," Marv advised me, and with that he turned and padded his way out of the room toward PB's office. The look in his eye told me that he was as fearful of breaking the news to The Coach as I would have been.

There were two doors to our training room. One went directly to a hallway which led to the coaches' offices. This was the one through which Marv Pollins disappeared. The other doorway led to the players' locker room. When I looked over to this one I saw forty quiet heads straining to see and hear what was going to happen. Right up front were the heads of Howard Fest, Chip Myers and Eric Crabtree. They were sweating profusely, as I was. If Paul bought the hiking accident story, they were scot free. If he didn't, we'd all go down the tubes together.

Marv had only been gone about forty-five seconds, but it seemed like a weekend. The training room was deathly quiet and at once seemed bright and stifling. My head ached something fierce.

Suddenly, from the direction of PB's office, came a piercing shout, and forty-one heads—mine and the forty others in the doorway—bolted stiffly upright.

"BULLSHIT." It was PB's voice, no doubt about it. "Bullshit," again, and then footsteps hurried down the hallway toward the training room. Instinct told me to turn and run at that moment, but I realized I wouldn't be able to get very far on my wounded ankle.

When Paul appeared in the doorway, his face was red and bitter. The veins stuck out on his forehead like cornfield furrows. He stopped short of entering the room and observed the injury from the doorway. "What you did was pure bullshit, mister," he yelled. "Look at that thing. God, that's awful." In seven years I'd never seen him any angrier than he was at that very moment.

"How could you be so damned stupid, Trumpy?" he screamed in a high-pitched voice. "I warned you—*everybody*—about being careful on Fridays and Saturdays. Now you do this to yourself."

84

"Coach," I began, weakly, "it's going to be OK. I'll be ready to go tomorrow."

"Bullshit," he said again. "You can't play on that thing tomorrow. Marv tells me you got about twenty-five or thirty stitches in there."

"Well, that was true, Coach," I offered, "but I'll be ready to play anyway. I'll have it padded up. You'll see. Just wait til tomorrow."

I didn't recall whether he said the word bullshit again, I guess it was entirely possible. But he did shoot me one of those icy stares he specialized in before turning and stomping away. The door to his room slammed shut with a jarring bang.

With sweat dripping from every pore, I sat back and sighed. The worst was over. PB apparently had bought the story about hiking in the foothills. Man, was he upset. He was a man who cursed very seldom, but on this occasion he was doing precious little to delete expletives.

Of course I didn't practice that day—I spent most of the time feeling sorry for myself. It didn't help much, and that night I put myself to bed in the downtown hotel early. I set the alarm for 5:30, and when it went off I got up and began to walk the hallways. Up and down, up and down, hour after hour, until, finally, I reached a point where circulation was beginning to come back to my ankle. It still throbbed like blazes, but when I entered the breakfast room about 8:30, I made a point of walking tall and happy. As I passed by the table where Paul Brown was sitting with some coaches, I displayed what I thought was a near-natural gait and smiled gingerly. "See, Coach," I said, "I told you I'd be good as new this morning."

He just looked up at me for a moment then went back to buttering his toast.

I was doing all right on that misproportioned ankle of mine until our pre-game meeting. The meeting lasted about twenty-five minutes, and when I finally stood to leave the room, it was as though someone had hit me in the ankle with a very large mallet. With no circulation moving through it for nearly a half hour, my ankle stiffened considerably and it buckled under the weight of my first step. Fortunately, a teammate—I don't remember who—was standing close by and I grabbed onto his shoulder for support. "For Pete's sake," I whispered to him, "help me outta this damn place. I can't walk a step on this ankle." With that, we threw an arm around each other's shoulder and bounded out the door under Coach Brown's everpresent gaze.

In the dressing room, a team doctor took a look at the ankle and whistled. It was bleeding all over the place. "I can't let you play today," he told me. But I wouldn't have it. "It'll be OK, Doc," I said, "just put a lot of tape and gauze on it." Against his better judgment, he conceded.

Concerned about my injury, a teammate—I won't mention his

name—approached me just before we went out on the field for warm-up drills.

"Hey, Trump," he said, "what's happenin', man."

"Not much," I replied solemnly. "I sure wish this ankle of mine would quit throbbing so. It's driving me up the wall."

My teammate smiled at me. "Well, you're in luck, my man," he said. "I'm going to cure all your ills. I got something right here that's just going to make you forget all about the lame ankle of yours."

"Yea?" I said, suspicious that anything could allow me to "forget" the pain.

"Yea." He opened his large hand, and in it I saw five oblong pills, bright orange in color. They were big pills, each about three or four times the size of an aspirin tablet. "Try some Wheaties, Trump," he said.

"Wheaties?"

"Sure, man," he grinned, "you know, Wheaties: the Breakfast of Champions."

My first reaction, of course, was, no. I had never taken a pep pill for football before, and I was fairly ignorant about the effects. I knew that some of the guys on the team used pills of one sort or another before games, but I didn't know what kind, what they were expected to do for you or anything else about them. I contemplated refusing my teammate's offer, but then I began to think: *What do I have to lose? I'm already banged up so bad I can hardly walk. The pills sure as heck aren't going to mess me up anymore than I am right now. Right?*

So, with slight reservation, I took a pill from my friend.

He wanted me to take two or three, said he usually took five or six before a game. I told him, no, I was a beginner and I thought I should take it easy the first time around. I ended up taking only half a tablet.

By the second quarter I was on cloud nine, really spaced out. It was a horrible feeling of not being able to control one's actions. I literally floated through the game, but I did make a few catches and generally contributed to a big Bengal win over the highly favored Oakland team.

After the game the doc looked at my ankle and said I had ripped out about a third of the stitches. (At one point in the game I had gone up for a ball and the defensive back made one of those gangbuster ankle-tackles on me—the kind that draws *oohs* from the crowd and gets replayed Friday nights on the *Johnny Carson Show*. I thought I was going to pass out, the pain was so great.) The doc did some quick repair work, but I really didn't recall too vividly what else went on in the clubhouse. I was in a deep haze most of the time.

As a post-script to this incident, I might add that my wife Pat had invited a high school friend of mine to our house for dinner that night. He was from Springfield and was then attending the University of Kentucky medical school. He brought three of his medical student friends—never opposed to a free meal—along with him. So, there we sat, six of us, talking about the game. I should say the five of *them*. Me? I was totally oblivious to what was being said. For all I knew there was only myself and my now-again throbbing ankle in our dining room. And I guess what happened next I will never be able to fully understand, maybe it's what they call "coming down hard." Because for no apparent reason, I sat there and began to cry. Uncontrollably. Tears just streamed down my face. Like a baby, I cried and cried and cried. Not once since that time did I take anything stronger than an aspirin before playing a professional football game, no matter how badly an injury was bothering me.

In the locker room before the opener against the Browns, the players were quieter than usual. I didn't know the reason; perhaps it was because suddenly there was the realization that *the season was about to officially begin*!

Players spend their pre-game moments mentally preparing in individual ways. In Bengal land there were no flamboyant speeches or pep rallies to get us psyched up. PB believed that type of thing was for college games and not the pros. "You all know your jobs," he advised us, "and as mature young men you ought to be able to get yourselves ready for a game."

He never mentioned why, if we were "mature young men," we all had to spend the night together before a game and see only "G"-rated movies. And none of us bothered to ask him.

PB swore to writers that the Cleveland game was "just like any other game," but he wasn't telling the truth.

The writers could have determined this just by watching him for five minutes—he paced uneasily amongst his troops, sometimes nodding his head to questions which weren't asked—he bit the corner of his lip in concern, and his eyes moved from here to there and back again, but they were distant. It was obvious—Paul was under a good deal of strain. He wanted to whip the Browns in the worst way, probably in much the same way Bill Bergey wanted so badly to beat us in the Philadelphia exhibition game. The Cleveland Browns were partially founded by Paul and were his employer for some sixteen years before they canned him in 1962. Yep, PB wanted that one—revenge is sweet at any age.

In his pre-game talk, Paul used the "Brass-Ring-representing-the-Super-Bowl" analogy again. "We've had a good exhibition season, boys," he said in a somewhat nervous voice, "but now we begin to play for real. I want all of you to stay with it today all the way. Let's make our first step toward the Big Brass Ring a successful one."

All I could think of was how many times Paul must have made similar speeches in his career. Really, it was mind boggling the time Paul had devoted to the game. He was responsible for so much—the full-time coaching staffs, the "classroom" concept of learning pro ball, the studying and analyzing of game films to grade players on performance, the messenger guard system, the face mask—for Pete's sake! Was there anything more fundamental to football than the face mask?—and so much more.

In all his years, the only thing he didn't bother to learn—or care to—was how to get his players up for a game. Because of this, most of the guys had their individual ways, particular methods of psyching themselves up, or down, in preparation for a game. Playing music to relax was the one pre-game activity almost all football teams have in common. Not in the Bengals' camp. "I frown upon it," said Paul.

An example of two different approaches to preparing for a game was Ron Pritchard and Essex Johnson. Pritch claimed he was more nervous in '75 than ever before, and it was so bad that he would come within a hair of loosing his lunch before each game. He said his new-found faith in God had put more pressure on him. "Before I found religion," he told me, "I was playing the game for Ron Pritchard and no one else. Now I'm playing it for God." Pritch went on to say that his talent as a linebacker was God-given, and he was now obliged to succeed all the more as a sign of his appreciation and belief. "Every time I make a good play out there," Ron said, "I thank God immediately afterwards. A person has to do this because Satan is here—all around us—at all times; the Earth is his domain. We must thank God and deny Satan in everything we do."

To see Pritch before a game, though, you wouldn't have thought he was denying Satan at all—you'd have thought he was one of Satan's henchmen. The guy went amuck, crashing his fists and helmet against walls and lockers just to psych himself up for contact. Remember: Pritchard was a linebacker.

On the opposite end of the spectrum was Essex Johnson. Unlike Pritchard, Essex, as a running back, had to avoid, not cause, head-on collisions on the field. "I think psyching yourself sky-high is the wrong approach to a game," Ess told me. "The more psyched you are, the more wasted energy you expend; therefore, you tire yourself out too quickly." Essex did whatever he could to relax his body and mind before taking the field, like listening to soul music (when Paul was out of ear-shot) and reading magazines, newspapers and comic books. "I keep it real low-key, man," he said, "I save my explosions for trap plays out between the stripes."

Kenny Anderson and Bob Johnson also had differing views on preparing for a game, which was funny because, as quarterback and center, they were the only two players on the field actually touching one another every play. Yet, their perspectives were yards apart.

"Before a game," Johnson said, "I studied my man. I wanted to know everything about him—who he was, how long he had been in the league, how well he moved to his right or left, how I played against him last time we met, his strengths and weaknesses. It was a tremendous personal challenge being an offensive lineman. The public didn't know or care whether you made a great block or not. With all that humanity stacked around the ball they couldn't see a block if they had to. The only satisfaction I got was inwardly knowing that I did my job well. I only hoped the coaches noticed it, too.''

For Kenny Anderson, it was a lot different. *Everyone* saw what he did every play, judged by 60,000 fans (and a TV audience of millions). He couldn't worry about just one man. His opposition was composed of eleven angry persons who had the collective goal of taking the ball away from him. "If someone missed a block up front," said Kenny, "no one saw it. But if I threw a pass interception or got caught behind the line everybody knew that it was *my* fault. Very rarely did they consider that the same missed block up front may well have been the reason I hurried a pass or got tackled for a loss.''

As a quarterback, Kenny suffered from the same malady as every one I've known who has played that position—insomnia. "On the nights preceding games," said the Rookie, "I'd wake up about 3:00 or 4:00. Right then my stomach started jumping, and I'd find myself going over each play in our playbook, over and over. The more I thought of it, the worse I felt, until the pit of my stomach felt as if I'd swallowed a lead football. That feeling stayed until the game *finally* began.''

Personally, I was a spitter—I should say, an attempted-spitter. In the locker room before the game my throat would be dry and cottony; I'd try my hardest to spit just to keep it lubricated, but nothing seemed to come out. I'd usually go over the blocking assignments and pass patterns one at a time in my head. I wanted to be sure that I didn't blow any of these or make any mental mistakes. The worse part of it, like Kenny, was the jumbling feeling I got in the pit of my stomach. It was the same feeling I got when I was a small boy and did something bad—a knawing, hollow pain of mixed anxiety and fear. It always came over me after realizing someone would find out what I did that was so bad and would give me a licking for it. Man, I hated that feeling, and I suffered it each football Sunday for ten years.

Before a game you could have found me in the shower stall. I was in shower stalls before games for ten years, in every stadium across the country. I walked, and I smoked, cigarette after cigarette. In 1968 I walked and smoked alone, and over the years various walking/smoking cohorts came and went.

For the last several years it was Bruce Coslet and Ron Pritchard. Like the three blind mice we paced around the shower stall, each lost in his own thoughts. We passed so close in the small area that our shoulder pads would come within a hair of touching. Yet not a word was spoken. I was really out of it—as they were—concentrating on the game. *We—I—couldn't afford to make any mistakes,* I'd tell myself, *the Browns were real opportunists and they'd convert every turnover into a score. Man, I hope I didn't fumble the ball.* Walk and smoke. *I had to cut the patterns sharper today than I had in practice. No doggin' it, not even for a single play. I had to get clear in the secondary. Clarence Scott could be tough. I had to CATCH THE BALL!* Walk and smoke. *Did I remind Marv Pollins to bring along an extra pair of contact lenses for me in case I lost one out on the field? I always lost one out on the field.* Walk and smoke. *Man, if only Herky were here leading us in prayer; this was the opening game of the regular season! This was for real! We need him!* Walk and smoke....

Then one of the players would come to the shower stall and say, "We're about ready to go out on the field; better hurry your asses up." Then: (cough!) "Jesus, it's like a factory in here." Cough! "Don't you guys know those damn things are hazardous for your health—they'll kill you." Suddenly we snapped back to some sort of reality, looked at one another then hightailed it for the field. Fortunately, as the first cleat hit the AstroTurf, the butterflies normally disappeared.

What a way to kick off a season! The Browns' game was one of the weirdest games I was ever in. It was like *two* games, really, one the first half and one the second.

The first half was all Bengals, completely dominating play. We were unbelievable, a fluid-running, precise machine. The first time we touched the ball we drove eighty yards in ten plays for a score. It was a typical Bengal drive: a short pass to Isaac Curtis...a three-yard draw to Boobie...a six-yard run by Boobie off left tackle...a seven-yard run by Lenvil Elliott...a keeper by Kenny for fourteen...a run around left end by Lenvil...a twenty-five yard pass to Lenvil out of the backfield...a five-yard burst up the middle by Boobie...Boobie again for two yards off right tackle...then— boom!—a sixteen-yard touchdown pass to Ike Curtis, who badly beat Clarence Scott. The point-after by Dave Green was good and the score was 7-0.

We scored the second time we had the ball, too—ninety-three yards in nine plays, the big ones being a fifty-yard pass from Kenny to Ike and a bruising fourteen-yard run to pay dirt by Boobie on a beautifully executed delayed draw play. (The play before Boobie's touchdown I ran a great route into the end zone and had my man beaten badly; Kenny overthrew me.) When it became 24-3, victory appeared certain.

But then fortune began to shift.

The Browns took a kickoff and, with Greg Pruitt and Hugh McKinnis leading the ground game and Mike Phipps hitting Reggie Rucker on clutch passes, they scored in ten plays to make it 24-10. After we received the kickoff and got the ball back to the 24-yard line, Kenny was thrown for a big loss and, on the next play, while fading back into the end zone on a pass play, the Rookie was hit by Jerry Sherk and dropped the ball. Lineback Charlie Hall pounced on it and the score was suddenly 24-17.

On the Brown's kickoff to us, Lemar Parrish fumbled the ball on our own eighteen and the Browns recovered. In three plays and a first down they were down to our one-yard line and it looked like it was going to be a tie game for sure. They had a second down and goal to go for a score, and on the first play runningback Billy Pritchard was stopped by the middle of our defensive line. And on the next *two* plays the ball was fumbled on the snap from recently converted center Bob Demarie to Phipps—and we took over on downs.

You could almost hear the collective sigh of relief in Riverfront Stadium, but it didn't last long. After we ran a few plays and punted, Cleveland took seven plays and were right back on our two-yard line again. Phipps tried a quarterback sneak and got about a yard, then on the next play—could it be possible?—the Browns fumbled the snap *again* and Phipps had to fall on the ball to retain possession. On the final attempt to push the ball over, runningback Hugh McKinnis put his head down and tried to get around the left side. He ran right into the outstretched arms of Ron Carpenter, and, unbelievably, our defense held again. Six times the Browns had a chance to tie the score from within our two-yard line and six times the defense rose to the occasion.

The final score was 27-17, and our defensive unit stole the show.

The hero of the game was Bob Brown, who anchored the middle of our defensive line. He played directly over center and was the man responsible for Demarie three times flubbing the snap to Phipps. He was smacking him with a very hard forearm behind 285 pounds precisely as he was snapping the ball. The sight of Bob Brown obviously gave Demarie a few things to think about other than getting the ball to Phipps. "I gambled in that situation," a happy Bob Brown said in the clubhouse afterwards, "I tried to hit the center just as he made movement on the ball. If they penalized me for jumping a bit too soon, who cared? We'd only be penalized an inch or two, and that don't matter a whole heck of a lot down there."

Funny, Suki and Johnson almost felt sorry for Demarie, I assume because they themselves are offensive linemen. "Demarie was in his first regular season game," Suki said, shaking his head, "there was no way he should be in on that situation against Bob Brown. It was a total mismatch."

Johnson, being a center, didn't have too hard a time empathizing with Demarie: "I was in that exact same situation going against Bob Brown when he was with the Chargers," said Bob, "and let me tell you it wasn't easy. You put your hands on the ball and your head down and think, 'My God, this elephant is going to blast my head off as soon as I move the ball." So you subconsciously become so concerned with him that you forget about all the good timing with the quarterback and you mess up the snap. He's the most fearsome guy I've faced in that goal line situation," Johnson said of Bob Brown.

We had several standouts in the game—Freddie Franchise was seventeen of twenty-seven for 287 yards...Ike caught six passes for 127 yards, and Boobie ran eighteen times for fifty-one yards (I even caught three passes for thirty-eight yards). But the unanimous selection as the star to receive the game ball was Bob Brown. He accepted it with a very large smile and said, holding the ball above his head, "Kids" (he always refers to us as "kids"), "I'll take thirteen more just like this." We would have been glad to give them to him, too.

Later, I read that across the way reporters swarmed all over Demarie to find out what the hell happened on those snaps from center. Fortunately, Demarie, being a nine-year veteran, was able to handle the situation. One guy asked him if he liked playing center now rather than his old position at guard or tackle. "Yea," Demarie answered, "except when it's third down and one to go for a touchdown." Another guy pointed out that centers are the most unknown players on the football field. Demarie looked at the reporter and weighed his own performance that day. "Geez," he said, "I hope so."

We all came out of that Cleveland game in good shape physically. We had a serious injury to only one player—me.

Somehow I managed to "hyperextend" the muscles in my forearm near the elbow. I don't know when in the game the injury occurred; all I remember was becoming aware of it toward the end of the third quarter and thinking, *Jesus, I wonder what in the world I've done to myself now!* The elbow area swelled to twice its normal size, and Monday, our off day, I went down to Spinney Field so the team docs could have a look at it. I felt rather ridiculous being seen in public since I couldn't straighten out my arm—I was forced to walk around with it cocked out in front of me at a right angle to my body. I felt like a portable coat rack.

X-rays indicated that, not only did I pull ligaments in the forearm-elbow region, but I also managed to spring loose some calcium deposits and bone chips which were wedged in around the elbow joint. The doctors told me the only remedial action was to undergo constant heat treatments for the remainder of the season. And, after the season I'd need an operation, which I eventually had, in Oklahoma City.

It was wonderful news. I guess Mondays are Mondays all over the world, even in the land of the professional football player.

On Tuesdays during the regular season, we watch movies— game films. To watch our movies we divided into two groups, the offense in one room, defense in another. Our offensive section was pretty much fun after the Cleveland game because we all had a good game. We all got a good laugh when the coaches kept re-running the play in which Suki Holland went after Walter Johnson and the two collided head-on. When these two immovable objects met the shock-waves could strip the hair off your arms. On that particular play the movies showed that Suki unquestionably lost out and he went down in a heap. As could be expected, the hecklers in the audience ate it up.

"Can't handle that little guy, huh, Suki?" said one.

"Hey, Suki, what were you doing down on all fours?" asked another.

"Maybe he was looking for his contact lense."

"Suki doesn't wear contacts."

"I know, but he should."

"Yea, then he could see to get out of Walter Johnson's way."
And so on.

Conduct during The Movies was patterned—it was an unwritten rule that players refrained from openly criticizing teammates for mistakes. The rationale went something like this: since we're all in the football brotherhood together, we better make the best of it. Criticism of teammates was non-constructive, bad for morale, destructive to the team and diminished pro football in general.

It was a philosophy of self-perpetuation and mutual back-scratching. Of course, there were exceptions to the rule.

Andre White, for instance. He was the most flagrant teammate-critic we ever had. The Bengals acquired Andre from Denver just before the first summer training camp in 1968. Because he had a year or two of experience, he was labeled right off as "THE Tight End for the Team." And he came to training camp driving a big car and wearing a big mouth.

He never really got a chance to show off his talent, though. Andre's injury had far-reaching ramifications because, now, free to analyze the situation from afar, he literally took over the sidelines, running it much the same way a general runs a war. You could count on one thing—wherever you went, Andre White's advice was never far away. He more or less put himself in charge of our special teams, telling guys how to play kickoffs and balling them out for missing tackles. And he appointed himself quartermaster in charge of Gatorade Allotment, warning players not to drink too much, or giving players coming back for seconds a look to instill guilt, much the way a scolding mother looks at her child for stealing an extra cookie. More than once during the first few exhibition games I saw Andre White actually slide up to Paul Brown and *suggest a play* the Old Coach might try! Man, to us rookies that really took some balls. However, after Andre had done this a few times I noticed PB quietly glancing over to where one of his coaches was standing and shoot him a stony look as if to say, "What the hell does this guy think he's *doing?*" Paul Brown had been in football for 40-some years. There was very little a second-year player with a broken collarbone could clarify for him.

Andre's worse offenses came during The Movies. When a player makes a bad play or commits a mistake during a game, he was sure to hear about it. The coaches enjoyed running and re-running that play again and again so everyone—especially the guy who committed it—had a fair opportunity to "evaluate" the error. The last thing you wanted to hear on these occasions was unsolicited criticism from one of your own teammates, especially one who was not even playing the game.

Try telling that to Andre White. Hell, during the movies this guy became the Clive Barnes of Bengal football. He'd critique everything. He'd do things like roll his eyes back in his head and gasp in horror, as if someone had just given him a shot to the kidneys. "A-h-h-h Gawd, Trumpy," he'd cry out, "not like that, man. You were doing it all *wrong.* When you were blocking that defensive end you should have popped him hard." Sometimes Andre threw a towel down in absolute disgust and whined something like, "Damn, man, that there was the worse excuse for football I've ever seen."

All of us first-year players didn't know how to react to this guy's histrionics. We thought perhaps veterans routinely did this type of critiquing in training camp just to shape up the rookies. But later we talked to some of the other veterans on the club and they assured us that this definitely was not standard operating procedure in the NFL. What was more, they said, they couldn't themselves figure out Andre White's program.

Nor, apparently, could Paul Brown. He cut "The Tight End for the Team" a few weeks into the exhibition season. Who knows—maybe those few plays suggested to PB by Andre White simply didn't work.

Once when we were watching The Movies, I noticed Vern Holland yawning. "Hey, Suki," I whispered, "these films aren't *that* boring are they?"

"They ain't too damn entertaining, neither," he replied. He shook his big head and said, "Man, I was so tired this morning I didn't even think my 'system' would work in getting me out of bed."

"Your system?" I asked.

Suki explained that the only way he was able to get his large frame out of bed early enough to make our 9:30 meetings was by employing a three-way wake-up system. "First," he said, "I have a wind-up alarm clock which I set for 8:30. When this goes off I just lay there without moving and let it ring itself all the way down. Next, my clock-radio goes off, first the radio, set loud on a soul station, then a few minutes later the alarm. It's a ten-minute snooze alarm so I keep punching it every ten minutes until the third element in my system goes into gear."

"The third element?"

"Yea, that's when I have a chick call me on the telephone and say, "Suki, baby, it's time to lift that big, bad, black, beautiful body of yours out of bed and share it with the world.' "

"That's some system, all right," I whistled with due admiration. Then: "But tell me something, Suki. Wtih a third step like that, why do you need the first two?"

His face went momentarily blank. After a shrug, he turned and walked away. "I'm goin' to have to work on that," he said.

Another guy who played a solid game against the Browns was our guard John Shinners. John had just been elected as our new player rep. I hoped John realized that his football playing had now to be beyond reproach. John often approached practices in a rather "relaxed" frame of mind. If he didn't put out then, though, management would undoubtedly attribute it to his job as player rep. I guess John was willing to take the chance of playing elsewhere the next year, just like his fellow guard Pat Matson was willing to do. John knew that because of his union ties, Herky would come to summer camp each year and immediately be demoted to third-string guard. He would have to work his butt off all summer long so that by the time the regular season opened he would be in the number one slot.

Offensive coach Tiger Johnson always said he was "icy" toward the players' association, so I asked him what effect Shinners' new role would have on him in the future. "When John comes to training camp next year will he be the third-string guard?" I inquired.

Tiger stopped and rubbed his prominent jawbone. "I was thinking more like fifth-string," he answered. "We have two first-round draft choices next year, and I was going to ask PB that both of them be left offensive guards."

Only the Texas twinkle in his eyes told me he was kidding.

John Shinners attended Cincinnati's Xavier University and was the New Orleans Saints' number one draft choice in 1969. His initial visit to New Orleans was a memorable one. His first night the team officials took John out and introduced him to what would become his new hometown, and to show New Orleans the packaged goods obtained by the Saints in the college draft.

By the time the fast-drinking crew had reached Al Hirt's place, John, not a drinker in his college days, was already three sheets to the wind. Despite this, more drinks followed, especially in toasts after each of Al Hirt's lively numbers. Finally, one of the club officials asked Al to introduce to the audience the Saints' number one draft choice and Al agreed. So, following a particularly robust number, he had the spotlights flash over to the table where John Shinners was sitting, rather white-faced and unmoving, and said, "Folks, we are honored to have with us tonight the first draft choice of our beloved New Orleans football team. The coaches told me he's one of the best football players around, so I wanted you to meet him. His name is John Shinners and he's an offensive guard from Xavier University."

As the crowd broke into a loud applause, it turned its attention to the special table where John and the club officials were seated. The table was above and slightly to the side of the stage where Al Hirt was performing. "Stand up and take a bow, mahboy," Al bellowed, and, against his better judgement, John wedged himself up out of the chair and took a singularly blurry step forward. Unfortunately, he failed to negotiate a railing. It caught him knee-high and, followed by some impressive spotlight work, John's body did a somersault and hurtled downward through the smokey atmosphere until it came to land with a thud near Al Hirt's feet. Luckily, John wasn't hurt; he had passed out before hitting the ground.

According to John, the high-dive act didn't faze Al Hirt a bit. The bearded, rotund man merely took a long belt of whatever he was drinking, shouted an enthusiastic, "Now that's what I call good ol' Catholic football player," and launched immediately into another rousing number. He barely missed a beat.

I didn't know whether John's role as a player representative had anything to do with the way he was eventually released by the Bengals. I knew that we left the same year, and in completely different styles. It was after the January, 1978, Super Bowl when Mike Brown called me in the office. (Decisions about returning players had to be made by February 1). "Bob," Mike said to me, "my dad and I think it's best if you retire. You don't want to get an injury this late in your career which could permanently affect you." I couldn't have agreed more and Mike told me to send an official "Letter of Retirement" to the NFL offices, informing them of my plans to retire, which I did.

The same suggestion was not made to John Shinners, despite the fact the team knew he wouldn't be back. John was simply waived out of the league. Rather than leaving with his head up as a "retired" veteran, he went out the back door as an "over-the-hill" player.

John was upset, to say the least. He later told me: "It was a kick in the teeth. It was as if they said, get the hell out, we don't need you anymore. That really hurt."

It's hard to discuss Bengal player representatives like John

Shinners without mentioning the very first one we had, back in 1968. That first year we rookies looked to those taken in the allocation draft for leadership, despite the fact that most of them had been in the league only a year or two themselves. Fortunately for us, there *was* one player who emerged as the team's players' representative, father figure and all-around undisputed messiah.

His name was Ernie Wright. And he was a dandy.

Ernie, an Ohio State product, was a nine-year NFL veteran, picked up by the Bengals from the San Diego Chargers. I guess his years of football experience and his sincere, soft-spoken manner for a big man (6'4", 270 pounds) made him a natural for title of "Elder Statesman" of the team.

Bengal management must have felt the same way, because Ernie, an offensive tackle, was the only guy in club history who roomed *alone* at training camp. We never figured how he worked that out.

I never forgot the time Bob Johnson and I sat down with big Ernie when he called Paul Brown to tell him of the strike in 1970. We sat on a bed across from him and got to hear only his side of the conversation. But it told us just how much against the players' association Paul Brown was. It went something like this: "Hello, Paul, this is Ernie. Yea. Well, the players have voted to strike, and—well, listen Paul, it wasn't that way at all. Well, we just wanted to—well, listen Paul. No, you were wrong, Paul. Now you didn't have to go and say a thing like that, Paul...." And on and on it went. Johnson and I laughed till we cried.

When I thought of Ernie Wright, I envisioned this mountainous sugardaddy outfitted in a blue terrycloth bathrobe, lying on his bed, smoking an *Anthony and Cleopatra* cigar and reading the morning newspaper. There was no hazing of rookies in our training camp, like there was in others, but every year Ernie Wright somehow persuaded a rookie to pick up the newspaper from in front of the dormitory and hand-deliver it to his doorstep each morning. It was the only case of training camp room service I could remember.

Ernie used to skip breakfast so he could get in a little extra shut-eye. So it was routine that, on the way back from our breakfast, we would poke our heads into his room to see whether he was up and ready for practice. There he'd be, lying in bed reading the paper, a purple smoke-cloud enshrouding him. "What's happening, Ernie?" we said, and he just looked over at us and sighed as if the weight of the world was teetering on his massive shoulders. "Just lying here readin' the paper," he said. "Just relaxin' some." You'd think from this that Ernie Wright would be rather docile on the football field. He wasn't. He was big and strong and smart. It was Ernie that really anchored our offensive line during those first struggling years.

I also remember the way Ernie loved to play poker. He was the self-appointed "banker" at all the games, and he prided himself on his knowledge of poker strategy and on the professional manner in which he mediated contested hands. In poker disputes, Ernie's law ruled. Once he made a decision, all lived by it.

I remember once that Ernie's cards were really running good. He took seventeen hundred dollars from one rookie and fifteen hundred from another—that was a total of nearly three thousand dollars in IOU's in one sitting. Problem was, both rookies were cut the next day and managed to slip away from training camp while Ernie was out on the practice field.

Poor Ernie. It was all he could do for a solid week to mope around training camp, shaking his head forlornly and muttering, "It jus' ain't right."

It makes me a little melancholy, looking back at those early Bengal years. Those were the fun days of the Bengals, the days when we weren't supposed to be good and we weren't. After a while it became different. The Cincinnati fans were clamoring for the Super Bowl; that meant the coaches drove us harder; it meant our mistakes were painfully run time and again during Movies; it meant young, thick-chested rookies were encouraged to push for your job; it meant the veterans, friends for years, were butting heads with a vengance in practice, and, it meant that the front office was more inclined to inform you that your high salary could be traded away to another team if you failed to produce as expected.

The whole atmosphere was different. It smelled of high-pressure big business, players' strikes, freedom issues, and courtroom battles.

I think I began to miss Ernie Wright.

In our second game of the season Kenny Anderson riddled the New Orleans' Saints' secondary with seventeen completions in twenty-two attempts for 203 yards and three touchdowns, two to Ike Curtis, including a beautiful fifty-two-yard bomb. We won 21-0.

The real stars of the game, though, were our guys on defense. Anytime you can shut out an NFL team, even the Saints, you are doing a real hardnosed job. Never during the game did the Saints penetrate our twenty-yard line. Ron Carpenter, Ken Johnson, Bob Brown, Sherm White, Bill Kollar—all played a great containing, team defense.

The standout, though, was indisputably Jim LeClair. The middle linebacker was credited with six unassisted tackles, five assisted tackles and his first pass interception as a pro. I had a feeling that if he kept improving and playing the way he did that day maybe he would make them forget Bill Bergey. Two injuries in the game. One was to Tommy Casanova who severely sprained an ankle and would be out a couple of weeks. You have three guesses who the other injured player was.

Right. It happened in the second quarter on a "90-double-go" from the "switch-open" formation. Basically this was a deep pattern on which I split out from the line about ten yards and ran in a straight sprint to the end zone. The intent was to have me one-on-one with a much smaller defensive back so I could use my quickness and height advantage to grab the ball over his head. I had rookie Jim DeRatt beaten on the play and Kenny Anderson threw a pretty nice ball. Unfortunately, just before it got to me I stepped in a small depression in the field and—snap!—the hamstring muscle in my right thigh tore apart like a worn rubberband.

The pain was immediate and intense, and I had to be helped from the field.

I was pretty depressed about it all the way home in the plane until two things occurred. The first was that our pilot announced over the PA system that the Buffalo Bills, behind a 227-yard performance by O.J. Simpson, walloped the Pittsburgh Steelers 30-21. This meant that we were now in first place in the Central Division, tied with the Houston Oilers, whom we would play the next week.

The second encouraging thing was the concern for my well-being displayed by my teammates. We kidded and poked fun at each other a lot, but when it came down to helping one another through anxious moments, we were really a close-knit group. "Take care of that thing, Trump," said my friend Chip Myers, "we need you in there, partner. My only advice is don't try to come back too soon, because it may go on you again. I know, I had it happen to me in '72."

The other guy who asked me to get healthy soon was my replacement Bruce Coslet. Not only replacement, but competitor. Bruce, like any other player, wanted to play full-time, but he was the second-string tight end behind me since his first year in 1969. There was a whole potful of NFL coaches who would have liked to have Bruce as their starting tight end, but Bruce was not unhappy with the Bengals. Because of my propensity for injuries and because we had a "two-tight end" offense on third-and-short situations, he actually did get in quite a bit of playing time. Considering the unusual circumstance, Bruce and I formed an unbelievably close relationship and he was probably the best friend I had on the team. (As I often told him, "Bruce, you and I have a strange and wonderful relationship—you're strange and I'm wonderful.") Bruce accepted his position behind me, but he also knew that if I slacked off or gave him the slightest opening he would do everything in his power to wrest the starting assignment away from me. In that respect, we actually helped each other; we were more competitive in our attitudes than many players and we pushed each other to top performance. We were about equal in blocking abilities, but I was three inches taller and a little quicker, therefore I was number one, and Bruce understood this in a professional manner.

Whenever I thought of Bruce I remembered the first touchdown reception he ever made as a Bengal. He came to us in 1969 a free agent out of the University of the Pacific. He fought seven other aspirants to become the second-string tight end, and during one game when I was injured he got his chance to prove himself. It was a home game at Nippert Stadium on the University of Cincinnati campus, where we played in pre-Riverfront Stadium days. On this particular play our then-rookie sensation quarterback Greg Cook faded back and uncorked a perfectly thrown bomb to Bruce, who caught it over his shoulder for a touchdown. Only trouble was that Bruce was so excited about it that he kept running with the ball after the play until he came to an abrupt halt against the concrete base of the grandstand. He shattered his kneecap and was out for the remainder of the season.

In his career, Bruce made forty-five receptions and nine TDs. Not bad for a back-up man.

In 1976, a year before I did, Bruce retired. He became a building contractor in California. When he left, a major part of my life left with him. For eight years we were best friends, competing for the same job, but helping each other every step of the way. His loss was a void impossible to fill. The Bengals tried, though, drafting *three* rookie tight ends to replace him. So now, rather than having Bruce Coslet chasing me, I had three wet-behind-the-ears kids with whom I had absolutely nothing in common. Suddenly I was the old man, the duffer, the impediment in the way of youthful progress.

It was an awful feeling, and many were the endless days of practice and long nights that I wished I had retired at the exact same time Bruce did.

After the Saints game, we got back to Cincinnati about nine. Pat and Susie Myers met Chip and me at the airport and we decided to go out for a pizza and beer before heading home. While we were eating I told Chip that when I got home I was going to finish insulating my garage because the 1929 LaSalle I bought a few weeks ago was supposed to be picked up the next morning. "You mean to tell me," Chip said, "that, hamstring pull and all, you are going to go back home and put in insulation?"

"Sure," I replied, "why not? I never get to sleep before three in the morning after a game anyway; besides, the work might be like therapy—help me keep my mind off the injury."

Pat and I got home about 10:30 or so and I got out all the utensils to go to work. My leg hurt like hell and I started to wonder if Chip hadn't been right about taking it easy tonight. Just then, two headlights turned into our driveway and I recognized the car to be Chip's. "Hey, what the hell are you guys doing over in this area?" I said, knowing Myers lived east of town, forty-five minutes away. Chip got out and grabbed a hammer from my toolbox. "Listen, my friend," he said, "I know how much those hamstring pulls hurt and how hard it was to move around on them. I figured if someone didn't give you a hand you'd be here until nine tomorrow morning, keeping up the neighbors and causing a general ruckus. With both of us working, we can lick this job in two or three hours."

Which we did. I'll tell you, one of the rewarding by-products of playing professional sports was the abiding friendships—a sort of athlete's love for one another, if you will—that was formed through years of living together through thick and thin. And I wouldn't have traded that for the world.

One of the most frustrating injuries I ever sustained was the one at the University of Illinois, in the seventh game of the season my sophomore year, when someone stepped on my hand in a pile-up and broke a few blood vessels.

On the sidelines, a doctor had taken a look at my hand and quickly applied a splint and bandages. And by the time I awoke the next morning, the flesh on the injured hand had completely swollen over the top of the bandages, so I rushed back to the doctor's office. "Here," he said, handing me a bottle of pills, "take one every six hours," and he sent me back to my room in the Sigma Chi fraternity house. I guess because of the pain I hadn't understood the doc too well, and I thought he said, "Take all these pills within the next six hours." Which I did. About 30 pills. I mean to tell you, I lost two days of my life completely. Later, my roommate told me how I laid in bed asleep when suddenly I raised up and screamed my head off. Or, how twice I told our fraternity president to go get screwed and challenged him to a fight, and how once I somehow ended up on the roof, and how several times they had to call the police because of my insane actions. Fortunately, I don't remember a thing.

When my head finally did clear, I found myself in a hospital room with a doctor curiously inspecting my left hand, which was now about four sizes bigger than normal. The skin was stretched so tight that it looked as if someone had polished it with Turtle Wax. When he finally punctured it with a sharp blade, pus sprayed out like oil from an oil can.

Immediately the doctor operated, drilling a hole clean through my hand in order to let the infection drain. I can remember waking up from the operation seeing myself bandaged from elbow to fingertip. My first impulse was that the good doctor had cut off my hand and I started to cry to the nurse, "The bastard cut off my hand, he cut off my hand. How the hell am I supposed to catch a football with one hand? Get that butcher in here. I'll kill him with my *good* hand." Finally, the nurse succeeded in quieting me down by unwrapping my arm and proving to me that my hand was intact, although altered to the point that I could see daylight through it.

My hospital stay lasted nine long weeks. Each day the routine was the same, a nurse came in and wrapped a very hot, wet towel around my arm in an effort to draw out the infection. When the towel became dry, another one went on in its place. Towel-wrap after towel-wrap for nine weeks; then, suddenly, overnight, the hot towels ceased completely. So abrupt was this change that the skin on my arm cracked right down to the bone. The wet towels had succeeded in drawing out every bit of moisture from my arm muscle and bones. As a result of all this, my hand was left partially paralyzed in a semi-fist position for the next two years.

I could have gotten out of my exams that semester at Illinois on a medical deferment. But I was depressed and decided to go ahead and take them anyway. I failed two of them and was flunked out of school. My football days at the University of Illinois had come to an end.

So many injuries had I incurred during my career, that the whirlpool at Spinney Field was dubbed the "S.S. Trumpy." That's precisely where I was a few days before the Houston game when Lemar Parrish approached me with a look of consternation etched across his face. "Say, Trump," he said, "maybe you can answer me a question."

He hesitated a moment as if to get his words in the precise order he desired. Finally he said, "When a dude gets married, does half of everything he owns belong to his wife?"

I had to stop to think, mainly because I was expecting a question that dealt a little closer to the subject of professional football. Secondly, I began to wonder why of all the guys on the team he would come to me with this question. Mentally I shrugged. "I have to confess, Leap," I pointed out, "I really don't know the answer. I believe it depends on the state laws involved." I took a moment to ponder the situation; all the while Lemar's eyes never left me. He stood his ground studying my every action. "I believe some states do have a community property arrangement whereby the wife is automatically half owner of all her husband's property. But beyond this I'm afraid that I'm a little hazy on the subject."

"Hmm-hmmm," responded Lemar. He stroked his chin in serious contemplation and added, "You say that under this community property arrangement my wife—uh, should I ever get married—that my wife would collect half of my total worth if she ever decided to split?"

"Well, don't quote me on it, Leap. But that's the way I understand it. Everything would be divided down the middle, fifty-fifty."

"Hmm-hmmm," repeated the small cornerback. Then with a final stroke of his sharp jaw he turned and walked away. I noticed a very strange—almost apprehensive, yet slyly evil—look on his face.

If I was a betting man, I would have bet that Leapin' Lemar

Parrish had something rather intricate cooking on the front burner. And it didn't take me long to find out what. Within twenty-four hours Leap was back again. "I got it all worked out, Trump-my-man," he said. He stood grinning like the village idiot.

"Got what worked out?"

"I'm gettin' married in a couple of weeks, and I got me a lawyer to draw up a contract."

"A contract between you and your lawyer?" I asked, posing what I thought was a logical question. But Lemar shot me a quizzical look and said, "You ain't listenin' to what I'm tellin' you, man. The contract is between me and the future Mrs. Leapin' Lemar."

"Oh?"

"Yea, and it stipulates that after we marry she must stay with me at least five years. If she leaves me before the five years is up she don't get nothin' that is mine."

Unbelievable, I thought. Nothing like having total trust in your marriage partner. Which brought up another point. "OK, Leap," I said, "you got this contract. Now what do you intend to do with it?"

"Well, I'm goin' to git my girl to sign it, of course."

"What the hell kind of girl in her right mind is going to sign a contract like that?"

"*She-et*, my man," said Leap, his thin lips breaking into a great smile of confidence. "If I tell my girl to sign it, she will sign it. That is, if she wants to get married she will."

As Lemar left I noticed how suddenly I had a headache.

And it lasted right through the movies of the Houston Oilers. Further, I suspected that after the game that upcoming Sunday in the Astrodome a few more players—on both sides—would have headaches of their own, and then some.

The Oilers' game meant a lot to us. Houston defeated us, embarrassed us actually, in 1974 on two occasions, 34-21 and 20-3. After that last game we vowed as a team that we would never allow that kind of humiliation to happen to us again.

One of the running backs who was sure to see action against us was Fred Willis. Fred, a former Bengal, hated Paul Brown with a passion, having for his former coach about the same amount of fondness that Alger Hiss had for Richard Nixon in the '50's. I understood Willis' animosity. It went back a few years. We drafted him out of Boston College in the second round in 1971, and he played gut-tough football for us. He was just getting accustomed to life in Cincinnati when all of a sudden PB up and traded him to the Oilers. What irked Fred most about the trade was the way in which it was handled. He was in a sporting goods store in downtown Cincinnati when the owner of the store, a man by the name of Eddie, walked over to Willis and said, "How do you feel, Fred?"

Fred looked at him strangely and replied, "I feel fine, Eddie.

Why do you ask?"

Eddie shrugged. "Well, I thought you might be a little upset or something."

"Upset. Why would I be upset?"

"I don't know. I assumed that when you learned that you were traded to Houston you'd be a little up—"

"I WAS WHAT?"

"Traded to Houston. I heard it on the radio...."

Upset wasn't the word. Fred Willis saw red and gave PB a good piece of his mind before leaving, I'll guarantee you that.

Waiting to board our plane for Houston, Lemar Parrish once again approached me with a big smile. "Well, my man," said Leap, "She's gone and done it. She's signed the contract. She really did it."

"You've got to be putting me on," I replied. "She actually signed it?" I looked at him to see if he were telling the truth. The way he was beaming with self-exaltation I knew that he had to be.

"I ain't jivin' you, Trump," Lemar said, "you know I ain't."

"Then you're a hell of a salesman, Lemar, that's all I've got to say."

"I cain't argue with that," he replied. "If my ol' lady takes off within the first five years, she don't get nothin'. The only thing she gets is G-O-N-E!"

Instant hero status was heaped upon our slightly built defensive back, and there were "Ooh-wees" and hand slaps all the way around. "I'm getting my ol' lady to sign one of those," said one teammate.

"I'm going to try for three years," said another.

Then, about half way to Houston the intercom came on and we recognized the voice of Father Connelly. Father has been a friend of PB's for forty-some years and he traveled with us much of the time. It was usually Father Connelly that led us in prayer before our games. He also made himself available for spiritual consultations. "Good evening, my boys," the Father said, "I want you all to know that at 7:30 tonight in Houston I will be holding a special chapel service. Each and every one of you is invited to attend this spiritual uplifting. You'll be interested to know that there will be no collection taken at the service. I repeat: *no* collection at the service. That is all."

We all broke up, but after a while I began to consider what Father Connelly had said. I hadn't had my spirit religiously "uplifted" since my parents sent me to Sunday school twenty years ago. Despite this, I suddenly got an insatiable urge to attend that night's service. After all, *someone* should have prayed for Lemar Parrish's future wife—she was going to need all the help she could get. By the way, whenever I saw Leap all dressed up I remember the time when he wore a bright tourquoise jump suit replete with Indian jewelry. Doc Cassanova called to him, "Hey, Leap, your mom a Navaho?"

"Nah, man. She was a Chicago 'ho."

Maybe something was lost in the translation.

In Houston I was paged at the hotel's desk, where someone had taken a telephone message. All it said was, "Call your wife. Son in hospital."

In a panic, I tried our home. No answer. Then I tried the hospital that Pat normally takes Jason to. They didn't know what I was talking about. I tried a few other hospitals. Never heard of her. Finally, I tried the first hospital again. Yes, a Mrs. Trumpy had admitted her son, but she couldn't be located. Don't know what was wrong with your son. Call back later.

Finally, I called Mike Brown. "Mike," I said, "Jason has been taken to the hospital in Cincinnati. I can't seem to find out what's wrong. If it's OK with you, I'd like to take the next plane out of here so I can find out what's happening."

"Fine," Mike responded, "the next plane is at 2:30 this morning. If you want me to get you on it, let me know."

I went back to the room and tried Pat one more time. This time I got hold of her. "What's going on back there?" I asked. "What's the matter with Jason?"

"He couldn't breathe after you left today," said Pat. Her voice was tired and worn and I could tell she had been through a real emotional strain. "I rushed him here and they looked at him immediately. They've diagnosed it as asthmatic bronchitis, whatever that is."

"How's he doing?" I asked, "should I come home?"

"No," replied Pat. "It was close there for a little while, but the doctors say he's resting comfortably now and he'll be fine in a day or two. There's really nothing you can do here."

In the end I agreed and hung up. Man, I'll tell you. This was just another aspect of being a pro football player that doesn't occur to the man in the street. Because we were gone from home so much of the time, our football wives had to be efficient crisis managers. They had to solve the emergency problems, and they had to learn to stay calm and make critical decisions, often times decisions that the man of the house would have made. If he were home, that is. But during the summer we were away for ten weeks and we were also gone at least seven weekends during the regular season. I'll bet if you took a poll among NFL families you'd find out that, uncannily, most crisis-type situations arise while the husband is out of town on "business." I know that in the times I was gone, Matt had to have stitches right above the eye and another time in his knee, had bitten his tongue nearly in half, and Jason had the tip of his thumb almost totally severed when a window fell on it.

I don't know why these accidents always seemed to happen when we were out of town, but they did. There must have been some sort of Murphy's Law lurking there somewhere.

As it turned out, that year's Houston game may have been, at least to that point, the most psychologically important game in the history of our franchise. We matured that Sunday afternoon, something Paul Brown had been patiently waiting for for eight years. We came from behind to win that one, and the number of times that feat had been accomplished by the Cincinnati Bengals you could have counted on one hand—not a human hand, a lobster's!

The first three times we had the ball we failed to move it, and the same was true for the Oilers. Both our ground games were gaining very little, and the passing was erratic. On our fourth possession, however, we got on the scoreboard, traveling seventy-five yards in eight plays. Boobie Clark, Lenvil Elliott and Stan Fritts handled the running while Chip Myers and Bruce Coslet grabbed clutch passes. The key play in the series was a little swing pass to Elliott who caught it and, bursting right through the outstretched arms of two converging linebackers, scampered thirty-one yards. Four plays later Elliott beat Steve Kiner to the end zone on a ten-yard pass play and we were on top 7-0.

It was short-lived. Dave Green kicked off to Billy "White Shoes" Johnson, a shifty second-year free agent, and he returned it fifty-five yards to the Oilers' 28. Only a last-second tackle by our rookie Marvin Cobb saved a touchdown. Not really saved, but *delayed*, because seven plays later Houston crossed our goal line. The ball carrier was our old friend Fred Willis. Oh, how Willis must have loved that one. I was on the sidelines and I could easily have shot a look at PB to see his reaction to Willis' scoring against him, but I chickened out.

We got the ball back, ran three futile plays and kicked again. And again it went to Billy Johnson. He got his white shoes to pumping and they didn't stop until they came to rest on our thirty-yard line. We held for seven plays, but Skip Butler kicked a thirty-seven yard field goal with 1:15 left in the half and the Oilers took a 10-7 lead into the locker room.

PB was visibly distressed when he addressed the team at halftime. "This is the turning point in our season," he said in a low, shaky voice. "Right now is the time to prove yourself, to stand up and be counted. I'm telling you, boys, that we have to beat this team and we have to beat them right now. It's going to take a supreme effort on your part in the second half, and I'll accept nothing less. You have to do the work out there, we can't do it for you."

Paul's emotional words didn't seem to make much of an impression on our guys, because when the second half began we traded ineffective ground games until little Billy Johnson took another Dave Green punt and scooted around, past and through would-be tacklers for a sixty-three-yard return and seven more points. It was now 17-7, Oilers, mid-way through the third quarter. Things looked dim—and dimmer still when we took the kickoff and ran three plays (Boobie lost two on a flare pass, Charlie Joiner picked up eight on a crossing pattern over the middle and Elliott lost two on an attempted run off right guard) and we punted again. Houston was moving at a brisk pace when receiver John Sawyer was hit by Ron Pritchard after a reception and fumbled the ball. Cornerback Ken Riley (called "the Rattler" because "he strikes quickly") scooped it up and returned it forty-three yards. On a pivotal third down play Kenny Anderson tried to hit Boobie Clark out of the backfield but it was hurriedly thrown and fell untouched. Fortunately for us, Houston's highly touted rookie linebacker Bob Brazile cold-cocked Boobie long after the play was dead and the refs assessed a very large penalty against him. That gave us an important first down, and in four plays Anderson hit wide-open Stan Fritts on a roll-out pass and it was 17-14.

To begin the fourth quarter we found ourselves in the familiar position of kicking to Houston, and it looked as if they were going to mount another long drive. But defensive end Ken Johnson really unloaded on Dan Pastorini, causing a fumble, and Al Beauchamp dived on it at our forty-one. In eight plays—including a twenty-five yard pass to Chip and a crucial defensive-holding call against cornerback Willie Alexander—we crossed the goal line. It was a little roll-out pass to Ike Curtis.

With 8:58 still left to play we knew our 21-17 lead was sitting on pretty thin ice, and, sure enough, on the fourth play of Houston's drive, Pastorini went long for his gangly 6'8" split end Ken Burrough and got an interference call at the goal line. Somehow our defensive secondary had gotten mixed up on coverage assignments, and Burrough found himself all alone near the end zone. Suddenly, from out of nowhere, came Lemar Parrish. Leapin' Lemar did what he did best—leap—and soon found himself riding on top of Burrough's shoulder pads before the ball had a chance to even get to him. Every official in the park threw a yellow flag, and, to be truthful, it was one of the most blatant cases of pass interference I've ever seen. And it turned out to be one helluva smart play by Leap. He knew that it was a sure seven points if Burrough were allowed to receive the ball over his shoulder in the end zone. The only thing Lemar could do was to purposefully interfere so Houston would get the ball, first down, on the one-yard line and pray that our defense could hold.

They did it two weeks before against Cleveland, true. But expecting them to do it again, this time against the tougher Oilers, was steep stuff. On the first play, Pastorini looked to handoff to one of his running backs, but both Willis and Don Hardeman headed for the same hole without accepting the ball from him, so the QB ate it for a yard loss. On the second play, a fired-up Fred Willis tried the right side and lost a yard when he was hit by Ron Carpenter, Ken Johnson and rookie linebacker Bo Harris. Next, Hardeman bolted around left end. *Almost* around left end. He was met hard by Jim LeClair and Bob Brown for no gain. Finally, in frustration, Fred Willis bulled his neck and busted through the right side, where he was met by LeClair head-to-head. When the dust cleared, Willis and the ball were left a half-inch from the white stripe.

For the second time in three games, the goal line unit held within the two-yard line, a total of ten plays. Unbelievable.

Houston did manage to dump Kenny Anderson for a safety when we took over on the half-inch line, but the Oilers' spirit was broken and we went on to win 21-19.

It was a big, big victory for us, and the locker room was charged with high voltage electricity after the game. All the guys were hugging one another and yelling at the top of their lungs, "DEFENSE, DEFENSE." Defensive captain Ron Carpenter said, "We've come a long way, man. We would have never done that last year." And everyone agreed.

Paul was so emotional he could hardly speak. "You, you guys are, are something. Really something else," he said. Actually, his remark was substantially inadequate. It was so damn hard for him to say *good* or *great*. Instead, we were "something else." Fortunately, the players were so super-charged that they ignored Paul's slight, and because he was so emotionally strung-out over the whole thing, some of the players finally decided to present him with the game ball. It was a magnanimous gesture, but it didn't sit well with everyone. An assistant coach standing next to me just shook his head and said: "Isn't this something. That old man gets the game ball and he has never once said to any of us, 'you are doing a fine job.' This is what makes coaching on this team so different from on other clubs. Here you never know where you stand."

While everyone else was whooping it up, our rookie tight end Jack Novak was sitting by his cubicle with his head hung down. I went over and gave him a nudge on the shoulder pads. "Hey, rook," I said, "don't take it so hard. The Old Man didn't mean anything out there. He was just all keyed up. He gets that way a lot."

"I know," Jack responded solemnly, "but it was so damn uncalled for. It made me feel like a fool."

What Jack was referring to happened on one of the last plays of the game. Boobie Clark had put a very hard, low roll block on defensive end Tody Smith, and apparently Tody figured that Clark shouldn't be blocking him so hard that late in the game. So as Clark was picking himself up off the ground, Smith drew back a cleated shoe and kicked him right in the face. Standing nearby, Jack Novak witnessed this and immediately ran up to Smith and began to wail on his body. The officials only saw Jack's response to Tody's unsportsmanlike conduct and quickly threw the rookie out of the game (an automatic fine of $200).

When Novak came running off, PB was waiting and immediately launched into him with a criticism not lacking severity. I couldn't believe what he was doing to our 12th-round draft choice so I stepped between them and said, "What the hell, Paul. He was just trying to defend a teammate from a guy who hit him with a cheap shot."

Suddenly PB turned on me and said, "SHUT UP. Don't you open your mouth again."

Then he started in on Jack once more, so I just took the rookie by the shoulderpads and moved him away from Paul. "Look, Jack," I said, "just get out of here. Go over there where the Old Man can't see you. In a few minutes he won't even remember this whole thing occurred."

Which is what happened.

Man, Tody Smith's cheap shot on Boobie was small beer compared with PB's shot on rookie Jack Novak.

Anyway that's my opinion.

As we were leaving the Dome to board our airport bus, a real figure from the past burst upon the scene. Screeching around the corner in a gleaming new El Dorado came the inconquerable Warren McVea. He wouldn't have made an entrance in any other way.

Warren, a tiny running back with us in 1968, was one of my best friends my rookie year. We were one of the funniest-looking duos around, me being 6'6" and white; Warren being 5'6" and black. When we moved down the street together we looked like an organ grinder with a pituitary problem taking his pet monkey for a walk.

The first time I ever saw Warren was my senior year when Utah played the University of Houston in the Astrodome. Warren McVea touched the ball only six times—and he scored *four* touchdowns, two on kick returns and two on running sweep plays. He was then—and into the pros—the quickest runner I had ever seen.

We used to say Warren was the only player on the Bengals who had to take a pay cut in order to play professional football. Let's just say he was treated rather regally at Houston. One story was that his father worked as a doorman at one of the city's fanciest hotels; meanwhile, Warren was living in the fancy penthouse suite on the top floor. And his wardrobe and expensive tastes would have pauperized John Bairdsford Tipton.

Contributing to his short stay with the Bengals, Warren retained his flashy individualistic ways in 1968, and I think they rubbed PB the wrong way. When you're building a new team you don't need any extroverts who might throw the system out of whack. The first chance Paul got he traded away Warren—to the Kansas City Chiefs for a German kicker named Horst Muhlmann. Too bad. Warren was a helluva runningback and he went on to add extreme explosiveness to the then-vaunted Chiefs' offense.

When I saw Warren drive up in his El Dorado, I hustled over to him and said, "Hey, Warren, if I knew you were coming, I would have brought some ice cream."

"You never forget, Trump," he smiled. Warren used to eat a quart of ice cream a day. It was the most amazing thing I've ever seen for a man his size.

"And if I knew I'd be seeing you," Warren said, "I'd a brought a pair of crutches."

"Son of a bitch," I responded, "you sure know how to hurt a guy."

He laughed and shook his head and said, "If you were any more delicate they'd stamp 'Fragile' across you and send you out to play in a package."

After a few more jibes at each other I asked Warren what he was presently doing. "Well," sighed the little man, "I guess you could say that I'm currently between jobs. I played a little WFL ball last year but I've given it up for good now. You know me, though, Trump," he smiled, "I ain't too worried. I'll pick up somethin' somewhere."

In my ten years of pro football I saw a lot of unusual players come and go. But of them all, only my friend Warren McVea would be driving around Houston in a brand new El Dorado while being "between jobs." He'll always be surrounded by class wherever he goes.

On the plane, the electricity from the locker room was still evident. The guys were really wound up about now being in sole possession of first place in the Central Division. I was playing a rubber of bridge with Bob Johnson and two other guys when all of a sudden we heard a commotion from across the aisle. I looked over and saw Tiger Johnson bent over double in his seat. He was clutching at his Texas midsection and gasping for breath. His seat-mate, fellow Texan Howard Fest, was hovering over the coach with a horrified look on his face. "Gawd, Tiger," Howard was saying, "you awright, you awright?"

I bolted out of my chair thinking, "Oh, Jesus, Tiger's having a heart attack." About the time I reached his side our strapping coach jerked upright in his chair and took one final voluminous inhale of air. His face was red as a branding iron and his eyes were watering unmercifully. "Howard," I shouted, "what the hell's the matter with Tiger?"

"Well," replied Howard Fest in his slow drawl, "you know how everytime we play in Houston my relations come on down to see us play?" I nodded that, indeed, I did, for who could forget the sight of fourteen or fifteen Texans, drunk as skunks, piling out of a Grey-

110

hound bus they chartered to loudly cheer on their favorite hero. "When I left them today," continued Howard, "they gave me this-here bag of jalapeno peppers to bring back home with me. Tiger took one look and said he hadn't had a good jalapeno pepper in years. So I gave him one and he popped the whole thing in his mouth."

A few seconds later Tiger began making motions as if he were going to pull through the ordeal. "How are you feeling now, Tiger?" I asked.

He nodded his great head slowly and in a broken voice that seemed to come from his sternum said, "That little buggar was so hot it popped one of my contact lenses clean outta my eye." He had managed to locate the lens and pop it back in before sitting back in his seat and taking a long, satisfied breath. "Now, boys," he announced, "that's what I call a damn good down-home Texas pepper."

The win in Houston put us at 3-0, the only undefeated team in the AFC. We were getting pretty reved up, but Paul had a way of not letting us get carried away. "I'd have to say," he admitted to us, "that, on the whole, you guys carried out team defense much better. Everyone seemed to be doing his job." Actually, the fact that Paul complimented us at all seemed, for him, a momentary lapse into unrestrained giddiness. He resorted to saying things like "on the whole" and "*team* defense." Only on special occasions did he single out players for praise. He could have stated, for example, "Carpenter, you and LeClair had an outstanding defensive day against Houston. Keep up the good work. And you, Bob Brown and Maulty Moore, you guys were marvelous at the goal line defense. No one got through you." But he didn't.

The charge had often been made that PB intentionally did not single out players for praise because outstanding individuals tended to become superstars, and superstars tended to ask for six-figure salaries, and they also tended to rise above the team as a whole, which could cause problems. Once, in Cleveland, Paul allowed Jimmy Brown to become a superstar (who could have stopped him?) and it eventually cost the coach his job. When it got down to choosing between Brown—Jimmy or Paul—Art Modell chose the former. And for Paul that hurt must have lingered interminably.

The one guy who did very little celebrating over the Houston victory was punter Dave Green. Paul chewed him out pretty good after the movies which, I guess, proved that compliments could have been spread like a thin blanket over the entire team so no one individual got more recognition than he was entitled to; on the other hand, criticism was to be meted out on an individual basis. Paul blamed Dave for the tremendous offensive show put on in the

Astrodome by Billy Johnson. White Shoes ran back six punts for 127 yards and four kickoffs for 136 yards. His 263 yards in these two categories accounted for nearly the entire Oilers' offense output. "Your job was to kick away from that guy," Paul reminded Green in front of us all. "You just didn't do it. You didn't get the job done." None of us expected Paul to throw in the fact that Dave's final punt of the game was one hell of a defensive gem that went out of bounds at the Oilers' five-yard line, virtually making it impossible for them to drive the length of the field and score in the remaining time. Like I say, we didn't expect him to mention it and he didn't disappoint us.

Seeing PB climb all over Dave Green reminded me of another punter we had. He upset PB so much that he actually cut him at *half time* during a game.

His name was Rex Keeling, and he would have fared far better had he stayed in the car selling business. That's exactly what he was doing in 1968—selling cars for his father in Samford, Georgia— when he got a call one day from Paul. The Old Coach explained that our regular punter, Dale Livingston, had just been called up for military duty and that the Bengals needed a punter for the final two games of the season. Rex, who, as a free agent, had tried out for the team in summer camp but because of Livingston's presence was cut, readily agreed.

Rex was really a nice kid, and it looked as if Paul Brown had pulled off one of his legendary coups by calling Keeling out of his forced retirement. Rex was really booting the ball all week in practice. But when it got down to the game itself, it was quite another matter.

I thing we were playing the Boston Patriots away. As fate would have it, Rex was called on to punt extensively during the first half. And, although I don't know the official statistics, I'm willing to bet that he didn't kick one ball more than a net distance of twenty-six yards.

Humbled in front of hostile fans, Paul Brown was livid. And at halftime he singled out Rex in the locker room. In a grave voice, he told him that he was disappointed—Rex had allowed the pressure of the pro leagues to get to him. "This game is just too big for you, Rex," Paul advised him. "You just can't handle it. You're gone." With that, Paul called over his shoulder to his ever present son, "Mike, write this boy out a check for what we owe him." And, then, loud enought for most to hear, "That's what I get for trying to make a kicker out of a used car salesman."

That was the last we saw of Rex Keeling, and I must say I felt sorry for him. He was really an awfully nice fellow. Considering the fact that Rex was the *only* punter the Bengals had, Paul's cashiering of him that day seemed harsher than usual. His dismissal meant that we would play the rest of the second half of the Boston game and the entire last game of the season without the services of a punter at all. I guess when you're a first-year expansion club with a 3-10 record, it just really didn't make much difference.

As I recall, that same year PB cut another Bengal at halftime.

His name was Dan Archer, a big kid, about 6'5", 250 pounds. A second-year player picked up by the Bengals in the allocation draft, he played mainly on our specialty teams, the punting team in particular. As such, he had but one responsibility: outside containment. The coaches made Dan's assignment perfectly clear to him: "Don't let the guy returning the punt get outside of you. Whatever you do, get wider than he does, even if it means running up into the second row of bleachers. Force the ball carrier inside so one of your teammates running around in the middle of the field looking for something to do can have a shot at tackling him."

Sure enough the worst thing that could happen did.

We were playing the Raiders in Oakland the eighth game of the season. As was frequent in those days, the punting team was on their field. Right before the punt one of our coaches yelled out to remind Dan Archer of his outside containment responsibility. Dan nodded and then proceeded to take an inside hip fake offered by a rookie punt returner named George Atkinson. A real speed-burner, Atkinson got outside of Archer and sprinted fifty yards to paydirt.

Paul Brown's farewell speech to Dan Archer at halftime was short and to the point. "Take your jockstrap off, son," said Paul, "you've just played your last game as a Cincinnati Bengal." The room grew perfectly quiet, and the players did anything possible to keep from looking over at the deflated Dan Archer. Most of us had our faces buried cheek deep in our towels, trying our hardest not to laugh out loud.

Another thing I observed about PB: it seemed as if whenever a word like "lose" was used, it was accompanied by the word "you," as in *"you* lost the game." When the word "win" was used, it was preceded by the word "we," as in *"we* managed to win the big one." To Paul, *we* and *lost* just didn't go together. It's like *political integrity*, words mutually exclusive.

Paul was continually threatening us or "warning" us about the upcoming opposition, as if we didn't know that any team, given the right circumstances, could beat any other NFL team on a given day. I really believe that one reason our guys played so hard in '75 was that they just couldn't bear the thought of coming in on a Tuesday following a loss to hear him stand up there and say, "See, I tried to warn you, didn't I? I told you they had a good football team, but you wouldn't listen to me. And *you* lost the game."

Believe me, we knew well enough that our next three opponents—New England, Oakland and Atlanta—were all stiff competition and we wanted to win so we didn't have to hear Paul say "I told you so."

For my part, because of my injury I was still uncomfortably far removed from the team. I felt like a newspaper reporter hanging around the guys, enjoying the atmosphere of a winning club, but not *really* being able to join in. It was terrible. My teammates were in the taping room before practice while I was in the training room getting a rub down. They would be in a meeting and I would be in the whirlpool. Crimine, I felt like the only kid on the block who wasn't invited to the party.

It drove me crazy during games—standing around on the sidelines as an observer, knowing full well I had the talent to be in there playing but because of the injury I wasn't. On the sidelines I walked, I stalked, I sat, I stood, I bit my nails. When I was nervous before a game I was playing in, it was a different scene. Then it was more of an adrenalin-pump nervousness, getting keyed up on purpose in order to play at a full psychological gallop. And the playing of the game was the *release* of that stored up nervousness. But when you knew you weren't going to be able to play, it was hell. You just had to digest that nervousness. I don't know where it went—I guess it washed out in the urine, like everything else. Man, I could never have been a second-string player. Or a coach. Neither of them got the chance to work off their anxieties. I'll amend that. Coaches got to holler at players and officials.

Paul was particularly edgy during those weeks. One of the reasons was that the World Football League officially folded after a year and a half of floundering. Paul said his phone didn't stop ringing. "I received about thirty calls the next morning," he told us, "players, coaches, trainers—they all needed jobs. I had to tell them we didn't have room for them on the Bengals. It was a bad situation, very bad."

I was kind of sorry to see the WFL go belly-up. The new league made it possible for me to negotiate a handsome salary with the Bengals, because they knew the WFL was after me. I'd be the first to admit that I asked the WFL for the sky just to see how far I could go. I was never totally serious about the negotiations, because I didn't want to leave the Bengals.

When this agent called me on behalf of some of the WFL teams, I told him, point blank: "before we even talk money I want these three things up front—I want the mortgage on my home completely paid off, I want a new Mercedes and I want a house rent-free in the city in which the WFL team is located."

There was a pause on the other end. Then the negotiator said, "I'll see what I can do. I'll call you back in three days."

It never occurred to me that a WFL team would even consider

the ludicrous demands I was making. But three days later the agent was back in touch with me. "No problem," he said. My head began to swirl, and I thought to myself, *OK, you're really going to let him have it now.* "In dollars," I said, "I want a five-year, no-cut contract calling for a half-million dollars."

"Mmmm," said the man on the other end. I looked over to where my wife Pat was sitting and shrugged. "And I want a $100,000 bonus for signing."

"Hmmm," again. Then: "I'll get back to you in three days."

By now I was beginning to think, "Hey, these guys are crazy! I'm not worth all of this." But, sure enough, three days later the agent called back; only this time he said, "The teams can't come up with that type of money right now." I looked at Pat and smiled, "I didn't really think they could."

"Yea," he said, "but here's what they *can* offer you..." and he went on to detail a four-year, no-cut contract calling for $75,000 the first year, $85,000 the second, $95,000 the third and $105,000 the fourth. Plus a $75,000 bonus for signing! Crimine! I had asked for a five-year package calling for a half-million; they were offering me a four-year package worth $425,000, plus additional benefits.

For days Pat and I walked around Cincinnati on a cloud. We really thought the whole thing was an absurdity, but who were we to argue? Finally, I went to see Mike Brown. "Mike," I said, "I don't want to take this offer from the WFL. Pat and I want to stay in Cincinnati with the Bengals. What can you do for me?"

He asked me what the WFL offer was and I told him. "Hell," he responded, predictably, "we can't match that."

"I know," I said.

"Well, how much will it take to keep you here?"

I thought a moment before answering. "Mike, I'm not going to be greedy. Here's what I'll accept"...and I named a certain salary figure in a multi-year contract package. My proposal was an extremely fair one for the team, and Mike recognized that fact immediately.

"Bob," he said, "you are the first person to come in here with any sort of reasonable offer. I'll accept the figures you just gave me. And because you demonstrated some restraint in you offer, I'll add a $20,000 bonus on top of it. Do you accept?"

I told Mike I would have to go home and discuss the whole thing with Pat, like I always did, and that I would let him know our answer in the morning. We really didn't have too much to talk about, we both wanted to stay in Cincinnati and the money the Bengals were going to pay me would insure our financial stability for the rest of our lives.

I guess, though, the best thing to come out of this negotiation was that *never again* in my football life would I have to go through the unpleasantries connected with bartering my personal worth with a professional football team.

That was worth a half-million dollars in peace of mind right there.

It only took three regular season games for Bob Brown to begin asserting himself as the Bengal Sugardaddy to replace Ernie Wright. It was a great sight to see players now routinely gathering around his monolithic body to listen to whatever he had to say about his days with Vince Lombardi and the Green Bay Packers. Big Bob told us he came in on a shooting star (winning the Super Bowl with Green Bay) and he planned to go out on a shooting star (when the Bengals won the Super Bowl).

Of Lombardi, Bob said: "He really was a great, great man. He had a volatile personality—he was very emotional, you know—but he was always very fair with his players." Bob got sort of a fond gleam in his eye. "Whenever we started to get big heads about our performance, Vince called a team meeting. Man, then all hell broke loose. 'You guys ain't nothin',' he screamed at us. 'You think you're something but you ain't. We—the coaches—are the great part of this team. There are no such things as great players, only great coaches. If you want to know the truth, you guys are no better than average football players. You win because we inspire you!' " Bob would sit back and smile. "He was a helluva coach," he'd say.

Bob Brown told us another story, too, this one not involving Lombardi. About four years ago, he said, he was traveling through Arkansas with a friend during the off season when they picked up a hitchhiker. "After a while on the road," Bob explained, "the hitchhiker wanted to go one way and we wanted to go another. We stopped the car and asked him to get out, and he got madder than hell. Then, all of a sudden, he pulled out a .25 revolver and fired at me point blank. The bullet got me in the neck." In fact, the bullet entered the right side of Bob's neck, traveled upward through the bottom of his mouth, continued on through the jaw and finally exited through the left cheek. "I mean to tell you," whistled Bob, "that little mothu' extracted four teeth, clean as you please." A doctor later told him that a quarter-inch in any direction and Bob would have been killed instantly.

Someone asked Bob what happened next. The big guy scratched his head and grinned. "Well, my friend, a real mean dude, reached back and snatched the gun away from the hitchhiker and then"—he stopped here momentarily and wrinkled his forehead in an expression of concern—"and then he treated him *real* bad."

Apparently, after "treating him real bad," Bob Brown's friend threw the hitchhiker out of the car and into a ditch along the side of the road. Then the two sped off to a nearby hospital where Bob was attended to. Later they called the police and drove back to the scene

116

For eight years my best friend Bruce Coslet (behind me in photo) chased me for my starting job. It finally came against Denver in 1975 but lasted only one game. His retirement a year before mine left a void impossible to fill. (Note: The photo reveals how closely officials can follow the action of the game.)

A

B

C

In '75, the Cincinnati Bengals had the most awesome passing attack in professional football. There were at least five good reasons....

A) We called Kenny Anderson "Freddie Franchise." In 1976, he was the best there was, and for five years, up until the '75 Buffalo game, we called him "Rookie."

B) With sprinter's speed, Isaac Curtis had those soft hands, hands so artistic they'd make a sculptor cry.

C) "Chuck" Joiner was a smooth, smart veteran, perhaps our most consistent receiver.

D) My good friend Chip Myers was called "Mr. Clutch"...he could catch it in a crowd.

E) Speed and quickness for a big man kept me in the pros for ten years.

E   D

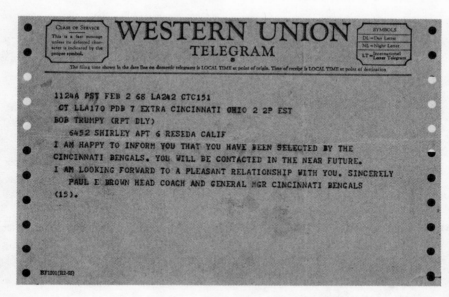

WESTERN UNION
TELEGRAM

The filing time shown in the date line on domestic telegrams is LOCAL TIME at point of origin. Time of receipt is LOCAL TIME at point of destination

1124A PST FEB 2 68 LA242 CTC151

CT LLA170 PDB 7 EXTRA CINCINNATI OHIO 2 2P EST

BOB TRUMPY (RPT DLY)

6452 SHIRLEY APT 6 RESEDA CALIF

I AM HAPPY TO INFORM YOU THAT YOU HAVE BEEN SELECTED BY THE

CINCINNATI BENGALS. YOU WILL BE CONTACTED IN THE NEAR FUTURE.

I AM LOOKING FORWARD TO A PLEASANT RELATIONSHIP WITH YOU. SINCERELY

PAUL E BROWN HEAD COACH AND GENERAL MGR CINCINNATI BENGALS

(15).

BF1201(R2-65)

This is it—the official word from the Mount, my first contact with the Cincinnati Bengals. When Pat said it was from the "Beagles" I thought I had been drafted by the SPCA.

The idea was to get my 6'6" frame one-on-one with the shorter defensive backs; it helped me become the fifth leading active receiver in the AFL.

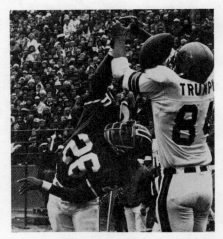

I knew my ability to play three positions would appeal to the business instincts of Paul Brown. Some guys would've been perturbed at learning all those blocking assignments...but it beat the hell out of collecting bills in Watts.

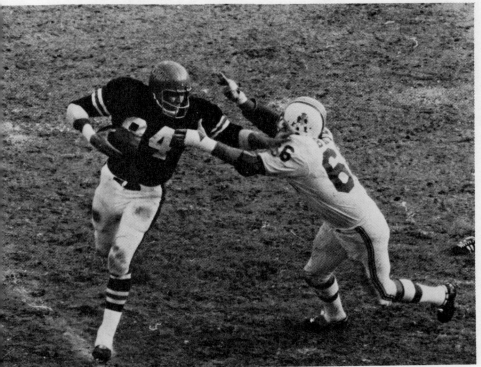

At 285 pounds and with Super Bowl experience, Bob Brown quickly became the Bengal sugardaddy to replace Ernie Wright. Bob said he "came in on a shooting star" with the Packers and he planned to go out on one with the Bengals. After our playoff loss to Oakland we collectively felt ashamed—we had treated Bob Brown "real bad."

A scout will tell you he knows everything about a player...but I was an oddball, a freak, a glove with six fingers; that I ever came to be drafted by the Bengals defies even the most lenient laws of probability.

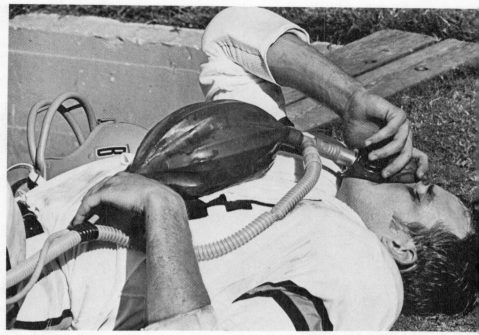

I should have listened to Paul back in 1969. I didn't, and ended up with thirty stitches in my ankle. To combat the pain, a teammate gave me some "Wheaties." I was on Cloud 9 most of the game, but afterwards I sat there and cried.

The one regret in my career is that I was not more durable. My injury list would have made a Blue Cross agent shudder.

In the mid-70's, the Bengals had the most intricate offense in the NFL. At times I needed a little help figuring out my assignments (that is not our 1968 running back Monk Williams instructing me).

I recognize that celebrity golfer in the center, but who are those other fellas? (Oh yeah, Bob Hope and Jack Nicklaus).

Not that I would want to take him on over the issue, but Ken Norton didn't like the fact that I was so much taller, so he stood on a 3" box to pose for this photo.

Here's a trivia quiz—only one of the four pictured above isn't wearing a pro sports championship ring. Is it (from left) Lou Piniella, New York Yankees; Billy Joe Dupree, Dallas Cowboys; Johnny Bench, Cincinnati Reds, or that tall kid from the Bengals?

In high school I was an all-around athlete—all-state in track and football, all-American in basketball. Here I was working on my tripping strategy so number 51 wouldn't get to the ball. I think the ref penalized me fifteen yards.

One of the unpleasantries of pro football life was the time spent away from the family. Football wives, like Pat, had to be efficient crisis managers. While I was away, Matt bit his tongue nearly in half; Jason had his thumb almost totally severed.

My favorite-son candidate to replace PB was Tiger Johnson (with the headset), which is what happened. Here, Tiger was practicing the icy stare his boss made a trademark. I only hope it wasn't me they were watching out on the field.

There was a general mystique about the man, and they said you either loved him or hated him. Greg Cook got along with Paul, but shoulder problems ended the career of the sure-fire superstar quarterback after only one year. Bill Bergey (l.) crossed Paul Brown once; now he's in Philadelphia.

As my roommate for nine seasons, team captain Bob Johnson was a saving grace for me—he added a dimension of security. My first (of six) roommates was cut because of the way he ate breakfast. If it wasn't bad enough that Johnson and I lived practically as husband and wife during summer camp, we also live within 500 yards of each other in Cincinnati.

Smiles from PB and Beau (58) notwith-standing, our surprise division champion-ship in 1970 was not in the Paul Brown scheme of things. Later he said being champions set the Bengal franchise back years.

This was our first team meeting in 1968. Paul, wearing the ever-present black hat, reminded us that Lou Groza sat through his opening remarks twenty-one times. We theorized that "Louie" was stone deaf, could sleep with his eyes open or had a very short memory.

It amazed me that he had been a head coach eleven years longer than I had been alive. He was a genius, and pro football, good or bad, was the child of Paul Brown. He shaped the "game" into what it is today—a sports conglomerate played within business, economic and scientific parameters.

My Bengal career opened other opportunities like, here in the 1978 Baltimore-Miami game, calling the action for NBC along with veteran sportscaster Stu Nahan.

where the confrontation took place. There they found the gun-toting hitchhiker, still laying face down in the ditch. He hadn't moved an inch. Bob Brown and his friend took one look at each other and hit the gas pedal, and they didn't slow down until they were somewhere north of the Mason-Dixon line. Instinct told them not to be in the area when the police learned exactly how "real bad" the hitchhiker had been treated.

As for activities on the field, the game against the Patriots was less-than-exciting. We were flat as a deflated football, due mainly to the fact that playing the 0-3 Patriots gave us as much dynamic inspiration as learning that our tax returns were being audited by the IRS.

Still, the previous year when we played a flat game we lost; in '75 we played flat and won, 27-10.

It was 7-7 at halftime and our locker room was like a madhouse. PB and his lieutenants were all over the place, hollering so loud... at so many people...about so many different mistakes...that it was impossible to follow everything that was said. I do remember Paul scolding us and letting us know that we should have been ashamed of ourselves because, "you don't have a bit of pride in what you are doing out there."

From the moment we left our locker room to begin the second half it was all over for our opponents. Mack Herron fumbled the ball, Ron Pritchard recovered, and shortly thereafter Dave Green kicked a twenty-nine-yard field goal. They came back with one of their own to tie it at 10-10, but that score didn't last long. We took the ball and quickly moved eighty-three yards—Kenny Anderson hitting Bruce Coslet, Ike Curtis and Charlie Joiner with passes—and scored a touchdown with the Essex Express skirting right end on a pretty twelve-yard run.

The Patriots ran two plays and Sam Cunningham was rudely introduced to Bob Brown—he fumbled the ball on their thirty-seven, where Al Beauchamp claimed squatters' rights on it. On the next play, Charlie Joiner put a hellacious juke on cornerback Ron Bolton—faking inside, faking outside, cutting inside—and caught the ball in the end zone. That made it 24-10, and Dave Green wrapped it up with a twenty-one-yard field goal.

The real difference in the game was the quarterbacks. Jim Plunkett and Kenny Anderson came into the league together five years before, with Stanford-bred Plunkett getting national fanfare. Kenny got nothing more than sportswriters scratching their heads and guffawing, "Who in the hell is this small town jerk Kenny Anderson? Look, he played his college ball at tiny Augustana College in Illinois, ha, ha."

117

Against the Patriots Kenny threw for 265 yards; Plunkett threw for fifty-nine.

And we were now 4-0, ha, ha.

Next up was the Raiders. It was always a big game. When we played west coast teams, our California guys—like Ike Curtis and Sherm White—played extra hard. They were playing for off-season "braggin' rights."

As for me, playing Oakland meant remembering the Bay area, location of my military career, such as it was. Military duty for me was underwhelming and short, very short.

Never had I contemplated joining the armed services, but when I flunked out of the University of Illinois in 1964 the Vietnam War was waxing hot; I knew that the dowdy old ladies in patched stretch stockings working the Springfield draft board were waiting with an arsonist's glee to reclassify my student deferment to 1-A status.

I decided right then that I would not give them that pleasure. So I signed up for the local Naval Reserve Unit, and I also put in for "Radioman" status. A Sigma Chi fraternity brother at Illinois advised me that a Radioman needed a top-secret security clearance, and that it would take months, even years, for the FBI to conduct the required thorough investigation into my background in order to grant me that clearance. I figured: what the hell, another year and the Vietnam War would be over; then they wouldn't even need me.

I was wrong there, by a long shot. The war was still going strong a year later, and in June of 1967 I found myself stationed at Treasure Island in the Bay Area. Understandably, I was a little upset about the whole thing. My reserve unit had been called up before my graduation at Utah. Plus, I had been married to Pat for less than a year, so I was faced with the unpleasant task of leaving her for two years and living with Uncle Sam.

I shouldn't have worried about it. Thanks to a military snafu, the Navy found a unique way of drumming me out—and it took only forty-eight hours. My second day there I was called into the medical officer's quarters to review my physical examination records. As ordered, I was standing at parade rest a few feet behind the medical officer when, suddenly, he attempted to stand up; he knocked his chair backward across the freshly waxed floor. As a torpedo slithers through the water toward its target, the chair slid toward me as if it were on greased ballbearings, and it caught me full on. Whack, CRACK. A direct hit, square on the kneecap.

Immediately I grabbed my leg and went down, "Jesus Christ, man," I hollered, "what have you done to my leg. I think you broke the son of a bitch."

The medical officer was paralyzed with fear. He was sweating terribly and all he could do was stand there and look around the premises to see whether anyone else had witnessed his clumsy move. Finally, he ran over to me and, in an attempt to quiet me down, began poking around my knee joint with worried fingers. "Can you bend your leg at all, son?" he asked, his voice cracking.

"No way," I said. "You've ruined me."

Later, after X-rays, it was determined that the impact of chair meeting kneecap had dislodged a large piece of calcium from behind my knee. The medical officer told me it would require some exploratory surgery to find out how to treat the condition.

Wonderful. The last time I was in a hospital I stayed for nine weeks and they drilled a hole clean through my hand. Given the same time and resourcefulness, there was no telling *what* the Navy could manage to do. So, immediate surgery was the answer, the doc said. Either surgery or....

Or...I couldn't believe it! The medical officer advised me that the Navy would *discharge* me right there and then if—and this was pre-eminent—*if* I agreed to sign papers releasing the Navy from any responsibility for the injured knee.

I didn't need to think twice about it. I recognized this as being one helluva viable alternative to a two-year hitch in the Navy. "Hand me a pen, man," is all I said. If I required a knee operation I would get it done on the outside, as a civilian. I certainly didn't need the Navy for that.

I signed the discharge papers and was evermore free of my military obligation. They didn't let me out right away, of course. As anyone connected with the military—or any governmental agency —knows, the processing of paperwork takes time. It's one of the truisms of bureaucratic life: the simpler the task, the more time-consuming becomes the processing of paperwork. It took about ninety days in all, and for that entire time I was assigned to be a buoy guard. In other words, I had the awesome responsibility of tossing out buoys from the bow of the Admiral's barge as we eased in for landings. What great satisfaction I had, a feeling of really beating the system. Here the government had spent ten or eleven months and probably about thirty thousand dollars in paperwork and manpower to grant me top-security status, and for what?—for me to spend three months babysitting for a damn buoy so paint wouldn't be chipped off the nose of an Admiral's barge!

My knee? Nothing really came of it. After some initial days of stiffness, the malady cleared up all together. I guess whatever pain or discomfort that sliding chair had caused me, if left the very day I signed my discharge papers.

Prior to the Oakland game, we anticipated a hard, close battle, one in which the "breaks" would win or lose it. We expected a high-scoring affair because both teams' quarterbacks, runners and receivers had quick-strike power. All the ingredients were there. Unfortunately, Mother Nature interceded. It rained in Cincinnati for three days before the game, and it was still raining at game time. The temperature had dipped into the low fifties, too, making the ball extremely heavy—hard to pass, and hard to catch. (The two high-quality QBs had eight interceptions between them.) Playing football on wet AstroTurf is like playing in socks on a freshly waxed kitchen floor. Thanks to a key interception by rookie cornerback Marvin Cobb, we found ourselves ahead 14-10 with only 2:58 on the clock. The fans felt victory was at hand because the Raiders had to go ninety-eight yards for a score.

I wasn't so sure. This queezy sort of knawing pain came over me and I began to pace the sidelines. All I could think of was the previous year's come-from-behind game which the Raiders won. My mouth became dry and thick and I saw Stabler hit two passes to Mike Sciani, one to Fred Biletnikoff and one to Clarence Davis and found themselves camped on our thirty-yard line with less than a minute to go. My heart leaped into my throat when, on the next play, I helplessly looked on as Stabler faded back to throw again and hurled the ball toward Cliff Branch, open on the right sidelines. By the grace of God, Jim LeClair saw Branch out there, too, and he hustled over in time to pick off the ball in mid-flight. We took over with forty-four seconds left, and, finally, the Raiders game was ours.

The locker room was in an uproar. Ron Pritchard was strutting back and forth saying, "I can't believe it, I can't believe it. I've never beaten the Raiders in my life. When I was with Houston we lost to them 55-0. I was beginning to believe they were invincible."

It was a big win. True, the game was no artistic masterpiece. The Rookie completed only four of nineteen passes for seventy-five yards. But he hit the big ones when they counted, and under the inclement conditions, that's all you can ask. By comparison, Stabler, an All-Pro, wasn't much better: eight of twenty-four for 113 yards.

The previous year we would have lost a game like that one; but in '75 we didn't. We were 5-0 now, and, strange, amid all the boisterous celebrating in our locker room, a re-occurring picture kept flashing through my mind. It was of Mike Reid, who, a few hours from then, would be playing the piano before a small audience at a restaurant only three miles away from Riverfront Stadium. All I could think of was, I wonder if Mike Reid still believes he made the right choice in retiring from the Bengals at age twenty-six? And suddenly I felt sorry for him because in his five years with the Bengals he never knew what it was like to be playing with the feeling of team love and unity, that special *togetherness* that only comes from having a 5-0 record. I knew one thing—Mike would have liked it.

Before the Atlanta game, I began working out again, and it was a sin how bad I felt, awkward. Everything I touched I dropped. My cleats felt as if they were constructed of poured concrete. Worse, before the game, Paul was sitting around telling anyone who would listen that Falcon tight end Jim Mitchell was "the best tight end in pro football." Geez, Paul sure knew how to hurt a guy.

One break we had was that Claude Humphrey, the iron-tough defensive end for the Falcons, had undergone knee surgery and didn't play against us. He was one rugged dude, and when he and Suki Holland matched up the Earth trembled. Suki and Claude were teammates in college, at Tennessee State, and whenever they faced each other they really put something extra into the hitting. I remember a pass play years ago when Claude really went after Suki and threw a big old fashioned round-house fist at him. Suki caught sight of it as it was making its way to his jaw, so he quickly ducked, allowing it to whistle briskly over his helmet. Then he stood up and unloaded a furious "bringin' death" forearm to Claude Humphrey's jaw. It really stunned him. On our next possession, Claude came after Suki again, but our tackle, figuring a good offense was a good defense, allowed the attacker to come within a few feet of him before merely taking a quick step backwards. This threw Humphrey totally off balance, and while he was staggering around Suki nailed him again—full force with another forearm directly on the face mask. Down went Humphrey a second time, so mad he could have ripped out chunks of AstroTurf with his bare teeth. When we all got back into the huddle, Kenny Anderson called a play in which I was supposed to block Claude Humphrey. I never wanted not to do anything so bad in my life. And I wasn't wrong. I went after him and he hit me a shot on the bridge of my nose so hard that it would have moved Mt. Rushmore a full six inches. My knees buckled and I came very near losing consciousness. As I was laying there, this black haze in my helmet, Suki came running up to me and asked in a worried voice, "You awright, Trump, you awright?" He pulled me up and I wobbled beside him back to the huddle. After catching my breath I turned to our tackle and said, "Listen, man, would you quit messing with that guy. I ain't as big as you, and he's going to kill me!" I certainly wasn't upset that Mister Humphrey was going to miss this game.

To say we played another flat game is an understatement of the facts. In our first five regular season games we hadn't permitted the opponent to cross our goal line during the first quarter. Our defense took this as a great source of pride.

That little impressed the Falcons, however, because they took our opening kickoff and promptly marched seventy-one yards in nine plays for a touchdown. So much for pride.

Our offense knew we had our work cut out for us. Playing catch up football on the opposition's home sod is a little like being a salmon trying to swim upstream. We knew we would have to give it our best shot.

We ran three plays and fumbled.

Indeed, on our second possession we ran eight plays and punted and on our third we ran four and did the same. At least Dave Green was getting in some valuable game-situation kicking practice.

It took our defense, specifically Rattler Riley, to turn it around for us. He jumped in front of a Pat Sullivan pass at the Falcons' thirty-four yard line, juked right then left, and ran the ball in for six points. It was Rattler's fourth interception in five games.

Then we pulled off one of the prettiest pass plays in Bengal memory. If there was a *Sports Illustrated* photographer on the scene worth his salt, a color photo of a diving Charlie Joiner would have been on the cover of the magazine that next week. Joiner lined up left and, when the ball was snapped, took off downfield as fast as he could go. He made one quick-step fake to the sidelines and then burst hell-for-leather to the inside and the goal line. Kenny threw a beautiful ball and Charlie made the diving catch right on the end zone stripe. He was in total, full sprinter's stride as he approached the ball, and at the moment of impact of leather on fingertips, he was so fully extended that if he had reached one more inch he may well have permanently increased the space between his upper and lower vertabrae. There was no way he could have hung on to that ball had he clipped his fingernails before the game.

At halftime it was 14-7, Bengals, and we got hollered at by the coaches. We came out for the third quarter geared for victory, and pulled off an eye-popping triple reverse pass that we ran five or six times a season. It was a real fan-pleaser because everyone was moving and it seemed as if half the guys on the offense got an opportunity to touch the ball at least once. Kenny took the snap from center Bob Johnson and headed right, handing off to halfback Stan Fritts running left, who handed the ball off to Ike Curtis running right, who handed it back to Kenny Anderson, who had spent most of the time between handoffs trying to appear to the defense to be innocent and unconcerned, who sighted me downfield on a come-back pattern and hit me with the ball on the numbers. I took the ball and headed upfield. Man oh man, what a play. Even the Atlanta fans loved it. Unfortunately, all the razzle-dazzle went for naught. I was carrying the ball one handed when I was hit from behind by Ray Easterling. He knocked the ball loose and a former teammate from Illinois, linebacker Don Hansen, pounced on it at our forty. The Falcons took over possession and the momentum that we had generated from the powerful running bursts and ending with the Mack Sennett pass play had been broken.

I didn't feel at all good about it.

Especially when, later, Atlanta got the ball with about eight minutes left and went to tight end Jim Mitchell on a beautiful thirty-one-yard screen pass play, and six plays later hit him again in the end zone to tie the game at 14-14. It was a real blow. Had it not been for a previous John Shinners' holding call that erased a touch-down and my stupid-ass fumble on the triple reverse-pass to stop a serious Bengal drive, we would have been way ahead in the game. But now we were fighting for our undefeated lives.

Finally we got a break, when runningback Haskell Stanback fumbled and Ron Carpenter recovered at our twenty-one. A pass to me fell incomplete when it was tipped at the last moment by East-erling, but a nice aerial to Charlie Joiner took it to the nine and then Boobie picked up five more, then two more, and finally Kenny, with 2:04 left, rolled out right to pass and decided to run it in himself. 21-14, and victory was salted away.

It was a frustrating game, though, the kind so full of mistakes and mental errors that even a win—and the fact that we were 6-0 on the season—wasn't much reason for jubilation.

The plane ride back to Cincinnati was mighty quiet.

WHAT'S A LITTLE HOLDING, MORE OR LESS?

This was the big one.

Cleveland was important because it was our opener and a personal grudge match for Paul Brown; Houston was a bitter conference rival, and Oakland was vital because they were the supposed next Super Bowl champions.

But this one was the biggest of them all. The Pittsburgh Steelers, defending world champions! If the Steelers lost to us they'd fall two full games behind in the loss column (they earlier had lost to Buffalo). If we won, we'd be 7-0, and well on our way to fame and fortune.

Pittsburgh-Cincinnati games were no ordinary football battles. They were full-scale wars. There was always controversy surrounding these slugfests. A few years back Steve Chomyszak crunched Terry Bradshaw on a pass play and separated his shoulder for him; Bill Bergey was called for a cheap shot when he put his helmet into Terry Hanratty's ribs. In '74, cornerback Glen Edwards closelined Kenny Anderson while he was standing out of bounds a full two seconds after the play had ended. The Cincinnati fans saw blood.

We should have been ready for the Steelers. Physically we were in top shape. And the Atlanta films showed that we could move the ball when we had a mind to. On a personal level, I was a bit disappointed with my showing in the Atlanta game. True, it was my first game after a four-week layoff, but I didn't think I did as bad as the films showed; but the films seldom lied.

"Did you see that ref in the Falcons' game?" asked someone. "Even with his authority he didn't want to tangle with Bob Brown." He was referring to an incident toward the end of the game. There was a three-foot white stripe around the playing surface which we players on the sidelines were supposed to stay behind when watching the action on the field. For one reason or another we had all crowded this line pretty good and one of the officials became upset with us. He started at the far end of our line of players and ran in front of each one of them, waving his hands madly. He began shoving people backward and saying, "Move back, dammit. Move your asses behind that white stripe." As he burst by the players one by one he suddenly came to towering Bob Brown. The ref pulled up short, bent his head backward and, much in the same way Jack must have sized up the beanstalk that first morning, looked straight up at Bob's facemask; then he shot a contemplative glance at Bob's massive chest and ample girth and said, real polite, "Excuse me, son. Could you please move back off of this white stripe. All the players are supposed to stand behind it, you know." Then he moved on, quickly, and one of our rookies said, "Man, Bob Brown even commands the respect of an NFL referee! *That's* respect."

By the way, Bob Brown soon put an addendum to the story he told us about being shot in the jaw. "I forgot to mention," he said, "that the time the hitchhiker plugged me down South was actually the second time I had been shot." The first, he said, occurred when he was a teenager and "I got into a scrape with another dude. He pulled a revolver on me and shot me in the chest." Bob Brown sighed. "I thank my lucky stars that the bullet didn't hit me flush. It would have hurt like hell, most likely."

I thought to myself: No wonder Bob Brown weighs 285 pounds. He's got more lead in him than a bullet-proof vest.

It was a miracle that on our road trips he was able to pass through those airport metal detectors without authorities impounding his body.

One of the quietest guys around the training complex the week of the Steeler's game was Dave Lapham, our guard. Only in his second year, Dave had the unenviable task of going against the Steelers' Mean Joe Greene. No one had to be educated about Mean Joe. He was big and strong and fast. The "Mean" label was really a misnomer, we were told, and I think it was originally coined because it rhymed so nicely with Greene. But then I'm not sure. We heard that Joe was almost trying to keep up with his bad-ass image that year. A few weeks previous, the story went, he had kicked a Cleveland Brown in the groin and put him in the hospital, and he had done something similar against Denver. I didn't know whether these charges were true. I couldn't imagine a player of Joe Greene's talent resorting to such street fighting. Of course, Mean Joe was only a part of the feared defense that had been coined "The Steel Curtain." There was also Dwight White (now *there* was a dirty player—after one play, Rufus Mayes, a black, came back to the huddle and announced, "Man, is that dude Dwight White a *nigger*!"), Fats Holmes and L.C. Greenwood. No doubt about it, this was one of the aggressive front-fours in all of football. And one of the most undisciplined in playing the game, which had actually benefitted them. You never knew for sure what they were going to do. Mean Joe, for instance, seemed to line up wherever he felt like it on a certain play and headed for whichever hole looked good to him. That made blocking severely difficult. If I had to summarize the Steelers' defense in a word it would be "intimadaters." They really taunted you, intimidated you, until you were so mad that you forgot about concentrating on your assignments. Then they'd blow right by you and sack the quarterback.

The Steeler linebackers were some of the best around: Jack Ham, Jack Lambert and Andy Russell. I got to know both Ham and Russell while shooting golf with them during the practice week preceding the All-Star game in San Diego. I considered them good friends and it seemed odd for me to go out and try to knock their heads off on a block. Really, though, you try harder against the guys you know. It's an ego thing.

Being campanions to the opposition is something that was hard for me to adjust to in the pros. Striking up a friendship with the "bad" guys seemed tantamount to providing the Russians with the blueprints of our nuclear reactors. In high school and college it was drilled into us that the guys wearing the brown jerseys, those guys on the *other side*, are the ENEMY! They are to be destroyed at all costs, for the good of the cause.

In the pros I learned fast: the way people moved from club to club, a teammate and best friend the past year may be on the opposition's squad the next year. And you didn't have to sever a friendship because of it. You just refrained from being friends for sixty minutes on Sundays.

The reason we pro players got along off the field was that we were really an elite corps of talented people practicing the same art. We had equal pride in our trade and mutual respect for one another. We viewed each other as executives in the same business. It just so happened that in our business we wore funny hats.

There were other misconceptions about pro football I picked up over the years. For example, most fans assume that our summer camps were made up of mostly bone-crunching, nut-busting drills and conditioning routines. Not true. High school and college players had it ten time worse than we did in this respect. That's because at Bengal camps there was no "shaping-up" program to get players physically fit. Once mid-July rolled around Bengal players were expected to report to summer camp *already in good physical shape.* From the beginning, summer camp emphasized the fundamentals of the game, not physical fitness. Actually, this caused the many injuries we had in '74.

Some of our guys reported to camp out of shape...and they didn't have the benefit of a comprehensive fitness program to work their muscles and bones into a pro football soundness before the season began.

It's funny how fans often form wrong impressions of pro football. I know that when I was a kid growing up in Illinois I thought professional football players were the best athletes in the world. In fact, I believed that they *transcended* this world. Pro football players —the Jimmy Browns, the Bobby Laynes, the Frank Giffords—were gods to be worshipped by common men everywhere, much as the Greeks worshipped gods before us. To me, a pro football player lived on some far Mt. Olympus where he lounged in togas and ate grapes from the cool hands of fleshy virgins. I seriously doubted whether these hero god-men, so vaunted and majestic, even deigned to urinate like the rest of us. I only knew that on Sundays they descended from their lofty homes and played football before an adoring throng and, once their superhuman work concluded, they returned to their mystical havens again. As a youngster, my three idols were 1) professional football players, 2) Superman and 3) my parents. In that order.

To be frank, I was a little shocked when I made it to the pros and learned first-hand about the type of players who comprised the NFL. Many of the players to me were unbelievably poor athletes. Not poor football players, but poor athletes. They didn't have the coordination for anything else, couldn't hit a baseball a mile, couldn't sink a corner jumpshot, couldn't cleanly return the tennis ball over the net. What they *could* do was play football—at least their one position— because they were built perfectly for it, and because they had trained for it for years. In the main, runningbacks could scamper but couldn't block; quarterbacks could throw, but couldn't dip and dodge or run over linemen; tackles could block, but in trying to catch a pass they looked like blindfolded prisoners pitching around in a courtyard.

Maybe it was because I was such an "all-around" athlete that I expected pro football players to be also. I don't know. All I can say is that I was truly disappointed when I learned that they weren't perfect in every way.

Now I looked back at my feelings concerning the elevation of pro football players to deity status and blush. I should have known all along that they were mere mortals, and that the status of god on the football field was non-existant—except, of course, for head coaches.

Looking ahead to the Steelers', Tiger Johnson was in rare form, running around the practice field cursing and rubbing his hands in glee. Tiger liked big games. "Get ready to lick your chops, boys," he told the offensive line, "The Steelers are a comin'." Then he turned toward Boobie and said, "Better be ready, son. Because when you get the ball and hit that line, all you're going to see in front of you is AstroTurf. The rest is up to you."

The fans were getting excited about the game, too. Believe it or not, I had 47 ticket requests for the game from family, friends and acquaintances. It appeared as if PB wasn't going to have to worry about a sell-out crowd. You could tell our players were gearing up: Defensive backs Rattler Riley and Leapin' Lemar pulled in to practice with brand new Cadillacs. Not to allow the offensive unit to be outdone, Ed Williams and John McDaniel wheeled in with gleaming Corvettes.

I think these guys were counting on whipping the Steelers. Either that or they were doing their patriotic part to help bolster the local economy.

Seeing all these new cars reminded me of the time several years ago when a black receiver we had named Speedy Thomas rolled into practice one day with a car you wouldn't believe. It was a new, green Toronado completely "flocked" in yellow felt. Flocked on the side of his car were his initials—*S.T.*, giganitcally—and in bold felt on top of the car was an expansive star.

When Paul walked into our meeting room that day, he was shaking his head. "I just saw an unbelievable sight in our parking lot," he said. "There's a car out there that's growing *hair* on it!"

We could hardly keep from breaking up. Sometimes you say to yourself, maybe the generation gap *is* as wide as they claim.

Since we were in first place, the press was paying a little more attention to us. When I was asked by an AP writer what it was like to be 6-0 for the first time in Bengal history, I told him:

"What this record has done has brought us close together as a team. We've always had good relationships with one another, but our undefeated streak has really made a tight-knit family out of us."

It was true. The guys were becoming each other's best friends. We hung out together, during football hours and after. Friendship and respect had gotten to the point that, after a victory, players didn't talk to reporters about their own performances; they talked to them about the good play of their *teammates*. Rattler Riley said he was having a good year because Ron Pritchard was playing excellent drop-back linebacking on pass plays, helping him out. Bob Johnson and Suki Holland compliment each other in key blocks. The whole defense, now called the "Big Orange Brotherhood," heaped praise upon Bob Brown.

It was really a great feeling, the only time in my ten years with the Bengals that it ever happened.

I guess player relationships analyzed most by the media back then consisted of black-white co-habitation. There were often innuendos, especially in a losing season, that this team or that team had a schism growing between players of different color. I remember we had a bad year early in the franchise's history and one of the papers indicated it was because some of our white players were not co-existing harmoniously with some of the black players.

Not true. To my knowledge up until Coy Bacon joined the team in '76 we never had a black-white problem on the Bengals. We never were able to afford that luxury. During the first years we all had to struggle *together* so our rag-tag team would not embarrass itself publicly. In our winning years, any prejucicial feelings were pushed aside because in order to win you needed total cooperation from each individual.

Everybody is familiar with the story of Gale Sayers and Brian Piccolo, a black and a white, who roomed together for the Chicago Bears. But few people probably realize that the Bengals may well have been one of the first teams to have a pair of interracial room-mates. Our linebackers Al Beauchamp and Ken Avery roomed together for seven years, since 1968, before being traded.

I suppose one of the most demonstrative black activists we ever had on the team was a second-round draft choice out of Lamar Tech named Tom Smiley. Tommy played with the Bengals in 1968, and, at 235 pounds, was the crunching-type running fullback for which Paul Brown teams are known. Unfortunately, as a receiver coming out of the backfield, Tom Smiley left a little to be desired; he had absolutely no hands at all. It was like he wore his fingers encased in cement gloves. We used to laugh at him in practice and say that Tom Smiley was the only player in professional football who had fore-arms extending from elbows to fingertips. Anyway, Tom had apparent-ly gotten into the teachings of Malcolm X. This was at the time the civil rights movements, Chicago riots and political assassinations were marking a new violent era. During training camp, it wasn't uncommon to hear, at any hour, the record-player in Tom's room blaring out Malcon X exhortations. Later, after Tom Smiley was traded, his roommate, Paul Robinson, another black runningback, told me that Tom used to recite Malcolm X passages almost every night. Paul said his roommate would open his Malcolm X books and pace the room reading incendiary paragraphs aloud with a zealot's fervor, eyes burning with passionate commitment.

Robinson, slenderly-built and one of the nicest guys you'd ever meet, told me he used to just sit silently on his bed and shake his head in agreement with every word Tom Smiley said. Not because he dug the teachings of Malcolm X, but because, frankly, Tom Smiley's zealousness—not to mention his size—scared the hell out of him.

Later, Royce Berry told me that Tommy Smiley was picked up by police in San Antonio, Texas. Berry said Smiley was standing on a street corner, dressed in body chains, and little else, preaching about the second-coming or something. They may have committed Smiley to psychiatric care, Royce said.

I recall the time when the media projected that the Bengals were going to have one of the all-time racial problems in football. That was in 1969 when we signed as a free agent a guy named Tommie

Smith, a wide receiver. Tommie was one of the fastest human beings in the world; indeed, he then held and still does, countless records for sprinting events.

In 1968 Tommie Smith became a household word, and he incurred the wrath of much of the nation when he and John Carlos pulled a sensational bit of infamy in Mexico City during the Olympics. Was there a more famous photo that year (I'm sure it appeared in most every daily newspaper in the world) than that of Tommie Smith and John Carlos standing to accept Olympic medals with shoulders bent, heads bowed, gloved fists defiantly raised while in the background America's national anthem was being played? Tommie Smith and John Carlos became hated men except, of course, for those people who were into The Movement.

We didn't really know what to expect when Tommie Smith reported to camp in 1969. Would he stir up the blacks on the team against the facist Paul Brown? Or, pass out black-movement literature? Perhaps make revolutionary speeches?

None of these things occurred. Tommie Smith was one of the nicest, most sincere, easy-going people I had ever met in my life. He was fun to talk to and almost never mentioned the subject of the black movement, unless, of course, someone would bring it up first.

I'll tell you something else, too, and this may well be a revelation to many people: Tommie Smith participated in the Mexico City demonstration for one reason and one reason only—he was *paid* to do it. By someone, some group, who wanted to embarrass the United States for some reason. Tommie told me, "Well, I was poor and I had to eat. I didn't have a cent to my name. Then, in Mexico City, someone came along with some *encouragement* for me to do what I did. I needed what they had to offer, so I jumped at it."

Tommie could have been a hell of a football player. The trouble was that he had never played the sport—he was strictly a sprint man at San Jose State—and he didn't know the first thing about running a pass pattern. From the day he was old enough to put on track shoes, Tommie had been coached that the shortest distance between two points was a straight line, and that's the way he ran, straight and hard, faster than anyone else. The coaches, particularly Bill Walsh, worked and worked with Tommie, but it was no use. The kid just couldn't learn to stop his legs from churning long enough to make a cut left or right. It was straight ahead speed or nothing at all.

There have been few players signed by the Bengals who *wanted* to play pro football more than Tommie Smith. But because of Tommie's inability to cut, Paul made a "cab squad" player out of him that first year, hoping that, by at least practicing with us, Tommie would one day learn how to run a good pass pattern. During those days the players on the Taxi squad did not travel with the team for away games. Except for Tommie. He wanted to see his teammates play the Jets and Joe Namath in New York so bad that he bought an airline ticket to New York with his own money; on the same plane in which we were riding first class, Tommie Smith was riding coach. In New York he stayed at a cheaper hotel across town, again, paying for the expenses out of his own pocket. He walked to the stadium. I doubt whether too many other players were so emotionally involved with a team that they'd take a personal financial loss to see them play a game.

Finally, late in the season, Tommie got a chance to play. Paul activated him because of injuries to other receivers. It was the Oakland game, and we were behind. Everyone in the park, including the Raiders' defensive backs, knew we were going to throw the bomb in hopes of putting some points on the board. The Raiders' defensive backs were playing so deep that it was physically impossible to run by them. Tommie Smith came in and at the snap of the ball took off in a straight line. He passed a sagging defensive back like he was a statue, and when he got fifty or sixty yards deep there was the ball waiting for him. He dived for it and made a spectacular catch. Unfortunately, on the play Tommie separated his shoulder. It was the last game he ever played in professional football.

By the time the Steelers' game rolled around the temperature was in the 70's. The sun was shining clear and bright upon the field and upon the sixty thousand fans wedged into Riverfront Stadium to watch the Bengals go after the Steelers. The scene, the *timing*, was perfect. It could have been the Bengals' biggest win in the history of the franchise.

The tone of the game was ominously set on the very first play. Steeler defensive end Dwight White broke through our offensive line and blindsided Kenny Anderson. The Rookie was down. And out. But not permanently. In came backup QB John Reaves, and two plays later we kicked. We never really seemed to get it totally together after that.

During the first half the game hardly proceeded at an artistic pace; after mistakes, penalties and interceptions it appeared that both teams would be heading to the locker rooms with a 3-3 tie. Hardly did it seem worth it, but we would have taken it; we could have regrouped and gone back at them in the second half. Perhaps we were looking *too* forward to Paul Brown's half-time advice or something; because with only sixteen seconds left and Pittsburgh not even close to field goal range, Bengal defensive back Lyle Blackwood fell and allowed Lynn Swann to cut across the middle, catch the ball on the ten and run in for a TD. Instead of going in with a 3-3 score, we were down 10-3. There was a big difference between the two, much bigger than seven points.

The locker room was deathly quiet. And our deflation showed in the way we played when we went back on the field. So much in shock were we that it was halfway through the fourth quarter before we were even able to pick up another *first down*!

Contrary to our disposition, the last-second first half touchdown really juiced up Pittsburgh, and they came out for the second half full of fire. They took the kickoff and drive seventy yards in ten plays to make it 17-3. The next time they touched the ball they went fifty-four yards in only five plays to make it 23-3 (the extra point was missed when Gerela's ball hit the goal post). The scoring play was a twenty-five-yard pass from Bradshaw to Swann, who found himself all alone when Lemar Parrish tried to cut and fell to the AstroTurf. He hit a wet spot on the turf, the only one on the field. Later we theorized that Pittsburgh had scouted that spot.

At 23-3 things looked dim.

Hold on a minute. This was 1975, not '74. This Bengal team was different. It had backbone, spunk, resiliency.

We were on our own fifteen. Boobie picked up ten around left end, Essex received a short flat pass for four more, Charlie Joiner hauled in a beautiful ball at midfield, Chip Myers caught one on the left side, Boobie ran for three, then, from the thirty-five-yard line, Kenny hit Charlie Joiner in the end zone, and now it was 23-10.

We got the ball back on the Steelers' forty-five and took only five plays to score again, this time on a fake draw to Boobie and a short swing pass to Essex. 23-17.

We had the ball again and were rolling. Pitch right to Boobie for seven, pitch left to Boobie for seven, Boobie up the middle for four, a big pass to Ike Curtis to the Steelers' twenty-five; we had a first down. Riverfront Stadium was coming apart at the seams. We had driven hard, mixing passes and runs. Certainly we could take it the remaining twenty-five yards, kick the extra point, and win 24-23. We would be 7-0, the Steelers 5-2.

Joy, we were goin' to the Super Bowl!

On the first play from the twenty-five Essex burst through right guard, streaking his way down to the fourteen, where we had another first down. Wait a moment! A flag had been thrown! A little yellow cloth lay against the turf like a wounded bird. Holding was called. HOLDING? WHO THE HELL WAS HOLDING ON THE PLAY? Everybody wanted to know.

The ref looked at the Bengals' Number 84. He was looking at the tight end.

Me.

I couldn't believe it. I was blocking Jack Ham on the play. He saw me coming toward him and at the last moment pushed out his hands to ward off my block. Somehow my hands, in front of me, got wound around Ham's just barely, fleetingly. But it was enough to merit a penalty, or so the ref decided.

The ball was moved back to the Steelers' thirty-five. Instead of us being first and ten at the eleven, we were now at the thirty-five.

On the next play, I went down the right side, put a fake on Glen Edwards and cut across the middle. I was open for an instant and Kenny saw me. He let go the ball and I saw a flattened, brown oblong missle spinning toward me. It was high, maybe overthrown. But I stretched out tall, with one hand, I touched it, but at the same moment Glen Edwards, who had recovered, hit me and the ball. It fell incomplete.

Third down. Kenny faded back and spotted Chip Myers on a down and out at the seventeen. He let go and. . . .

The ball was intercepted by safety Mike Wagner.

He ran it back sixty-five yards to our eighteen-yard line, from where the Steelers scored again, in four plays.

With a minute left, and the score now 30-17, the game was salted away. We had had our chance. We blew it. My holding penalty hurt more than anything else. It was a weak call, one undeserving, in my opinion. But then again I didn't wear a black and white striped shirt. My opinion and a dollar fifty would buy me a gallon of gasoline.

If anything good can be said of those final few minutes, it was this: After that disasterous interception and Steeler touchdown, on the last play of the game Kenny hit Chip Myers in the end zone for a twenty-five-yard touchdown to make the final score 30-24.

Even though we were beaten we didn't give up.

That was a good sign, though of little consolation at the time.

I expected our clubhouse to be one of shouted cuss words, kicked lockers and thrown helmets. But it really wasn't. The guys had fought hard, and we came this close to beating the world champions. Even Paul was in a pretty good mood. He congratulated us for "the effort," and added, "you played good out there, really tooth and nail. You didn't give up, that's what's important. I don't doubt for a minute that if it weren't for that key play of the game"— he stopped a moment and shot a cold look in my corner of the room—"that *holding penalty*, we could have won." I just sat and shook my head. I really couldn't argue with the Coach. My mistake had hurt us bad, there was no denying it. I suppose something like that happens to every player in his football life, and that day it happened to me. But against the Steelers, for Pete's sakes! And I had forty-seven friends and relatives in the stands!

I felt miserable.

Paul continued, "The season's now only half over. There's a long way to go yet. We are now in a three-way tie with Houston and Pittsburgh for the league lead, so we're far from being out of it. We have to pick ourselves up and be counted. As far as I'm concerned it is now a new season."

Pretty encouraging words from a man who seldom took defeat lightly.

The other guys sensed this, too, and I think it helped life their spirits a little. "Shoot," said Bob Johnson, "did you see how quiet

Pittsburgh was out there today? They were just thinking they were going to get beat. We should have put it to them."

"Yea," added Chip Myers, "we should have gotten them when they were down. We will next time."

"We still got a helluva good team here," offered Lemar Parrish. "We'll keep pushing."

"Look," said Jim LeClair, "We're 7-1 now, one of the best records in football. This loss is hardly the end of the world."

They were all right.

It was great to see the guys so up and confident again. I had never seen it before on a Bengal team. In previous years we would have taken the loss as a personal bereavement and would have blamed it on our own professional ineptness. But not that team. Despite the defeat, the guys were still together and confident as ever. This was the type of cohesiveness and maturity that could take us a long way. That realization made me feel a little less lousy. But not much.

The thing is, when you rack up a net three hundred sixty-seven yards, score twenty-four points, recover two fumbles and intercept two passes, you are supposed to win the game.

But mistakes and missed opportunities killed us. If there was one thing I learned in ten years it was that, in professional football, when opportunity offered itself in a game, you grabbed it and capitalized on it.

In a way, the films partially vindicated me on the disasterous holding call. The entanglement of hands was so momentary that it definitely did not warrant a penalty. The aggravating thing was that the Steelers were constantly yelling at the officials to make penalty calls against their oppenents, and the refs were intimidated by them. The Steelers were worse than professional lobbyists. Next to them, the National Rifle Association pressure groups would pale.

The problem with a holding penalty is that the infringement itself, the *interpretation* of it, was so imprecise. "If they wanted to," guard Dave Lapham told me, "they could call holding on virtually every play of the game. If you look hard enough you can see a little holding each time the ball is snapped."

Holding in football was a little like white collar crime— everybody did it and for the most part authorities looked the other way. Except for the one time I tried it. Then, sure as hell, I got caught.

A problem re-surfaced in the Pittsburgh game—our running attack. It hadn't really gotten consistently untracked, and it befuddled us all. We gained only sixty-nine yards on the ground against the Steelers. Statistics showed that after seven games we had only 787 yards on the ground, which was dead last in the AFC.

One guy came up with a reason for our poor rushing efforts, and, of all things, he wasn't a Bengal, but a Steeler—Andy Russell.

He was quoted in the paper as saying, "Bob Trumpy is the key to the Bengals' running game and he has been hurt. We think he's the best blocking tight end in pro football. While studying the films we could see a big difference in the way the Bengals ran when Trumpy was playing and the way they ran when he wasn't." All the while I was blushing, I noted the Steelers also had some pretty nice words for Bob Johnson.

Linebacker Jack Lambert told a newspaperman, "Bob Johnson is probably the best center I've played against." Now that's what I call pretty high praise for a pair of roommates. Kind of frustrating though: The Steelers whipped us and then complimented us to death.

I guess when you win you can afford such generosities. Unfortunately, PB must have missed the paper that day. Because on Wednesday, Nov. 5, at approximately 10:30 in the morning, I hit rock-bottom in my football career.

I was demoted to second-string.

We were on the Spinney practice field. Bruce Coslet and I were huddled together, going over some new plays we were trying to learn for the Denver game. Suddenly Bill Walsh appeared. He walked over to where we were standing and said, "Bruce, you are starting this week."

Then he turned and hurried off.

Just like that. I guess in the Bengal organization that was the way you informed a player who, when healthy, started every game in the history of the franchise, that he had been relegated to second-class citizenship. You told the backup man that he was starting and walked away. Later, going over our offensive plays, Tiger Johnson turned and said, "Now on this play, *Bruce*, I want you to...." It really sounded strange. For eight years Tiger had been turning from his diagrams, looking at me, and saying, "Now on this play, *Bob*, I want you to...."

My entire professional football life flashed before my eyes. And I could tell by Bruce's face that he was as confused as I. It put him a quite a compromising position. For the first time since 1969 he would be starting a game in front of me even though I was actually physically sound enough to be playing. I was sure the prospects of being made a starter thrilled him, and yet I was sure he realized that since 1969 our very good relationship had been predicated on the fact that he was my backup, I was the starter.

To put him at ease I merely said, "Give 'em hell Sunday, Bruce. You deserve to be starting."

I meant it, too. If there were any doubts in my mind about that, all I had to do was take another look at the films of the Pittsburgh game. It was a matter of semantics: I don't know whether it was more accurate to say Bruce deserved to play Sunday, or I didn't deserve to play.

Either way, it was a downer for me.

The idea of being a bench jockey when healthy was going to take a little getting used to. I knew what Paul was doing, what really was behind it. He was punishing me for my pitiful performance, and looking at it objectively, I guess I couldn't blame him.

But I couldn't totally agree either. I especially took exception to the manner in which I was informed of my demotion. I came to learn, though, that The Man, PB, often moved in strange ways. This was just one of them.

I'd really have been upset if I thought it was going to be a long-term proposition. But I didn't think it was. I saw it as a one-game penalty assessed against me, much in the way the ref assessed those fifteen yards for holding. In my opinion, both were open to debate. I knew one thing: I'd be busting my butt to get back in there as a starter. Being healthy and on the sidelines was like being in a sexual revolution when you were out of ammunition.

Funny, one of the gruesome ironies of that whole thing was this: two days prior to the loss to the Steelers, I was selected to appear on a local TV program as the Bengals' "Star of the Week" on the day following the game.

So what happens? The day before the show, I am called for holding Andy Russell and I become the goat of the game. And we get knocked out of first place. And our six-game winning streak comes to an end.

Sometimes irony could be hilarious.

That next week was one of the longest weeks I spent in my career. I just couldn't get over that fact that my mistake had cost the team so much, and that it upset Paul to the point where he would second-string me. I'll tell you one thing, I was determined to be on my best behavior during my probation period.

And that's why what happened next, in Denver, scared the hell out of me. The Denver Nuggets of the ABA were playing at home against the New York Nets that Saturday night. Dan Issel played for the Nuggets, and we knew Kenny Anderson used to live next door to Dan, so we asked The Rookie to get us some tickets.

That was our first mistake.

The second was misjudging the two-hour time change between Cincinnati and Denver.

Following the team movie, five of us—myself, Freddie Franchise, Bob Johnson, Bruce Coslet and John Shinners—found ourselves in the best seats in the Denver Coliseum. Issel had gotten us five seats in the glass enclosed governor's box. We sat next to Colorado Lieutenant Governor George Brown, a black who seemed to be a nice fellow.

We were watching warmups when one of the guys commented

that it was only 8:15. "Good," said Kenny, who had never before gone against the rules, "we can see the first half or so before getting out of here. We have to be in by 10:30."

We all sat back and nodded. It took about five seconds for the comment to register. Oddly, we all seemed to get the flash at the same time.

"My God," Coslet shouted, "I just remembered. Paul said that we were to continue to function on *Cincinnati* time."

"Yea," added John Shinners, "that means it is 10:15 Cincinnati time. We have exactly fifteen minutes to get back to the hotel."

We stared at one another blankly. Then we looked over at the Rookie. He was in the process of turning sickly pale. "We'll be traded," he said. "All of us. Or waived. Or cut."

"Or worse," someone chipped in, "we'll be fined $500."

In seconds Kenny Anderson was out of the governor's box and running helter-skelter through the hallways looking for a phone booth. He located one, picked up the directory and ripped through the pages until he found the number of a cab company. He was shouting into the phone as I approached and I heard him saying, "If you're here in five minutes we'll make it worth your while." He listened for a moment and then, slowly, hung up the receiver. His shoulders slumped in defeat. "It's no use," he muttered, "they can't make it here in less that fifteen minutes." He leaned back against the wall and closed his eyes. "We're dead," he said.

Just then two girls in their '20's, dressed in Levis and ski jackets, walked by. They were heading for the ticket window to complain about their seat location.

I had an idea.

I approached them with an offer. "We'll give you girls these ticket stubs," I told them holding the evidence aloft, "if you do us a favor. They're the best seats in the house."

There was a pause. One of the girls looked at me, and my four football friends, and took a skeptical step backwards. I got the feeling she thought I had something sort of kinky in mind. (I did notice, however, that the second girl kind of smiled at the suggestion, then cracked her gum.)

"Nothing like that," I assured them. I explained the situation as best I could and finished by saying, "so it you take us to the Denver Hilton right now we will give you tickets to sit in the governor's box."

In a flash we were down two flights of Coliseum stairs and out into the night. It had begun to snow, and the route to the girls' car was through a swampy area six inches deep with mud. Despite this treacherous terrain, we made good time. Kenny Anderson was moving faster than I had ever seen him. He was way out front.

When we finally arrived at the girls' car we discovered we were in trouble. The car was a Ford Mustang. Bucket seats in front, precious little room in back.

It didn't matter. Grunting and shoving, we piled in—three guys and a girl in back, two guys and a girl up front—and headed out. Before we even got out of the parking lot someone had calculated that there was, exclusive of the girls, about thirty feet and twelve-hundred pounds of humanity squeezed into that little car.

At any rate, we were on our way. Or so we thought. As we were heading up the northbound ramp to the Interstate, the girls informed us that they had lived in Denver for only three months, and they didn't really know where the Hilton was located. "That's OK," said Bruce Coslet, "I do," and we all gave a collective sigh of relief. "We have to get on the Interstate heading south."

A surrendering gasp came from the back seat, from the general direction of Kenny Anderson. I think he put his head in his hands. "We'll all be cut," he reminded us.

Outside it began to snow harder. And I guess it was only by the grace of God that we finally made it back to the Hilton. When we pulled up to the front door an explosive "Hoo-ray" resounded from inside the Ford Mustang. I should say all the other guys yelled. I didn't. From the Coliseum my Adam's apple had been supporting someone's elbow, and my voice box refused to function.

We began piling out systematically, which is to say every man for himself, and accidentally someone hit the girl who was driving. She yelled something about a contact lense having popped our, but my friends—led by the Rookie—had long disappeared into the hotel. I tried to apologize and say thank you, but I still couldn't speak. So I just pushed $50 through the window and took off.

All things considered, the girls earned every cent of the money.

Later, at breakfast, Kenny looked haggard. "I wasn't in my room for 60 seconds," he said, "before Bill Walsh knocked on the door for a bed-check. He took one look at my tee-shirt which was soaked with sweat, and asked me what I had been doing."

"What did you tell him?" I asked.

Kenny tried to smile. "I told him I had been doing some exercises, preparing for the game."

Good ol' Freddie Franchise, I thought, a quarterback who keeps his cool under fire. For my part, when I hit the bed, I set a new record for thanking God a hundred times in less than a minute.

As it turned out, Paul kept his word, and I didn't start the Denver game. But it was only two plays old when I got in on a third and short situation.

We ran a "Halfback Solid-8." On this play Boobie led around my end and put a block on the safety. Charlie Joiner and I were supposed to double team the outside linebacker, in this case a guy named Joe Rizzo, and drive him backwards. I was so juiced up to look good that, when the ball was snapped, I fired out and hit Rizzo so hard that I drove him out of the play before Charlie even had a chance to advance on him. In fact, I popped him so good that his feet never had a chance to leave the turf, and the cleats on the bottom of his shoes cut two inch-deep tracks in the sod for a full ten yards. "Jesus Christ," Charlie Joiner said to me, "you *buried* that guy. Take it easy, will you? I didn't even get a chance to touch him. Made me look like I was just standin'around here doing nothin'."

On the basis of this drive, our offensive unit thought we were going to put on a real show for the fans. But the seven points we scored in that initial drive turned out to be the only ones we put on the board in the entire first half.

In the fourth quarter we worked the ball to the Broncos' thirty but Dave Green missed a field goal. That really hurt because minutes later Jim Turner converted one from the twenty-eight and the Broncos drew within one point. Greenie had a chance to redeem himself with 2:07 remaining in the game, but he again blew a sure-shot, this one from the eighteen, and Denver had two minutes in which to drive in for a score; fortunately they failed and we earned a hard-fought come-from-behind victory.

Actually, a few days from then nobody would remember that we won by only a single point. They just knew that against Denver we put a "W" in the win column. And, they noticed that we were 7-1, back on the winning track and tied for first place with Pittsburgh in the AFC Central Division.

After the game, Bob Johnson was still seething over the officiating. There was a holding call on a play that saw Ed Williams pull off a nice run to the Broncos' fifteen. The penalty called the play back. "At first they called it on me," Bob said. "So I went up and asked the ref for some clarification. He told me, 'I didn't really know who it was on. It was the guard or the center or *somebody*.' "

Real good. If Christopher Columbus had been equally precise we'd probably all be living in Nova Scotia.

The officiating got to Dave Green, too. On a twenty-eight-yard field goal that he missed Dave claimed to have been disturbed by a snowball. (From the beginning of the game the fans had been pelting the field, the sidelines and the players with snowballs.) "Just as I was in my motion to kick," Dave said, "a snowball exploded in front of me. I thought it hit Ricky Davis (the holder) so I expected the refs to call a time out. They didn't, though, so I hurriedly looked back down at the ball and continued on with the kick."

The films verified Dave's story, and Paul said he thought a timeout should have been called. After he missed it, Dave Green walked over to an official and said, "What the hell was that?"

The ref answered, "It was a miss, that was what it was."

The refs always had things under control.

After the films I noticed Bruce Coslet sitting there shaking his head. "I really blew it," he said, referring to a pass play in the first quarter. He was wide open down the middle and Kenny hit him right in the numbers. Bruce dropped it. (By the same token I had two receptions.)

"After that mistake," said Bruce, "you could bet that you would be off probation and I'd be on. Now I've got to find a way to get my ass out of this jam." Bruce certainly knew what he was talking about. Because two days later Tiger Johnson was drawing X's and O's on the board, and he turned to me and said, "Now on this play, *Bob*, I want you to...."

Hot damn. It was official. I was starting Monday night against the Bills.

But, though I personally was excited about the prospects and despite the fact that Monday night football had become as American as Coca-Cola, our guys were looking forward to the game with the same enthusiasm a diabetic looked forward to a Hershey bar. "I hate it," said John Shinners. "I'd rather play at 9:00 in the morning." "Heck," added Bob Johnson, "I was usually in bed by 10:30 at night. On Monday that will be about halftime."

The problem was, Monday games really mess up a team's schedule, its discipline. Not only for the week of the game, but also for the following week, because it gave us one less day to get over aches and pains (which was important at that late point in the season) and to prepare for the upcoming Sunday game.

Despite that, the Monday night game did promise to be quite an explosive show. The Bills were the NFL's number one team offensively, by a mile. Going into our game they led the league in points scored, net yards per game and rushing yards per game.

In the main, of course, their offensive attack was a nuclear warhead named O.J. Simpson. The guy was a true phenomena, a superstar in every sense of the word. It made us a little leery of his potential for breaking a game wide open when we learned that he had already rushed for more yards that season than had the entire Bengal *team*.

Doing his part to prepare us for what was ahead, Paul gave us a nugget of wisdom to contemplate: "To beat this club," said Paul, *"we are going to have to score more points than they do."*

Defensive line coach Chuck Studley then chipped in, quite simply, if mysteriously, "The toughest thing about the running of O.J. Simpson is that where he starts isn't where he finishes."

To think, professional football coaches get paid high salaries for thinking heavy thoughts.

And so we waited.

God, it was awful.

Chip Myers said, "Of all the aspects of professional football, to me waiting is the worst. It's harder than the traveling, harder than negotiating. It's just a total waste of time. It'll drive you up a wall.

Professional football players are geared for hitting our psychological peaks at about 1:00 on Sundays. But that week Sunday came

141

and went. Most of Monday, we had done nothing but exist in a timeless vacuum, playing a little bridge or trivia with a group of rookies. The hours dragged. We sat and thought about the game that night. It was perhaps the most disadvantageous thing we could do. You can think too much. Football is a game of instinct, of responding, of reacting, of *executing*.

We were becoming nervous. Pittsburgh won on Sunday, as did Houston, upsetting the Miami Dolphins. The Dolphins' loss added incentive to Buffalo—they could pick up a game on them by beating us. We needed a win to remain tied for first place with the Steelers at 8-1. It we lost we'd go into second-place tie with the Oilers.

It was nail-biting time. Worse, Buffalo players were saying that this game was their *season*. If they allowed us to beat them, their record would fall to 5-4 and their hopes of a playoff spot would vanish like so much smoke. No one had to tell us that it was no fun to play a team that was in a must-win situation.

And too: There was the Monday night jinx, two previous humiliating Bengal losses on Monday night games, nightmarish defeats, public embarrassments. And it was visions of these dancing in our heads that we took on the field with us that fated Monday night.

Damn. Why did we worry so much. Because that very game was, if I may be permitted a biased evaluation, the most excitingly awesome display of offensive explosiveness in the history of Monday night football.

O.J. Simpson was running brilliance personified, busting inside, finding a hole jammed, juking to the outside, shedding tacklers the way a snake sheds fangs, and sprinting for forty, fifty and sixty yards at a time. He ran for a spectacular 197 yards on the night, and Buffalo scored twenty-four points.

O.J. was *not* the star of the game.

A quarterback by the name of Anderson hit thirty of forty-six passes for a mind-boggling four hundred forty-seven yards. He broke or tied five Bengal records. We scored thirty-three points.

You could imagine the scene in our locker room. The aftermath of such exciting football games were unbelievably inibriating, almost sensual. Not unexpectedly, one of the most emotional guys was our pressure cooker linebacker Ron Pritchard. Since he was also our resident Bible-beater, he gathered us about him and said, "I think we should offer a prayer. Somebody up there has control over us and I happen to believe it's God. He's helping the Bengals this year, I know it. Let's show him some respect." It grew quiet for a moment and Ron proceeded to thank the Lord for the night's victory. He also prayed that we stay healthy and get into the playoffs and that Isaac Curtis' ankle, which he sprained in the game, healed itself quickly.

Even me, not being the religious sort, had to say a loud "Amen" to all of it. What the hell, if General Patton had the audacity to pray for clear skies, why couldn't the Cincinnati Bengals pray for a healed ankle and a shot at the playoffs?

We awarded two game balls, one to Kenny and one to Chip Myers, who had seven receptions, all of them tough ones, for one hundred-nine yards. Chip couldn't say enough about his quarterback. "I had never seen a guy who was so precise. He was by far the best quarterback in the game. Every pass he had time to throw was perfect."

As could be expected, reporters were all over our quarterback like drones around a queen bee. And how did The Rookie take this adulatory attention? When I overheard him he said, "Really, the coaches upstairs called an excellent game. And our receivers did a great job getting open."

Kenny Anderson was too good to be real. When I asked him how he felt after the game he said, "Well, my arm's kind of tired."

Of all the guys who were celebrating I think Dave Lapham, who played another fine game, was the happiest. "Eight and one," he kept shouting in the shower, "eight and one, do you believe it?" Other than the obvious fact that an 8-1 record tied us with the Steelers for first place, I couldn't understand why he was so all-fired excited by it. "Trump," he smiled, "I have never been on an 8-1 team in my entire life. This is an absolute first for me."

I nodded acknowledgement and then thought for a moment. Hell, except for high school, I hadn't either. I responded with a whoop worthy of an attacking Apache warrior.

Only two guys on the team weren't going absolutely bananas. Dave Green, who had missed two field goals and two extra points, was a little down. "I was hoping," said Dave, "that Chip Myers would give me his game ball. I'd like to take it home to practice with."

The other guy was Al Beauchamp, who was still steamed about a run-in he had with Jim Braxton at the end of the game. Apparently with about thirty seconds left Beau made a good tackle on Braxton, and the Bill's fullback got up and said something like, "Shit, you guys were lucky. You ain't got half the team you think you've got. You were just plain lucky."

The comment really got the dander up on our eight-year linebacker, so he warned Braxton to keep his mouth shut. But Braxton persisted in this line of maligning banter so Beau told him, "The next time you open your mouth I'm going to spit in it."

Braxton opened his mouth and Beau kept his word. I'll say one thing, it was a true championship spit—through Beau's face mask and into Braxton's mouth, at six paces.

I guess one of the most dramatic things that resulted in that game was this: Kenny Anderson everafter would no longer be known as The Rookie. His performance that night easily took him far out of the rookie status, and he wouldn't get our vote for the Bengals'

Rookie of the Year award for the fifth consecutive time.
Passing for 446 yards will do that to you.

DEEP THROAT
SYNDROME

"You know why we are so tough?" after the game Chip Myers asked me, rhetorically. "Because we have the most innovative offense in football. We run and pass in literally hundreds of ways because of all the different formations we use."

Chip was right. We threw more formations, variations, and motions at the opposition than a catepillar has ribs. For example, we had the basic "pro set" with a tight end, a wide receiver on each side and two runningbacks behind the quarterback—and sometimes the basic pro set with *three* wide receivers (one of them in the backfield replacing a runningback) and a tight end. We ran a two-tight-end offense, and a no-tight-end offense (by using three wide receivers).

On and on it went. And in each of those formations, any one of our men could and would, while the QB was barking out signals, go in motion to the other side of the field. Lord, studying Bengal game films must have given opposing defenses the feeling of viewing the choreography of a Harlem Globetrotters routine.

Our running attack showed signs of life in the Bills' game. Junebug Elliott ran for twenty-nine yards and Boobie added another fifty-six. After he watched a replay of the game, Paul said that Junebug was robbed of additional yardage by two poor calls by the officials. On the first call, Lenvil Elliott had run back a kickoff for a hundred-two-yard touchdown, but an official ruled that there had been a clip on the play. Paul asked the official the number of the player who was supposed to have perpetrated the sin, but the official said no one was able to identify the violater. Paul said the replay showed no evidence of a clip.

The second bad call was when Lenvil broke several tackles and had a man beaten for another touchdown when the official stopped the play. He ruled that Junebug's knee had touched the ground. The replay, Paul told us, showed that Lenvil had started to go down after being hit, but he put a hand down to block the fall. Without ever having his knee touch the ground, he managed to catch his balance and take off again.

The officials cost us a minimum of fourteen points that Monday night. That was probably about par for a night's work.

As for the upcoming Cleveland game, we were all a little leary. It was tough to play a team that hadn't won a game all season. A team with an 0-9 record had nothing to lose and that made them a very precarious foe to face. It was hard to figure out Cleveland's record. Maybe Cleveland's problem was that losing, like winning, became a habit, a habit as hard to break as chain smoking.

"Don't let the Browns' record fool you," Paul advised us, "you have to beware of them. From a psychological standpoint they are a very dangerous team to play. If they lose, people will say they should have lost because they have a lousy team. If they should win, it would make their season for them."

I suspected what Paul said was true, and I knew the Browns would really be gunning for us. Whenever PB returned to Cleveland the whole ballpark worked itself into a gigantic sweat. The team and its fans loved nothing better than whipping the man who founded them and for whom the team was named. I imagine it was the same satisfaction a son gets the first time he beats his father in arm-wrestling.

We needed a victory over the Browns in the worst way. The Steelers would be home in front of their sets watching us because they didn't play until the following Monday night. If we won—and won impressively—maybe it would give the Steelers that much more to think about Monday night. If they lost and we won, we would be in sole possession of first place.

We had to keep applying pressure.

I learned ex-Bengal Neil Craig would start for the Browns, and nothing could have made me happier. Neil and I never saw eye to eye, mostly because of our separate parts played in the players' strike of 1974.

I would have enjoyed really sticking it to him—popping him good on some blocking assignments or beating him badly on a pass pattern. I never have been a vengeful person, but this was my one exception. I had been carrying around this ill feeling for a year and I had to get it out of my system.

Neil Craig was a real strange football player for us. The Bengals drafted him as a defensive back out of Fisk University in 1971 (Neil used to tell us that Fisk was so small that one of the football field goalposts was painted on the side of a campus building), but he just wasn't tough enough to cut it. He was a fine athlete all right, but a lousy "support" man when it came to stopping sweeps around the ends. Neil liked to tackle guys high, which is something you don't do a lot of, and get away with, in the NFL.

My first run-in with Neil occurred during the '74 training camp. I was one of the first (if not *the* first) player to report for camp that year in spite of the strike. It was a real tense situation, so we all tried our best not to make any big waves between teammates. Except Neil Craig. A few days into camp he was walking the players' picket line at Wilmington as I was heading back to the dormitory following a practice. Suddenly he pointed to me and yelled out, so everyone could hear: "Now there goes a real Paul Brown man. Paul Brown does all of his thinking for him. He does whatever Paul Brown says."

I don't know why, but those remarks always stuck with me. I vowed then that I'd like to someday get back at Neil Craig, not in a criminal way or anything, but on the football field.

When the picketing players finally decided to come into camp, we called a meeting. We were supposed to decide whether we wanted to go ahead with the season or strike again. I got up and made some comments against going back on strike. I said something like, "I don't believe it would be a wise move to strike again. The first one showed us that our strikes generally fail, and I think we'd be committing occupational suicide." I added that, if the NFL owners desired it, they could get rid of us all and re-stock their teams with other players, guys from the WFL or the Continental League. "If we strike and, therefore, do not get paid for this season," I concluded, "who is it going to hurt more—us, whose livelihoods depend on those nice salaries, or the NFL owners, who are already millionaires?"

Now it was Neil's turn. He got up and began a speech so full of legal phrases and terminology it would have made Perry Mason quake. Neil had been attending some law school classes during the off season and I guess he was now featuring himself as some sort of locker room lawyer. It sounded like he was merely using legal definitions strung together, with no real cohesiveness. Of course no one understood a word he said, but when he finished there was an effusive "O-o-o-w-e-e-e" from the players.

Mike Brown, himself a Harvard-graduated lawyer, stood up and scratched his head. "The way I see it," said Mike, "you guys can go the way Trumpy said or you can do what Neil Craig said, whatever that was. The choice is up to you."

We voted not to go back out on strike, but even though this minor victory was mine, Neil Craig's comments stayed with me.

Unfortunately, it didn't help much, because in Cleveland we did something no other NFL team seemed likely to do in 1975. We lost to the Browns. It was not a distinction we enjoyed.

I don't know what went wrong, really. We were ahead, handily, when all of the sudden the roof caved in. It happened right after Kenny Anderson got hurt, so I guess that had a lot to do with it.

Perhaps we were doomed from the beginning, because Billy Lefear took the opening kickoff and sprinted ninety-two yards before John McDaniel caught him from behind and hauled him down at the Browns' two. Greg Pruitt scored on the next play (extra point was missed) to make it 6-0. All this before the people in the upper deck had a chance to make it to their seats. And before they had a chance to get their flasks uncorked, the Browns made it 9-0 on a field goal from the seventeen by Don Cockcroft.

From our viewpoint, it was not an ideal way to begin a game. Kenny Anderson quickly went to work, though, leading us fifty-three yards in just three plays. We scored on a thirty-five-yard touchdown play—to me! It was my first touchdown of the regular season and I was naturally jubilant over it. And we were back in the game, at 9-7, so that made me happy, too. But the greatest thrill of all was *how* the TD was scored.

I beat Neil Craig on the play.

It was like when you were a kid and you dreamed of getting a sparkling new bicycle for Christmas...and you woke up Christmas morning and there it was, sitting there waiting for you under the tree. I had dreamed of beating Neil Craig for a year.

Had we not lost the game it would have been one of the highlights of the season for me.

We were up 20-12 at halftime, in command of the game, and there wasn't a great deal of emotion in the clubhouse. Our showing in the second half really cannot be attributed to a general letdown. Especially when you realize that we took the Browns' opening third quarter kickoff and promptly drove eighty-five yards, with a forty-one-yard pass play from Kenny to Charlie Joiner placing the ball at the Browns' five.

It was a costly gain. Jerry Sherk hit Kenny with a helmet in the chest just as our quarterback was releasing the ball. We could tell Kenny was hurting but he refused to leave the game. From the five we ran two running plays which got us to the three, and then on third and goal Kenny tried to hit me on a three-yard rollout pass. Even from this short distance, Kenny threw it behind and short of where I was. We could tell his day was over.

Kenny's injury was the turning point. Before he left the game, Kenny was eleven of sixteen for 237 yards and two touchdowns. Those were hard statistics to replace. You might say his presence rather dominated play.

We just didn't seem to have any fight left in us. Our offense, behind reserve QB John Reaves, just clunked along, and our defense tackled as if the Browns' runners and receivers had a contagious disease they didn't want to catch.

The day's frustration ended at 35-23.

I really don't know what else to say about the game. The trip to Cincinnati was the quietest in years. A cloud of black silence hovered over all of us on the plane. We knew that what we did that day reduced our chances of winning the AFC Central, and perhaps even our chances of making it to the playoffs. Said one player, sitting

148

behind me, "Shit, we really blew it big-time today."

"Yea," said another. "Even Linda Lovelace would've choked on that one."

It rather nicely put our performance in perspective.

All in all, the Browns' game was the worst game we played all season. It was unfortunate that it came at such a critical time in our bid to catch the Steelers.

To say PB was a little down in the mouth over our loss to the Browns was being generous. It was such a big game for him, there in his home town, and we made him look silly. He took such things very personally.

"It was a total team breakdown," he told us, voice trembling. "Everybody did something wrong at some point." He took a breath and added, "Your performance could have *ruined* the season for us."

It *was* a total breakdown; a real team effort of ineptness. Guys usually surehanded fumbled away the ball—Lemar on a punt return, Junebug Elliott on a kickoff return—the defense failed us, and the running game reached a level of futile impotency.

It seemed as if the harder we tried to make our running game go the more we screwed it up. Perhaps we were just *overly* geared for the passing game so we could take full advantage of Freddie Franchise's marvelous mechanical accuracy and our flock of gifted receivers. (And perhaps rightfully so! We were, after all, leading the entire NFL in passing offense, and that wasn't too shabby an accomplishment.) Against the Browns, we once more used seven different receivers—including me (two receptions, 44 yards).

What the Browns' victory really did was force our backs firmly against the wall. With Houston upcoming our mettle as a team was going to be put to the test. Fortitude was at stake, and, as one of our defensive backs simply put it, "the time has come to get our shit together."

Our immediate concern was the physical well-being of Kenny Anderson. Freddie was walking around in a great deal of pain, unable to lift his arms above his head. Even the staunchest of optimists would have had to agree that this condition would make his effectiveness as a passer suspect.

As if the possibility of Kenny not playing wasn't bad enough, we had something else to ponder. Pittsburgh absolutely mauled Houston on the Monday night game, so we trailed the Steelers by a full game. The coaches told us that the Steeler-Oiler contest was such an important game to us that PB stayed up until *midnight* watching it, notebook and pencil in hand. When the Old Coach wasn't in the sack by nine you knew even *he* was feeling the pressure of a long season.

Worse, the cold, wet, miserable winter weather had now set in.

Temperatures were in the 20's winds whipping sufficiently violent to muss the hair of a statue. Believe me, playing football in weather that prohibited the slightest bit of circulation in your extremities was not a pleasant experience.

On our squad, the winter weather was hardest on the guys from California, guys like Ike Curtis, Sherm White and Bernard Jackson. Having grown up in the moderate climate of the West Coast, their constitutions were acclimated to warm days and balmy nights. They looked forward to Ohio's blustery weather with the same enthusiasm a child looked forward to a trip to the dentist.

I wasn't too fond of it myself, but whenever the bad weather began, I employed a psychological trick to make its presence partially bearable. In those few moments of silence permitted to a combination pro football player, husband and father-of-two, I would close my eyes and mentally project myself to the West Coast, back to the sunbaked beaches and ocean breezes. I sat and recalled those blissful six months I spent there in 1967. Somehow this mental transporting provided me a modicum of inner peace; it allowed me to cope with the pain of catching bullet-shaped leather projectiles on Sundays with hands blown sensitive by sub-freezing winds.

Although my stay in California was a relatively short one, it would always have special meaning to me. For one thing, if I hadn't attended Glendale Junior College there before entering the University of Utah, I never would have had the opportunity to meet the lovely Miss Patricia Ann Feith, the young lady who became Mrs. Pat Trumpy. We met one night at a beach party (which there are a lot of in California) and we hit it off right away. She was living with her parents in their beachfront home in Playa Del Ray. We dated for nearly my entire stay in California, and I actually ended up moving in with Pat and her parents, Larry and Marge, for about three weeks prior to leaving for Utah.

Prior to this, I roomed with three guys in a big old six-room house near campus. Listen, to a lad from the conservative Midwest, these three guys really opened my eyes to the way of things on the West Coast.

One of my roommates was attending Glendale Junior College on a football scholarship, was working as a carpenter's apprentice at about $12 an hour and at the same time was drawing regular unemployment checks from the state. Six days a week you could see him spinning around town in his new, red Jaguar XKE. On the seventh day, the day he had to go downtown to pick up his unemployment check, he drove a 1952 Chevy.

One day toward the end of the quarter my roommate decided he needed a lot of money right away, so he offered to pay a second roommate $500 to push his XKE over a cliff. That way he could collect a handsome sum in insurance money. Sure enough, two days later the owner of the car took a date up to the San Angelos Forest,

150

parked the car and walked off to absorb some of the environment. By the time they returned to their parking spot, the XKE was gone.

They later found it below, splintered into a thousand pieces.

The owner collected $6,000 from the insurance company, paid our roommate the $500 he owed him, and took off for a tour of Europe.

There was another rip-off adventure they introduced me to, and I took part in it frequently. Compared to the XKE-over-the-cliff scheme, this one was small potatoes; however, it was not without its good points. After all, it combined criminality with the necessity of having steady nerves, key timing, quick feet and a large appetite.

It was called "tennis-shoeing."

Tennis-shoeing was the fine art of going into a restaurant, ordering and eating a big meal and then running out on the bill. It was hard to explain the reason for it, but I must admit the expectation of being caught at this trickery never failed to make the meal taste that much better, at least more exciting.

The closest I ever came to getting caught was the time I tried a solo performance. It was at Bob's Restaurant in Montrose, California, about three miles from home. It was late at night, and I was hungry. I went in, sat at the counter, and ordered a $6 meal, knowing full well I only had pocket-change on me.

As the waitress was placing the meal in front of me, I looked up to see eight highway patrolmen filing into the restaurant. I thought, *Jesus, these guys are on to me! I've had it.* I watched in horror as, one by one, these officers of law took up residence on stools along the counter. Finally, in the second to last stool, next to me on my left, sat a stocky, thick-necked partolman with reddish hair. I was scared stiff. What the hell was I going to do when I finished the meal? I certainly didn't have the money to pay for it.

I had to think fast.

I decided to strike up a friendly conversation, and I told him that my father was also a highway patrolman, back in Springfield. I said that seeing this uniform next to me made me a bit homesick; then I went on to talk about my father and how I respected him because he was risking his life every day for an ungrateful citizenship and so forth.

All in all, I was doing nicely. Then, when I finished my meal, I said, "I really want to thank you for talking to me tonight. You really made me feel better about being so far from home." Then I told him that, as a token of my appreciation, I would pick up the check for his cup of coffee, to which he profusely objected. I insisted, of course. "I'm going to tell the cashier," I explained to him, "that I'm going to pay for your coffee. So when I get up there, just wave your hand toward her so she knows you're the patrolman I'm talking about."

When I got to the cash register I said to the cashier, "One of

151

those nice highway patrolmen had insisted on buying my dinner."
She looked at me rather skeptically, so I pointed across the room. She
looked down the counter until she saw my stocky, thick-chested red-
haired friend smiling and nodding affirmatively to her and waving
his hand.

Once my tennis shoes hit the pavement, they didn't stop for an
hour. And I never once tried tennis-shoeing again.

Back at wintry Spinney Field, I had rarely seen so many medical
men in one place at one time. You'd have thought that it was a
Wednesday and the Bengals' training complex was a golf course.

They were everywhere.

The object of all their attention, of course, was our quarterback.
Kenny Anderson had had more diathermy therapy, X-rays, rub-
downs and whirlpool baths than any two Bengals I had known. His
right shoulder was now a permanent bright red color from all the
treatment.

Kenny said his upper torso was extremely tender, but he vowed
he'd be able to go against the Oilers, two days hence.

I didn't know whether he was right or not. I *did* know one
thing: suddenly John Reaves' stock had soared, and, next to Kenny,
the coaches were spending more time with him that anyone else on
the squad.

All I could think of was, gee, it must be nice to feel needed.

Despite the pressures of the drive for the playoffs that year we
still found time to perpetrate our annual Turkey Charade. We had
been doing it for years. We set it up by telling all the rookies during
Thanksgiving week that, as a promotional gesture, one of the
Kroger Supermarkets in town was giving away free butterball turkeys to all Bengal players. All you had to do, we claimed, was go the
the store the day before Thanksgiving, tell them you were a Bengal
and they would hand over a turkey.

We were dealing from a stacked deck, of course, because we had
already worked out the gag with the store manager. And when the
expectant rookie went in and asked for his free bird, he was handed a
note saying, "The only thing free is the air you're breathing. The
biggest turkey here is *YOU*!

On the whole, I'd have to say we had a smarter bunch of rookies
in '75. Many of them called the store ahead of time to find out what
size turkey they were to receive, so they were told about the Charade.

But there were a few who took the bait. One was our specialty
team expert, Brad Cousino, the little linebacker who, with his cocky
attitude and haughty mannerisms, reminded me of our former linebacker coach Vince Costello. Because of his small size, Brad seemed

to take himself very seriously, and he didn't appreciate being made fun of. (He was the only guy I knew who could stand in front of a mirror and take 45 minutes to brush his hair.) Anyway, the day before Thanksgiving he got caught being the dummy in our free turkey scheme and, quite naturally, felt the fool for it. As he was turning around to leave the turkey counter, having been handed the note by the store manager, Brad happened to see two of his rookie teammates, Al Krevis and Champ Henson. They were there to get their free turkeys, too, so Brad hustled out of sight and looked on as the manager handed the rookies the note. Having been duped, they hung their heads, cussed, laughed, and began to walk away. Just then one of them spotted Brad Cousino scurrying around an aisle or two away. They hurried to catch up with him.

Brad played dumb to the whole thing, too embarrassed to admit he had also been taken in by the ruse. He tried to convince his two teammates that the only reason he was in the store was to buy a can of *Drano*, which he miraculously produced in his hand as proof.

The Turkey Charade provided us endless moments of mirth over the years. Like the time Doug Hafner, a Bengals' scout, somehow found out about the free turkeys and flew in from down South somewhere to pick it up. And last year Evan Jolitz, who was supposed to spend Thanksgiving with his wife and all their relatives, announced that he was going to provide the turkey feast for everyone. He was informed that, in order to feed them all, it would have to be an 18-pound bird. No problem, said Evan which, when he found out the day before Thanksgiving he wasn't really entitled to a free turkey, didn't turn out to be an accurate statement.

Then there was Ken Johnson as a rookie. Just as he was heading into the store, two of our veterans, Steve Chomyszak and Ken Avery were walking out. They were there for legitimate shopping reasons and had a basket full of brown bags. When they saw Big-Un heading in for his free turkey they really laid it on thick, and told him to go in and pick out whichever bird he wanted.

Which he did. Ken Johnson grabbed a bird large enough to warrant a stretcher to carry it out. But our big defensive end merely tucked it under his arm and headed for the door. The store manager had been watching, of course, so he ran up behind him and said, "Hey, what do you think you're doing?"

Big-Un pulled up short and turned to face the man. "My name's Ken Johnson," he said, "and I play for the Cincinnati Bengals. I'm gettin' my free turkey."

The manager tried to explain that the whole thing was a joke, and the store really didn't have turkeys to give away. Big-Un really got mad. He drew up close to the manager, whom he towered over, and looked at him with spiteful eyes. "That's bullshit," he snarled. "Two white guys just walked out of here with all sorts of free food. You don't want to give me this turkey cuz I'm black. Well you ain't gettin' away with that, man!'' With that, he turned and headed for the front door. Chomyszak and Avery had been watching the whole thing by peering through the front window, and they were on the sidewalk in laughter. When Big-Un came out in a huff and headed for his car they intercepted him and explained the annual rookie Charade to him.

I guess Big-Un was mad enough to fight, and the next day, when Avery was relaying the details to a few teammates, Big-Un walked in and pointed a finger at him and said, "Shut your mouth or I'm going to break your nose." Then he turned and walked out.

No one ever accused Ken Johnson of having a great sense of humor. I remember another incident earlier that year, when our runningback Doug Dressler let it slip to a newspaperman that his teammates' nickname for Ken Johnson was "Big Daddy Dirtpile." He was bestowed with that moniker because of the way he dressed— wild, flashy, mod duds that more times than not clashed hideously with one another. Put clothing like that on a 6'8" frame and you have a real visual pollution on your hands. Man, Big-Un was fit to be tied when he read about his nickname in the papers, and he ran searching for Dressler with mayhem on his mind. Fortunately, for Doug, Paul had just traded him to New England and he was already packed and standing in line at the Greater Cincinnati Airport. The trade may well have saved Doug Dressler's life.

Back to the Oilers' game: fifteen minutes before game time, we still didn't know who our starting quarterback was. Then, as we were about to take the field, someone went over to Kenny's locker and informed him that he was wanted in Paul Brown's office.

He was back within minutes with a disappointed look about him. "I won't be starting today," he sighed. "The Coach has decided to go with John." Our team physician, Dr. George Ballou, told Paul that Kenny *could* have played that day, but if he was again hit hard in the same place, he'd be out for the remainder of the year.

That was all Paul needed to hear.

John Reaves became the man on the spot.

And quite a job he did.

In a driving rain John hit thirteen of twenty-three passes for 162 yards and two touchdowns.

We won 23-19, a big, big victory, virtually knocking Houston out of any chance for the playoffs.

Had John Reaves been Noah himself, he couldn't have guided us any more effectively through the rain-sloshed seas on the River-front Stadium AstroTurf. It had rained virtually non-stop for days, and there were standing pools six and eight inches deep and yards in circumference from one end zone to the other. Added to this topo-graphical problem was the fact that the rain beat down unrelentingly throughout the entire game, making the ball slippery and footing treacherous.

We had a whole slew of heroes. On defense Bernard Jackson made seven tackles, rookie Marvin Cobb (filling in for Leap) had six and veteran Bob Brown, holding ground in the middle of the line much the way a captain held sway over his ship, had nine tackles. He was ecstatic. "This team," he said afterwards, shaking his head, "this team reminds me of the old days, our championship years with the Packers. Back then we had Bart Starr and Zeke Bartkowski. When Bart was hurt, Zeke would fill in." The big guy smiled widely and nodded over to John Reaves. "Now we got Anderson and Reaves. When Kenny can't do it, John can."

Jim LeClair also played a great game: ten tackles and two passes deflected. On the last series of plays, though, it appeared as if Jim was seriously injured. He had gotten kicked in the head and was knocked unconscious. For a full five minutes he lay on the sloppy field without moving a muscle. Finally Marv Pollins signaled toward the bench for the stretcher and we thought, uh-oh, there goes our starting middle linebacker for the stretch drive against the Steelers. Even as they carried him off he wasn't moving a great deal; but I guess after a few minutes they brought him around on the sidelines. "Shit, I wasn't hurt that much," he said in the clubhouse. "I just wanted to throw a chill into the fans."

With all of these stars (I shouldn't leave out my own four receptions for forty-two yards) this game really belonged to one man—John Reaves, who came over in a trade with the Philadelphia Eagles. It was great to see all the reporters gathered around him after the game, firing questions at him. I didn't know whether he would ever again have the opportunity to be in the center-stage position he was that day, but I'll guarantee you this: John Reaves will never forget the thrill of that Sunday in Cincinnati in the driving rain when he threw two touchdown passes against the Oilers and helped his team virtually cinch a playoff spot. A thrill like that you carry to the grave.

And I think it was safe to assume that John was similar to W.C. Fields in one respect. All things considered, he would have rather been there than in Philadelphia.

Come to think of it, we all would rather have been here than in Philadelphia...but we had little choice in the matter.

We played the Eagles there that next Sunday.

It was a game of which we had to be careful. The Eagles possessed an embarrassing 3-8 record but they had that extra emotion when playing us because of Bill Bergey, Horst Muhlmann, Stan Walters and Mike Boryla—all once Bengal property. Beating their old boss, Paul Brown, could have made the season for them.

And who could forget August. During the exhibition season, they kicked our tails 30-20. Bergey wore the mantle of hero by recovering a fumble, intercepting a pass and making tackles all over the field. Horst kicked three field goals. You might say Paul was pissed.

We *needed* the Eagles game, no doubt about it. We figured that, if we could win two of our last three games (we played Philadelphia, Pittsburgh and San Diego), we were a cinch for the playoffs. If we could win all three and the Steelers lose two (say, to us and to the Rams) then we would be the Central Division champs. Not half bad.

The possibility of us going all the way had not escaped our guys. Defensive end Sherman White gave a speech to us that would have done Martin Luther King proud. "I have a dream," said Sherman, "I have a dream that we are going to come out of nowhere; I have a dream that we are the Cinderella team of the NFL; I have a dream that we are going to scratch and claw our way to the playoffs. And I have a dream that we are going to win the Super Bowl! We, the Bengals, are the chosen team. I have a dream...."

What's the line sung by Harry Nilsson? *Dreams are nothing more than wishes and a wish is just a dream you wish to come true?*

Right on, Sherm White. We all dreamed then. Worked hard. Fought hard. We were convinced that we could do it.

To relieve the pressure of all this, I used to lead trivia battles for the rookies. Some of them got hold of our old Bengal yearbooks and had become interested in the unknown players of yore, those misguided castoffs who at one time represented the Cincinnati Bengals on the football field. The idea was that my teammates would call out a name and I would tell the most vivid impression I had of that particular player.

Any Bengal fan worth his salt will have no trouble remembering some of these early-year players. Like:

JIM BOUDREAUX, tackle, 1968. Jim was the recipient of the Bengals' first Johnson & Johnson Award for taping over and above the call of duty. Somehow Jim managed to attach adhesive tape, gauze, foam rubber and Ace bandages to virtually every moving part on his body—and a few that didn't move. For games as well as practices. It boggles the mind that with all of this cumbersome protection that he could even walk out of the locker room under his own power. By comparison to Jim Boudreaux, a hockey goalie would have appeared naked and unprotected. He was really a sight to behold; he wore so much tape he looked more like an Egyptian mummy than a football player. When I saw Jim Boudreaux limp across the locker room encased in his adhesive tape suit, I didn't know whether to say "Hi, Jim" or offer him a tana leaf.

JOHN GUILLORY, safety, 1969-70. Because of his proclivity

for getting leg cramps, John used to carry around a bottle of Gatorade at all times. For some undetermined reason John Guillory believed that Gatorade had hidden powers to ward off cramps. He used to introduce himself to rookies by saying, "They call me the Gatorade kid," but all of us admitted that, to the best of our collective knowledge, John Guillory was the only person on the team who ever referred to him as "the Gatorade kid." One day as I was standing on the sidelines in practice, John approached me and said, "You sure have a funny-looking stomach." I've always thought his comment a little strange for two reasons: first, I have never considered, nor had anyone else, my stomach to be particularly funny looking; secondly, the comment was coming from a guy in his 20's who was bald, stood about 5'8", weighed roughly 165 pounds and, according to some, was a mulatto. To this date, John Guillory is the only 5'8" bald mulatto-looking dude ever to call me funny-looking. I had often considered it a possibility that John Guillory never had any mirrors in his house.

HARRY GUNNER, defensive end, 1968-69. Harry, at 6'8", played basketball at the University of Oregon. He was one of the few 6'8" men I've met in my life who could not dunk a basketball. He did have a claim to fame, however, and that was he once held the former Lew Alcindor to three points in a UCLA-Oregon basketball game. When he got to the Bengals, Harry helped form our first off-season Bengal basketball team; he appointed himself treasurer. We used to play the faculties of different high schools in the area and split the take with them 50-50. We would have fans hanging from the rafters to watch our show, and our share for a night might be as high as $3,000 or $4,000. Split among 15 players that's a pretty good chunk of bread. However, somehow it never worked out that we'd get as much as we should. Harry would pass out the payments and it would average something like $20 a man. We were all rookies then and he was a veteran, so we never questioned his handling of the funds. Looking back on it now, we were stupid. And I guess Harry Gunner laughed himself all the way to the bank.

SHERRILL HEADRICK, linebacker, 1968. A real veteran, Sherrill played on the Kansas City Chiefs' fine Super Bowl teams before being picked up by the Bengals in the special allocation draft. The thing I remember most about Sherrill was that he was the first, last and only pre-game barfer we'd had on the team. Right before our first game in 1968 I was smoking in the shower stall prior to going out on the field when I saw this player bolt past me and dive for the urinal. It was Sherrill Headrick and he proceeded to toss his cookies all over the place. If you want to know the truth, I was impressed by this. Here was this fantastic football player at the end of his career and he was still nervous enough before a football game to vomit. It wasn't until a week later that my admiration for this feat diminished somewhat. Before our second game of the season I sat next to Sherrill at our pre-game meal. We eat at nine in the morning, and the standard fare consisted of steak and potatoes (which sounds great but was not really all that palatable at 9 a.m.). As the waitress began to place the plate of food in front of Sherrill he motioned her to take it away. Then he whispered something in her ear. A few moments later she returned with a glass of orange juice, a raw egg and a bottle of tobasco sauce, which she placed carefully in front of the big man. As I looked on in dismay, Sherrill routinely cracked the egg and poured it into his glass of orange juice. Then he added liberal dashes of tobasco, swooshed it all together for good measure, and quickly downed the wretched stuff. Why Sherrill Headrick did this I never knew. But it sure as hell went a long way to explain why he got so all-fired ill before our games.

CHARLEY KING, safety, 1968-69. Charley is the only man I've *used* to advance my own personal worth. I'm not particularly proud of the fact, but, like in any big business, in professional football there are the users and the usees. The reason I used Charley was this: through the grapevine, I had come to learn that during the summer camp try-outs in 1968 the coaching staff's evaluation of rookie Bob Trumpy was something like this: "Exceptional speed for a big man, runs patterns crisply; has fine hands, but what about *toughness*? Has yet to demonstrate a fighter instinct needed to survive in the NFL." As soon as I heard this I knew I had to do something fast. That afternoon I selected, unbeknownst to him, my fall guy, Charley King, an allocation draft choice from Purdue. Charley was a nice, quiet player and, though we weren't great friends or anything, we had gotten to know each other well since he normally defended against me during our passing drills. I suppose I felt a twinge of guilt for what I was about to do, but I was convinced that I *needed* Charley to prove to the eagereyed coaches that I was mean enough to stay in the big leagues. It was during our routine passing "skeleton drill" for quarterbacks, receivers and defensive backs. Normally, we went at this fairly competitively, but not in a real blood-and-guts manner. So it surprised the hell out of Charley King when I caught a pass, turned, and rammed full force directly over his body, pumping my legs as if I were attempting to stomp out a brush fire. Charley flattened out like a collapsable ironing board; I was 6'6" and then 210 pounds and Charley was all of 5'10" and about 185, wet. After the surprise of the sneak attack wore off, he really got pissed, and he bounced up off the ground, cursing and pumping his fists. This was exactly the reaction I wanted to provoke and I went at him with all I had. Because of my distinct size advantage, it only lasted a few seconds. But in that short time I noticed the coaches had gathered around to tacitly nod to one another, as if to say, "Well, now, there's the toughness we've been looking for in our big 12th-round draft choice." It made me feel pretty good, I have to admit. Of course I didn't enjoy making Charley King look bad that day, but as it turned out it couldn't have hurt him too much. He stuck with the Bengals through summer camp and played for us for a couple of years. I must say, though, he never was too friendly with me thereafter. I guess I could have sat down and tried to explain to him that there was nothing personal in what I did, but I doubt whether it would have made Charley any happier.

DALE LIVINGSTON, punter, 1968-69. "Sweets," as we called him, had a hard time adjusting to professional football. More than anything else, I think it was the contact in the sport he disliked. One time Dale was called on to punt in a game and, having failed to cleanly negotiate an ill-snapped ball, he took off running for the sidelines. Someone shoved him just as he was going out, and he landed in a heap. Sweets didn't get up. Finally, Marv Pollins burst all the way across the field to see what the problem was. He had been on such errands before. "Where do you hurt?" he asked our man. Dale looked up at the trainer and groaned and said, *"Everywhere."* Marv shook his head; "Well, you *better*," he said and summoned for a stretcher. Once back to the Bengals' side of the field, having successfully held up the game for five or six minutes, Sweets continued to lay there unmoved, with all of us now gathered around him. We felt a sudden shoving at our backs and turned to see Paul Brown pushing his way through the wall of human flesh. Successfully reaching his punter, Paul eyed him skeptically once, twice, then he said, real spiteful, "I'm *glad* you're hurt." His comment finished us for the day. It was hard to concentrate on the field when you're giggling.

And, on the topic of giggling, well, we beat the Eagles 31-0. A laugher all the way. And Bill Bergey, Stan Walters, Mike Boryla and Horst Muhlmann—if they hadn't showed up at Veterans Stadium at all their presence would have been only barely less felt.

The Eagles' play was ludicrous. They gave us our first touchdown when Spike Jones couldn't cleanly handle a center snap in our end zone and Bill Kollar wrapped him up on the one. Then, a few series later, Boryla hit our Marvin Cobb at our eleven and he returned it to our thirty-four. On the next play Joe Lavender interferred with Ike Curtis and it resulted in a forty-yard penalty. Kenny Anderson, back at the helm, faded back to pass, saw his receivers covered and took off up the middle, coming to lite twenty-four yards later on the six-yard line. Believe it or not, that run by Kenny was the second longest run by a Bengal that year!

On our third TD Kenny hit Ed Williams on a ten-yard TD pass. On the play, Ed beat Bill Bergey. Paul Brown was not unhappy.

I suppose the most encouraging thing about that game was our running attack. It really came together, aimed right at the famed Bill Bergey, too! We really rolled over him—258 yards, a club record.

All in all it was a terrific win. It was a great momentum generator to take with us into Three Rivers Stadium the next week. Against the Steelers we were going to need all the help we could get....

BLOOD ON THE TURF

Our attack seemed to become *balanced*, and it couldn't have come at a better time. So important was the Steeler game that Paul set the stage in this manner: "You can't afford to fumble the ball away four times like you did against Philadelphia," he said. "You can't afford to allow two interceptions. You do and you'll pay the piper. Pittsburgh's got a good ballclub."

Paul never went out of his way to get us up emotionally. He was a *practical* man—his whole existence built on no-nonsense, grey flannel, dyed in the wool pragmatism—and he approached games, even big games, from that perspective. We couldn't fumble four times, true. Couldn't throw two interceptions, either. And Pittsburgh *did* have a good team. Couldn't argue with a thing he said.

I'll bet Coach slept well at nights, knowing he was never wrong.

The whole *world* knew how tough the Steelers were. In fact, the famed front four of the defense was the cover attraction in that week's issue of *Time* magazine. There they were in real-life color: L.C. Greenwood, Joe Greene, Dwight White and Ernie Holmes. National coverboys. If I didn't hate them so much I would have been happy for them.

The year before when we played the Steelers in Three Rivers Stadium we came away with our tails between our legs. They didn't beat us as badly as we humiliated ourselves as professionals.

It was awful. It was played on a Saturday before a national television audience. We had a dozen or so players injured and had Wayne Clark at quarterback. Paul *allowed* him to throw only eight passes all day long. It appeared as if the Old Coach they called "The Great Innovator" was actually throwing in the towel. Giving up in the NFL was not, then or now, an admirable quality.

I wasn't even at that game, and, looking back on it, I suppose it was one of the more fortunate things to have happened in my career. There's no way I could have stood mute on the sidelines and watched as my friends and teammates performed more like Emmett Kelleys in orange helmets than professional football players. Some of our guys *didn't* remain silent. They blasted PB's tactics in the press. A year later they were no longer with us.

The decision to keep me at home was upsetting. I had asked Paul on a Thursday whether or not I was going to make the trip with the team, despite the fact that I was too injured to actually play. Paul told me he didn't know, that he would think about it and give me his answer later. The next day, a Friday, while I was in the whirlpool he walked in and said, simply: "You won't be going to Pittsburgh with us."

I shrugged and said OK.

But the decision hurt.

I realize I couldn't have helped my teammates execute out on the field, but at the least I could have lent some encouraging lung-power from the sidelines. Had I made the trip, of course, I would have taken up unneeded space on the plane and in the motel. I would have been an additional mouth to feed. In short, my presence would have cost the team a few extra bucks.

In corporate fiscal matters, such superfluous expenditures were seldom tolerated.

As far as Pittsburgh was concerned, it still galled me to think about the first meeting with Pittsburgh that year. They looked quick and strong, but we had had a chance to beat them and blew it. An official stopped us on our own eleven-yard line when he called that unfair holding penalty on me.

It was a tough year for the officials. For the first time, coaches, owners and fans became more vocal in their criticism of the job they were doing. Civilians became all too aware of what some players knew for a long time—guys who worked at officiating as a part-time occupation were not going to be able to do a consistently superlative job in their work. In my opinion, NFL officials must be fully paid *full-time* employees of the NFL, much the way umpires are for professional baseball. What they *cannot* be is grocery store operators and dry cleaning entrepreneurs six days a week and expect to do a credible job of evaluating an athlete's performance on Sunday, simply by putting on a striped shirt.

The official's call against me in the first Pittsburgh game hurt our chances of going to the Super Bowl. Carrying the call to its logical conclusion: the call cost us the game; the game could cost us the division championship, which could cost us the home field advantage in the playoffs (the wild card team is always the visiting team); historical data shows that visiting wild card teams rarely win in playoff games. A loss in the playoffs meant no trip to Miami for the Super Bowl, which deprived our city of much national limelight and financially cost us players dearly.

All because of a single lousy call in November.

It didn't seem right—a group of part-time workers having so much control over our very livelihoods, What if the official was tired game day, or hung-over? Or he hated Paul Brown so much that he'd subconsciously make calls against him? (This happened, by the way. There was one ref who couldn't stand our boss and he purpose-fully made calls against us; there was another NFL official who liked to see thrilling games played so he made calls in crucial situations that would make the games closer in score.) One official interprets holding one way, a second another. In the end, it is the players (and fans) who suffer.

The bad call against me didn't make national headlines. But others that year did. The St. Louis Cardinals' Mel Gray caught a pass in the end zone with eight seconds left, but he fumbled the ball before his feet hit the ground. The official ruled that Gray had maintained sufficient possession and called a touchdown. The deci-sion enabled the Cardinals to tie the game against the Redskins, go to overtime, and eventually win. Washington's head coach George Allen really blasted the officials and demanded that NFL owners look into ways of using instant replays to help decide controversial calls.

A second misbegotten decision involved an all-important game between Buffalo and Miami. Mercury Morris appeared to have fumbled the ball deep in the Dolphins' territory toward the end of the game. The official ruled the play dead before Morris lost the ball, however, and the Dolphins were able to retain possession and win the game 31-21.

It knocked Buffalo out of playoff contention, something owner Ralph Wilson didn't take sitting down. Publicly he stated that the head linesman who called the play should be fired from the job and never allowed to work another game. "Anyone that incompetent," he said, "shouldn't be allowed to officiate."

Others also came out against the officiating, despite Pete Ro-zelle's automatic fine for such action. (Paul Brown kept silent to the press; but I saw him take down the name and number of an official and immediately call in a complaint to the league office.) Ram's former owner Carroll Rosenbloom had some choice words for the men with the whistles as did Viking coach Bud Grant, who claimed that NFL officialdom was "a multi-million dollar operation being handled by amateurs on Sunday afternoons."

No pulling of punches there.

Our Rufus Mayes knew the frustration of poor officiating first-hand. When a certain official was doing our games Ruf counted on being called for holding four or five times. Interpretation of the rule varied greatly from official to official. Ruf did have an unusual way of carrying his hands into a block, but our films showed that more often than not he was not holding the opposition. But that little mattered to the official who saw only what he wanted to see.

To be truthful, I never did fully understand exactly what consti-tuted holding. Each year the league office sent around a guy to explain some of the key rules to us players. I was in the league ten years and I swear I heard ten different definitions of holding. That was hardly the kind of consistency that was going to help us prepare for playing penalty-free football games.

I can remember one time a few years ago when a ref erroneously called holding on me and I approached him for an explanation. He just ignored me, typically, and began pacing off the penalty. It burned me up so I ran around and got in front of him, blocking his path upfield. He stopped in my shadow and looked up at me. "Get out of the way," he commanded.

"Not til you change your call," I informed him. "I'm not moving an inch til you admit you were wrong."

He remained firm. "No way am I changing that call," he stated.

"Then we'll be here all day." It was a momentary standoff until finally one of the other officials interceded. He took the ball and, placing his leg defiantly between mine, continued the counting of hashmarks for the full fifteen yards. The first ref and I just stood there unmoving, staring daggers at one another until we decided that the matter was out of our hands. The fans ate it up. But I doubt whether I got the benefit of an impartial call from that official again.

Generally I tried to keep aloof from officials. I didn't want to know who they were or what they liked to call. If you find a guy who is a stickler for calling holding and you hesitate to think about it each time you block, you're not going to do a very effective job. You have to shoot out and get your man with everything you have—and let the chips fall where they may.

I didn't know what the answer was. At first I thought that by hiring two more officials per game you could somehow have people positioned more judiciously to get a better look at what was going on. But the more I considered this the more I realized that two more striped shirts out there might just compound an already untenable problem. They may start haggling like rug merchants with *each other*! I guess in the end the final solution is to go ahead and hire full-time guys, pay them very well and, as George Allen and others have suggested, use instant replay on some limited, formularized basis to settle calls in question.

Something has to be done, though.

The way I figure it, the official who called holding on me in that important Pittsburgh game should have been prosecuted as a criminal. Grand theft. His decision stole a swimming pool paid for with my Super Bowl check right out of my back yard.

The officials notwithstanding, we had to show up against the Steelers. We were ready.

You could tell by the mood on the plane. There was the proper mix of nervousness and looseness among the players. We went into Pittsburgh fully expecting to beat the Steelers. We thought we had the best team. All we needed to do was prove it.

164

Paul Brown was even in an uncharacteristically easy mood. When I saw him he was laughing and telling reporters what it was like playing football in Pittsburgh. "There were," said Paul, "more thugs per square inch there than in any stadium in the country." He said the crowds at the Steelers' game were like "a Mafia convention." Pretty vivid language for a man who seldom opened up.

And there was a quote someone read aloud attributed to the Steelers' All-Pro defensive end L.C. Greenwood. L.C. said, "Tell ladies, old men and the faint of heart to stay away, because there's going to be blood spilt on the turf.

To this, there was a rousing response by everyone on the plane. The guys *wanted* the Steelers.

It promised to be a heady confrontation to pique the tastes of football connoisseurs everywhere.

Well, it could've been. Should've been.

But it wasn't.

What should have been vintage football turned out to be nothing more than Ripple.

The Steelers rolled 35-14.

The game was virtually over before we got ourselves untracked. The Steelers took the opening kickoff and marched sixty-eight yards in eleven plays to make it 7-0.

The second time we had the ball we handed Pittsburgh the game. In four plays we had driven into Steeler territory and it looked as if we had everything going. Then, suddenly, on a sweep left, Boobie Clark fumbled the ball and linebacker Jack Lambert picked it up. He ran twenty-one yards before lateraling back to J.T. Thomas, who ran an additional twenty-one for a touchdown. It was 14-0. The play crushed us. We had counted on really taking it to the Steelers, to beat them on their home turf for the first time; instead we were behind by two touchdowns, and the Steelers never looked back.

It was a mighty depressed group in our dressing room. We had given Pittsburgh their third Central Division championship in four years. Paul was disappointed and bitter. "They blew you out of there today," he said, gratuitously reminding of us of something we already knew. "They really overpowered you."

And finally there was a rather apropo comment by John Shinners. "If you want to know the truth," said John, "the way we played today, I'm embarrassed to go home."

We all were.

The blood on the turf was ours.

Well, what it came down to was this: If we could beat San Diego on the final day of the season, we would go to the playoffs. Should we lose, our season was over. All that work we put in since mid-July wouldn't mean a thing. Paul Brown told us he saw the game as a *challenge*, and, in a moment of charity, reminded us that "the burden is all yours."

"I know," he added, "I don't need to remind you that if you go to the first playoff game each player receives as additional payment one-fourteenth of his regular season salary. That should be some incentive to do a good job Sunday." Let it be said that the years taught Paul how to appeal to our basic instincts.

Of all our guys, no one wanted to beat the Chargers worse than Bob Brown. It was the Chargers who waived our 285-pound defensive tackle in summer camp, enabling PB to pick him up for $100. According to Bob, Chargers' head coach Tommy Prothro told him flat-out: "We don't think you can play the game any more. We are releasing you."

"I guess you could say," Bob acknowledged to the players who now commonly gathered around his mountainous frame for advice, "that I've got me a few vendettas to settle Sunday. They embarrassed me and I didn't appreciate it. I'm *ready* for this one."

Bob said the decision to cut him came as a complete surprise. As a matter of fact, Bob Brown and Tommy Prothro had spent much of the summer together before training camp at a "fat farm" in North Carolina. They spent hours together talking, mostly about football, gooey deserts and bridge, a game that they say Prothro admired with devotion bordering on the fanatical.

"He gave me absolutely no indication that he was going to waive me," Bob sighed. "I guess I just got caught in the youth movement. Man, it was rough when you were thirty-five years old."

Then he looked up and smiled, rather slyly, at the rookies around him. "Tell you what, kids," he winked. "Come Sunday, Bob Brown will play some *football.*

I had a feeling. I had a feeling that Center Ed Flanagan, the guy who would be playing across from Bob Brown Sunday, was going to wish he never made the trip to Cincinnati. I had a feeling Bob Brown was going to *treat him real bad.*

To us veteran Bengals, there was a very special memory evoked whenever we played the San Diego Chargers.

The image was of an ex-Charger who came to us in the allocation draft of 1968. His name was Frank Buncom and he played linebacker.

Ask Beau, Bob Johnson, Essex, Howard Fest or me about Frank Buncom, and we'd all have given you the same answer—he was the classiest guy in professional football; quiet, polite, intelligent, always a nice word for everyone. While the rest of us were running around in Wilmington bars drinking beer during summer camp,

Frank was over in the Union talking to the students about life, brotherhood and the importance of an education.

Frank was a seven-year veteran when he came to the Bengals, and he was picked by Paul Brown to be our starting linebacker. He had a great first year, giving much-needed leadership to all us rookies, and he had a good summer camp in '69. Frank and the rest of us were really looking forward to opening our second regular season against the Miami Dolphins at home. As was our custom, we had spent the night at a downtown hotel, and about 7:30 in the morning Frank's roommate, Ernie Wright, our veteran tackle, was awakened by the sound of belabored breathing. Ernie rushed over and tried to awaken his roommate, but to no avail. He then hurried off to get Marv Pollins, who was one floor below. By the time they got back to the room it was too late.

Frank Buncom was dead. He was twenty-nine years old.

The doctors later told us the cause of death was a blood clot that had formed in Frank's left lung, causing extreme shock to his body and eventually heart failure.

Paul was subdued in the locker room before the game. He had witnessed many incredible things in his forty years of coaching, but never had a player died on him. With the game just moments away, a lesser man could have used the occasion to deliver a legendary "Win One for the Gipper" speech, but Paul had the good grace to refrain from doing so. Instead, he just said that it was an extremely unfortunate incident and that the game must still go on. Each of us would have to deal with the tragedy in his own way, Paul added, then he turned it over to Father Connelly who delivered an on-the-spot eulogy. Finally, Frank's best friend took the floor.

Ernie Wright spoke in soft tones, barely moving his lips: "I'm not going to make any 'This Game's for Frank' speeches to you," Ernie said. "That would be Hollywood, and Frank Buncom was not Hollywood." He paused a moment for a deep breath. I saw his eyes mist over. "Frank was the type of guy everybody wished they were," he said, "but because of moral weaknesses or circumstances they never could be. If they passed out an award for the nicest, most gentlemanly human being, it would have gone to Frank Buncom. I have two sons, and if they grow up to be like Frank, I'll be very proud."

I guess Ernie said what we all felt, really. There just wasn't too much more we could do.

We went on to upset Miami that day, but it didn't seem to matter much. Afterwards, we awarded the game ball to Frank Jr., who was the absolute shining light in his father's life. Frank had married late in life—to a wonderful girl named Sarah. We used to rib him in the clubhouse about the late marriage, saying the general things about him being too over-the-hill to perform connubial duties and all. Frank just took it in stride, and he used his son as evidence of his prowess ("not older, my friends," he'd said, "just better"). I've never seen a prouder father—all he wanted to do that last year of life was talk about his boy.

Giving the game ball to Frank Jr. was all we could really do by way of recognizing our love for his father.

For some reason I think we all felt a little responsible for his death; the game ball was to assure Frank Jr. that his dad's teammates would never forget him, that he had affected each of our lives in some small way.

The boy deserved better, I know. But how do you begin to compensate a child for the loss of his father at age twenty-nine?

Weeks later we saw Frank's attorney and he told us he had never seen such a well thought-out will in his life. "It was a masterpiece," he said, "as thoroughly planned as any I've seen." He said Frank had gone to such great lengths in designing his estate that Sarah and Frank Jr. will never in their lives have financial burdens to worry them.

You'd have expected that from Frank Buncom.

There were certain things that came to mind when we played the San Diego Chargers.

Wheaties, for instance. And Greenies. And Bennies and California Reds.

Drugs, in other words.

It was in the early '70's that Commissioner Pete Rozelle fined and put eight Chargers on probation for using drugs. He also fined the club and its general manager Harland Svare.

Much of the trouble began when a defensive end for the Chargers, Houston Ridge, sued the club, team doctor and the league because, he alleged, the club gave him pep pills to kill pain so he could continue to play while injured.

It was also claimed that the Chargers' trainer used to leave packages of bennies or greenies in players' lockers before games; afterwards he'd give them "downers" so they could get to sleep at night. Further, it was revealed that a druggist had sold 10,000 amphetamines to the Chargers' business manager. Houston Ridge collected in the neighborhood of $300,000 to settle the suit.

To say the least, the publicity gave pro football a black eye. But it did manage to bring to light a then-growing problem in the NFL. Drug use was prevalent on many teams; but these indulgences gave the public the impression that *all* football players were drug freaks, bennying up on Sundays so they could hit the guy across from them in full fury then laugh at the resultant pain.

It simply wasn't true.

There were, of course, cliques of guys on each team who took something to stimulate them, but by no means were they in the majority.

On our team, I'd say the peak years for uppers were 1969 and '70. At that time maybe twenty-five percent of our players popped pills before games. But their activity was so undercover, so secretive, that had I not suffered my ankle injury I never would have known it existed.

When I accepted the Wheaties for the injury, I tacitly became part of the inner circle of users. Although that one time was the only time I ever took drugs, I somehow became known as a man who understood and accepted what was going on, and I became privy to conversations about drug use.

I was shocked to learn about some of my teammates who were pepping up before games. One of them in particular knocked me out, and it was safe to say it would blow the minds of every Bengal fan, too. This player was one of the most respected and well-thought-of individuals we had ever had on the team, an All-Pro lineman.

He was also one of the biggest drug users.

He never missed playing a game without greenies. It became part of his routine, as much as the habitual pre-game donning of shoulder pads. All you had to do was look at him during a game and you could tell he was flying high. There were the dilated pupils and the shallow breathing, the hyperintensity. Even during the hottest of games, he seldom bothered to take in liquids.

I remember a plane ride back from Los Angeles in 1973. We had lost a close game to the Rams. This player was so bennied up that he couldn't stop talking the entire flight home. On and on he rambled, nearly incoherently, hardly pausing to catch his breath. The plane ride lasted three-and-a-half hours. Teammates who made the mistake of sitting next to him would tolerate the incessant chatter for a few minutes then hastily move on to quieter quarters. By the end of the trip he was sitting in a section all alone.

Another game, this one in Denver, a player, another one of our all-American types, had taken so many amphetamines that he began to hyperventilate. He spent his flight home with his face buried in an oxygen mask.

It boggles the mind that Paul Brown and our coaches didn't realize what was going on right under thier noses. But they didn't. It wasn't just a matter of them looking the other way, either. Paul Brown would have never in this world allowed his players to take anything as unprofessional as bennies and greenies. As for allowing the trainer to pass pep pills out among players, Marv Pollins wouldn't know a Wheatie from a California Red. If there's a large B imprinted on the tablet, Marv understood that it was Bayer aspirin. After this he was hard pressed.

I don't believe PB even deigned to consider that his players would be involved in such illicit activities as pill taking. Perhaps he was just too wrapped up in his own concerns to notice.

Back in those early years there was an expression frequently heard among members of the drug cabal. It was "going for sixty." As in: "Big game today, Trump. Think I'm going for sixty." *Sixty* was milligrams. *Going for* was synonymous with ingesting, as in amphetamines.

Most of the drugs on our team came from California. They were brought to summer camp by the teammates who lived on the West Coast and who seemed to have easy access to them. They came by the thousands. Mounds of pills in all shapes and sizes: long thin green ones, round orange ones, oblong red ones. I didn't know their names or what they did for you.

I don't happen to want to indict all players from California. It just so happens that, on the Bengals back then, some of our California guys seemed to have the connections. Many of them said they just had their wives get a couple of hundred uppers from their diet clinics, which were popular on the West Coast. The purpose of these diet pills was to make you so hyperactive that you didn't care about eating a meal. We had guys taking ten or twenty of them before games.

You saw them on Mondays following a game and they looked terrible, and felt worse. You'd ask them if they got any sleep the night before and they looked at you through blank pupils and say they took so many pills they wouldn't be able to fall asleep until Tuesday night. We had one guy who crashed on a Tuesday night in downtown Cincinnati. The police found him early the next morning stretched out on a park bench. His body was covered with newspapers.

Following our last Houston game, I talked to some of the Oilers' players about a guy who at one time had a substantial drug problem. He had played for three or four teams, and was known throughout the league as a real "hop-head." His Houston teammates told me that he was now straightened out and a real good football player for them. At one time, though, he was taking Mescaline—a *real* mind-blowing drug—before every game. He was also taking another pill that he didn't even know the name of. He just took it because someone said to do so.

That sounds incredibly ignorant, I know. I mean, the two chemical combinations could have mixed negatively in his body and killed him instantly. I guess it didn't matter. He was so high that he spent his career playing under the grandoise hallucination that he was one great football player. I heard that he once told a teammate about a time he was so tripped out that he "could hear the sweat dripping off the tight end's nose." And I also heard that the constant drug taking had affected his internal organs so much that he had lost the faculty of bladder control. He'd be walking down the street when all of a sudden he'd realized that he had wet his pants.

One of the most unfortunate results of what the drug abuse publicity did to the NFL in those early years was to affect the outlook of the kids. You could hardly blame a high school or college football player, believing pro players ingested uppers as a way of life, who though to himself, "Geez, I better begin taking some of those pills now. When I get to the pros I'm going to be expected to know how to *handle* them."

And drug use in the NFL must have been a financial haven for pushers. All they had to do was corner a kid on the school yard and say, "Listen, you ought to try one of these pills. I just sold some to so-and-so of the New York Jets and he says he had never played a better game in his life."

No, I'm not a believer in using drugs to hype oneself for a game. I made the mistake of taking Wheaties once. That was enough. I ended up that night crying myself to sleep.

The week of the Chargers' game, the temperature dipped to frigid levels. The California guys were walking around muttering under their breaths. We suggested they try to view Midwest winters as "an experience."

What's the expression—cold hands, warm heart?

If that's not it, it should be. Because that was just the way San Diego played. At game time the wind chill factor brought the temperature on the field to zero and it was obvious that the Chargers hadn't prepared too well for the severe climatic change. Every time their frozen fingers attempted to grasp the football they had the good-heartedness to drop it, allowing our side to claim possession.

You want to know how ridiculous it was? The Cincinnati Bengals scored three touchdowns *before the San Diego offense ran even a single play from scrimmage*!

In ten years, it was the most ludicrous display I had ever witnessed.

We received the kickoff and promptly traveled sixty-eight yards for a TD. We kicked off and Ricky Young fumbled at the eleven. Later he was moved to say, "It was so cold my hands were like sticks out there." Johnny Mack pounced on it and three plays later Stan Fritts went on a six-yard scoring run to make it 14-0. We kicked off again and Mike Fuller got his chance to catch it. He fumbled at the thirty-two, Johnny Mack once more playing Johnny-on-the-spot, and eight plays hence Stan Fritts dived over from the one. Dave Green missed the point-after, and the score read 20-0. San Diego's offense and our defense, could've been collecting unemployment benefits—neither had yet seen any action.

When San Diego's offense finally did get on the field to show us their stuff, it ran three plays and punted. We took five plays, including a tight-end screen to me and a beautifully executed fifty-two-yard bomb to Ike Curtis, to make it 27-0. We were still in the first quarter. At this point the bench began feeling that the possibility of going to Oakland next week for the playoffs was becoming very real.

By halftime we had forty-one points, nineteen first downs and 316 yards on total offense.

The final score was 47-17.

"From a confidence standpoint," said my roomie Bob Johnson, "this was a helluva game."

I sort of felt sorry for San Diego, really, as did several of the guys. The handful of original Bengal players knew what it was like to be humiliated before millions of viewers. Even Paul Brown showed some emotion, such as it was, for the opposition. As the clock was ticking off the last painful seconds for the Chargers, a band in the stands struck up a tune for Tommy Prothro. It was "Auld Lang Syne." PB heard this and looked over at his counterpart; then he trotted across the field and shook Prothro's hand. It was the only time I ever saw Paul Brown do that.

Our locker room was exploding, not only because of the big win (in which we set three club records), but for the fact the Bengals were *officially* going to the playoffs.

One of the happiest was Bob Brown. "Listen, kids," Bob told us. "That one felt mighty good. Thank you all." We awarded the game ball to Bob Brown. Bob played a very super-charged game, but not the great type of game that usually earned a game ball. But we all knew how much it meant to him, so we gave him the ball anyway. It was little things like that that shows you just how much my teammates loved this guy. What's so amazing was that Bob Brown gained all this respect in just a few short months. Many of us had been on the Bengals for many years, but none of us could hold a candle to Bob when it came to possessing the respect of teammates. I remember a game when Bob was really feeling the aches and pains of playing pro football at age 35. He was standing in the defensive huddle with his big frame bent nearly in half. One of our defensive backs, who could probably pass for one of Bob Brown's sons, saw the big man huffing and puffing. He went up to him and—not saying a word—reached over, took Bob Brown's chin strap, and snapped it in place for him.

"You boys were up in the bit and showed it," Paul told us. "We did it (making the playoffs) ourselves and we can all take pride in that." Words like this from Paul Brown bordered on near jubilation.

Freddie Franchise had another one of his computer-like days. Playing only the first half, he hit eighteen of twenty-three for 216 yards and three touchdowns. Such statistics were becoming old hat, taken for granted. Only when Freddie *didn't* perform with mechanical precision equal to this did we notice him. No doubt about it: more than anything else, that golden arm of his got us where we were that day: the wild card team of the American Football Conference, going to the playoffs.

It was with this very goal that we had begun our season six months previously.

Said our quarterback, by way of summing up our season and bringing our clubhouse celebration to a close: "Starting right now it's a new NFL season. There are now only six teams and we're all starting out even. If we go three-and-oh we'll be Super Bowl champs."

Really, it was as basic as that.

PLAYOFFS, PANIC AND PAUL

And so it began.

We were to take the first step toward Paul Brown's "Big Brass Ring."

It wouldn't be easy. We would be playing a) in Oakland, b) in warm weather and, c) on natural grass. Each of these would be an adjustment for us. And the fact that no wild card team ever made it to the Super Bowl didn't help our odds much.

There were probably not two more evenly matched teams than the Raiders and Bengals. Right down the list the squads were comparable. Kenny Anderson had his dangerous receivers—Ike, Charlie, Chip, myself; Kenny Stabler had an equal corps—Branch, Biletnikoff, Siani, Moore. The offensive and defensive lines were man for man an even match up.

In our short existence we were in two previous playoff games; we lost two previous playoff games. The first was in 1970 when we were in only our third year as an expansion club. We finished with an 8-6 record, winning our last seven games in a row, and were matched with the Baltimore Colts in the playoffs. The Colts beat us soundly, 17-0. They went on to win the Super Bowl.

In 1973 we again advanced to the playoffs, this time facing the perfectly honed Miami Dolphins. They whopped us 34-16. Miami also went on to win the Super Bowl.

PB was actually upset that we went to the playoffs in those years. Not in his wildest expectations had he anticipated his young club finishing as high in the standings as we did—it just hadn't been in the Coach's scheme of things. "It set our franchise back years," Paul told the press. And he was serious. The problem was that, not only would the city now come to expect such spectacular feats from its still fledgling team, but the Bengals, because of the high finish in the final standings, would draft precariously low in the college drafts.

You couldn't get outstanding talent to build a franchise when you're 18th in line at the drafting table.

Both the Bengals and Raiders finished the year with 11-3 records. Oakland had been in the playoffs eight out of nine years, though, so to them an 11-3 record was old hat.

To us it was much more. It was our best record ever.

The guys were loose, except for Ron Pritchard. He sucker punched Chip Myers in the locker room. Chip had three white footballs he was autographing for presents. Pritchard came in and began tossing one of them in the air. Chip asked him to be careful not to get it dirty and Ron got very upset. He intentionally threw the ball on the ground and Chip called him a disparaging name. That's when Pritchard sucker punched him. Then about a half hour later Chip was standing by his locker talking to a teammate. Pritchard walked by and surmised that Chip was talking about him. Pritchard walked over and sucker punched him again.

The pressure of the playoffs seemed to be getting to our linebacker.

During our last game he picked a fight with another teammate, rookie linebacker Glen Cameron. Pritchard didn't like Cameron's attitude after he ran off the field after a kickoff. He called Glen some names on the sidelines and then tried to provoke a fight with him in the locker room at half time.

Most of us thought Ron Pritchard was beginning to become psycho.

For example, game day in Oakland. It began ominously.

Reggie Jackson, then of the Oakland A's, led the team in prayer during the morning chapel service in the hotel. Sitting right up front at the service was Reggie's onetime college roommate at Arizona State, Ron Pritchard.

Reggie asked the attending players, "How many want to be saved by Christ?" Several players raised their hands. Then he asked, "How many players already *have* been saved by Christ?"

Ron Pritchard raised his hand.

I don't know whether Ron was saved before or after he sucker punched Chip Myers.

And in the end, he probably became the victim of his own intensity—his career ending in pain and frustration. The end began on the practice field halfway through the '76 season. Bruce Coslet blocked Ron on a play and Pritch went down hollering, grabbing his knee. X-rays disclosed calcium deposits and bone spurs, and surgery was prescribed. After the surgery Ron was convinced he would come back to play during the season, and he was encouraged by our weight trainer Kim Wood who kind of made Ron Pritchard his personal reclamation project. Kim proudly told all of us that, because of a special program he had put Pritch on, our linebacker would be back playing with us in five weeks. Never been done before, Kim apprised us, it would make medical history. Ron believed him and busted his butt, and, sure enough, by the last game of the season against Oakland, Pritch was in full uniform. He didn't start, however, and it bothered him. Finally, in the fourth quarter, the game well out of hand because Oakland was romping us, Ron Pritchard took it upon himself to run out on the field. He lasted one play. A sweep, Marv Hubbard leading. It cost Pritch three more operations in the next thirteen months. After this, the Bengals were through with him and he was traded to Houston, where he lasted but a moment. Later he tried to hook up with Oakland but with no luck. The last I heard of Ron Pritchard he was trying to get up enough money to build his own church in Lake Tahoe. Yes, his own church. In Lake Tahoe. Well, Ron Pritchard was, afterall, a linebacker.

As for our playoff game—well, I heard Perry Mason say it on television a thousand times.

"The defense rests."

That's exactly what happened to us in the playoffs. That, and the poor kicking game. And the failure to seize the opportunity when we had it.

Combined, these factors earned us a 31-28 loss to the Raiders. Which meant we wouldn't be going against the Steelers the next week. Which meant we wouldn't be going to the Super Bowl.

It was hard adjusting to that realization. Our season was *over*! Since mid-July we had been busting our butts, working toward a singular goal. Suddenly it all ended. Frustratingly. The vision faded. Sherm White's "dream" dissolved.

We came up short.

It should never have happened the way it did. Our defense gave up 228 yards on the ground in the first half alone. The Raiders ran almost exclusively to our right—a lot at Pritchard—and managed to pull ahead 17-7 by halftime.

And the score went 21-7 with only four minutes gone in the third quarter. The game was beginning to look the world like a rout.

But we came back. How we came back! Like we did in so many other games that year.

We scored on a six-yard Lenvil Elliott run after driving nearly the entire length of the field in only eleven plays. (A big play was a pass interference call against Jack Tatum, who hit me too soon. It was good for a gain of twenty-seven yards.)

The Raiders made it 31-14 to begin the fourth quarter, but still we failed to give in. With 9:13 to go Rattler Riley stepped in front of a Ken Stabler pass and two plays later Kenny found Charlie Joiner in the end zone.

It was 31-21. And we were moving.

There were five minutes remaining and we used only seven plays to go forty-three yards, one of them being a thirty-seven-yard strike to clutch-handed Chip Myers. Then Kenny got the ball to Ike in the corner of the end zone, and our receiver made a circus catch, taking the ball away from Neal Colzie. It was only Ike's third reception of the game.

31-28. Four minutes fifteen seconds left on the clock. And we were only three points away—a field goal!—from tieing the game.

But we needed the ball!

God. We got it! Unbelievably.

Stabler missed a handoff to Pete Banaszak and Ron Carpenter recovered the fumble at our own thirty-four yard line. The guys on our bench went crazy. It was as if our own collective prayer had been answered, granted by some unseen force. At one point we were down by seventeen points; now we had a mere thirty-four yards to go in four minutes and the playoff victory was ours.

What a storybook finish. A Cinderella team with a spectacular come-from-behind victory. An expansion team of untried rookies and over-the-hill castoffs just eight short years previous, came of age, beating the veteran Oakland Raiders on their own turf.

It had all the elements of a front-page drama.

But we blew it.

We panicked. Absolutely fell apart. Instead of taking our time, using all four minutes to go the requisite thirty-four yards, we tried to go for it all at once. On the very first play Kenny went for the bomb (the play was called from the sidelines). Mad Stork Hendricks shook a weak block by Boobie in the backfield and sacked Kenny for a loss all the way back to the forty-three. It was Hendricks' fourth sack of our quarterback on the afternoon. And it put us out of field goal range.

Still, we fought. Kenny hit Bruce Coslet for a five-yard gain, making it third and eleven. To get the first down Kenny came to me, on a short sideline route, but at the very last nanosecond, defensive back Charlie Phillips snapped out his arm and tipped the ball out of bounds.

Fourth down came. We needed eleven to get a first down at the twenty-eight.

That'd be field goal position right there, to say nothing of a fine spot to begin another series of plays for a touchdown drive with three minutes still left on the clock.

Kenny faded back and looked deep. Ike appeared to be covered, so did Charlie Joiner. Kenny did exactly what he has been trained to do for five years: "When your primary receivers are covered, dump the ball off to one of your backs!" Kenny saw Lenvil on the right flat and his mind clicked. He let the ball go.

Even as it was in the air Kenny realized he had made a mistake. Lenvil was only three or four yards deep, with a defensive man coming up hard. At best the completed pass would have gone for a very short gain—and the ball would be turned over to the Raiders.

It was a mental miscalculation, perhaps the only one Kenny made all season.

178

It didn't matter, anyway. The ball was the slightest bit high and Lenvil let it slide out of his hands to the turf. Incomplete pass.

It was the game. A crushing loss. We had been given a once-in-a-lifetime opportunity and couldn't convert. As someone said on the plane going home, "We had all the marbles. We just didn't shoot 'em."

The atmosphere in the locker room would have made a mood ring quiver.

"When I recovered that fumble," moaned Ron Carpenter, "I thought it was an omen. I thought it said to us, here you are; here is your ticket to the AFC championship game. But we just couldn't cash it in."

"What a disappointment," agreed Charlie Joiner. "After my touchdown reception I knew we were going to come back. I sensed we were really going to win this one." Chuck Joiner shook his head and buried his face in a towel.

Ike, too, was unhappy. "I thought they should have thrown to me more," he told reporters. The Raiders had played him plenty tight. But Ike looked around at his quiet teammates and sighed. "We sure tried to come back tough, though," he said. "It just wasn't enough."

It was a disillusioning afternoon. We had one fine ballclub there, and we just didn't put it together when it counted. It was natural that the guys should feel bitter and disappointed. We really felt we could have gone on to Pittsburgh the next week and given them a real tussle. But we never knew. It had been a hell of a year, but we simply fell short.

Of all the varied reactions to the loss, the one which surprised me the most was the one by Paul Brown. Normally PB's not overly charitable after a loss, and a playoff loss is no exception. But after reminding our front four that "you allowed yourselves to be blown right out of there," Paul paused to catch his breath and regain his composure. Then he told us: "I was proud of you. You gave it your best shot. You tried hard. You came back. You did the best you could."

Then he told us that this was the best Bengal team he'd ever had.

It was an eerie reaction. I had been with Paul after each Bengal loss since the club's inception. Never before had I seen him so easy-going and high-spirited after a defeat. He actually seemed satisfied. For Paul, that's really weird. And perhaps that should have told us something Paul had in the back of his mind. Like retirement.

If I had to single out a player who was affected most by the loss it was Bob Brown. There was, at best, some doubt as to whether his veteran body was willing—or *able*—to be put through the gruesome tortures of summer heat and two-a-day workouts at Wilmington

College another year. (Apparently the spirit was willing, but the flesh was weak—Big Bob was waived the next year.) Besides, Bob had had a vision. He had seen himself "going out on a shooting star." But that year's star fizzled out.

"The worst part for me," Bob softly uttered, "is saying that this year is over." He was sprawled across the clubhouse floor, his body wet and swollen and caked with mud. "You all can say 'wait till next year.' But I hate waiting till next year. I thought we had the kids here to do it *now*."

The big guy sat there in silence. Each teammate who passed by gave him a meaningful tap on the head or shoulderpads, as if to say, "Thanks, Bob, for giving us everything you could this year." Finally Bob Brown wiped the sweat from his face and threw the towel out in front of him. "I'll be damned," he said, and struggled to his aching feet. As we sat and watched his frame hulk off to the showers, I think we all felt a little sad. And guilty. We had a bona fide chance to get into the AFC championship game and we blew it, shattering Bob Brown's "vision." We had let Bob Brown down.

We had treated him real bad.

The flight home was a somber one.

The feelings of anger and frustration and the individual self-persecutions of letting down each other subsided. Strangely, there was an almost collective shifting of blame for our loss.

It fell squarely on the person of Paul Brown.

"All week long he told the media that he was treating the Oakland game just like any other game," one player complained.

"Yea," another agreed, "that was a mistake. The playoffs just ain't another game."

A third teammate said: "You have to give our opposition ten points just because of our coaching philosophy."

The prevailing theory was that Paul just didn't adequately prepare us for a game mentally. He *had* treated it as if it were any old game, which it was not. Anyone who believed that John Madden treated the playoffs as "just another game" wasn't being rational.

Our players felt that we should've gone out to Oakland at least a day or two early, not only to acclimate our bodies to the change from cold to warm temperatures but also to practice at least one day on natural turf. The ground was frozen solid in Cincinnati so we had prepared ourselves for playing on grass by practicing all week on AstroTurf. And because we waited until late Saturday to leave for the West Coast, our pre-game meal for the important playoff game consisted of an airline's flight dinner, Swiss steak or something.

Hardly rib-sticking fare.

Despite the importance of this game, Paul's "inspirational" message before going out on the field consisted of low-key things like "all those on the kickoff team raise their hands; all those on the receiving team raise their hands." Even an optimist would have had to admit this type of presentation lacked a certain amount of flare.

His insistence on non-fomenting speeches was a Paul Brown shortcoming; it was a glaring weakness I found in his coaching make-up. There were no inspirational words, no emotional monologues, no rah-rah oratories. The closest he came to raising our emotional levels was when he threatened us with "you can be replaced if you don't do your job."

Paul said we were mature young men; therefore, each player was left alone to pique himself psychologically. That made great theory, but lousy winning percentages in big games.

It simply didn't work. PB had forty-three individuals from forty-three backgrounds and forty-three different mental constitutions. When he insisted that each one psyche himself up before a game, Paul ended up with forty-three *different* levels and pitches of psyche. And that ran counter to the predication that professional football is a *team* sport, with *team* defense, *team* offense, *team* everything.

I can remember a game in Baltimore several years ago. The Colts were having a rough year and the fans were staying home. PB's pre-game remarks went something like this: "It's cold and miserable out there today. This stadium is old and delapidated. It seats about 60,000 fans, but we don't expect there'll be more than 25,000 or so here today. But don't let that worry you. Go out and play football."

Knute Rockne would've turned in his grave.

After Paul's message, we went out and "played football." Badly. We lost.

Paul couldn't understand why.

One thing about Paul Brown, there was a general mystique about the man. And they said you either loved him or hated him.

I don't know whether that was true. But I *did* know one thing: you had to *respect* him.

Foremost, Paul Brown was a coaching genius. Professional football was, good or bad, the child of Paul Brown. He shaped it into what it is today—a sports conglomerate played within business, economic and scientific parameters. It remains a thriving entertainment showcase for our competition-demanding nation. The "game" had evolved because Paul Brown caused it to do so.

You've heard the allegations about Paul—as a coach he was aloof, cold-hearted, business-oriented and conservative; he allowed the game to pass him by; he shunned superstars on his team and he held tight purse strings when it came to paying his players.

There may have been *some* truth in each of these. But there were also a lot of built-in misconceptions.

One of the annual charges against Paul—and this was a complete falsehood—was that Paul called all plays from the sidelines. It wasn't true. To be sure, the Paul Brown "system" utilized the messenger guard method of relaying suggested plays to the quarterback, but Paul took no part in calling those plays. This was strictly up to our offensive coaches, like Bill Walsh and Tiger Johnson on the field with headsets, and J.D. Donaldson in a booth high above the playing surface.

I doubt whether Paul *could* have called our plays. Not only was he too involved in other day-to-day business matters of running the team to develop play-by-play strategy, but, to be frank, Paul hadn't really known and understood the intricacies involved in each individual assignment for all our plays.

Let me give you an example. A few years ago I ran into Paul during the off-season and he told me that he had his eyes on a tight end—"a real great blocker"—for the upcoming college draft. His name was Al Chandler and he played football for the powerful University of Oklahoma team. "This Chandler boy," said Paul, "is the tight end who's going to take your position away from you." I looked at our coach for a moment, then smiled. "Paul," I advised him, "Oklahoma had a potent offense, but Al Chandler's blocking at the line wasn't the reason. Oklahoma ran from the Wishbone. This meant the tight end didn't have to tangle with those big defensive ends, the way he had to in the pros. Most of the time the tight end released downfield to block those tiny defensive backs."

Paul wrinkled his brow. "Oh?" he said, as if I had just let him in on a hidden fact.

I simply nodded and added, "Go ahead and draft Al Chandler. You'd have the highest paid third-string tight end in professional football."

As a matter of fact, Paul *did* go ahead and draft Al Chandler. And Al played behind Bruce and me for a couple of years before being released to the San Francisco 49ers.

As for Paul being aloof and unemotional, I don't wholeheartedly agree here either. I have on several occasions seen him break down and weep openly—once in 1970 when we beat the Browns at Riverfront and two years later when we beat them in Cleveland. And on numerous other occasions he came close to tears. And if you were gullible enough to believe Paul Brown was unemotional on the sidelines during a game I would like to show you some wristwatches for sale. The TV cameras always seemed to capture him that way, but let me tell you, he was a bundle of charged-up nervous tension out there, forever yelling—at officials, at players, even at his own coaches. (Countless times coaches quit right there on the sidelines after being chewed out by Paul; only to remain with the team after the passion of the game had passed.)

His so-called aloofness I credited to shyness. Really. Even Paul's intimates said it was true. Like Jackie Raynert, probably PB's closest friend. Jackie was in the sportswear business in Atlanta and frequently went to Cincinnati to be with Paul for particularly big games.

Jackie liked to talk to us players about Paul when the Old Coach wasn't present. He claimed that Paul Brown was one of the most misjudged men in America.

"People paint an image of him as being stoic, aloof," Jackie said. "But that's really not true. I have known Paul for more years than you boys have been alive and I can tell you that he is a very warm, very personable man."

He told about how, when his sons were young, Paul used to dress up as Santa Claus. He waited until the boys were asleep, and then went into their rooms and woke them up about two or three in the morning. He talked to them, asked them what they wanted for Christmas and whether they'd been good. Then he held each one of them for a moment, gave them a kiss and scurried out of the room.

"I'd scolded Paul about not opening up to people more," Jackie said. "And I'll tell you why he didn't. It was because he was *shy*, one of the shyest men I've ever met. His shyness was often misinterpreted as coldheartedness. It hid the fact that he was an extremely warm man."

I didn't doubt Jackie then, and I don't now.

But I thought it was unfortunate that I never really saw that side of Paul Brown. I guess we were too ingrained in the player-coach, employer-employee, master-slave relationship.

I found that a little sad.

They had charged, too, that Paul Brown was too conservative in his football technique and that the game had passed him by. Yet, under Paul, the Bengals had *the* most intricate offensive system in professional football—ask any opposing defensive coach. The *run*, not the pass, was a conservative weapon. And the Bengals had the leading passing team in the NFL for several of the PB years. As for the game passing him by, Paul was, is, and always will be the singular most successful coach on the pro football field—a lifetime record of 351 wins, 134 losses and sixteen ties. Paul also shaped one of the most successful young franchises in the country—the Cincinnati Bengals—in eight short years. And he did it despite the fact that all the other jealous NFL team owners ganged up on him in the original allocation draft to ensure Paul possessed the very worst material possible to begin building his franchise with.

If there *was* a part of the game that passed Paul by it was not on the field but in the locker room. Player relationships. Too much had happened to America since Paul's championship years in Cleveland. Hippies. The Vietnam War. The 60s decade of revolution. Individual freedoms. No longer could you just command a player to do something and he'd do it without hesitation. Players suddenly asked, *why?* And saying, "because I am the coach and I said so, that's why" no longer put the fear of God into employees.

People were different in the 50s and early 60s. They understood the Paul Brown way of things. They obeyed. Football used to be a simpler business for Paul. But it would never be that way again.

They also said Paul Brown didn't allow superstars on his team and he underpaid his players. True? I'm not sure. There was Greg Cook, Mike Reid, Bill Bergey—superstars all. And, Kenny Anderson and Ike Curtis have emerged as current-day NFL superstars, their names known to football fans everywhere. As for the salaries, I believed Paul was at least "competitive." He paid his players what he felt they were worth, and worth was determined by the going market rate as well as PB's personally devised grading system. There was a much travelled story about this when Paul was head coach of the Browns. Reportedly, a guard came in and Paul paid him a certain figure, based on how he graded out. A second guard, one who had the exact same grade, than sat down at the negotiating table and somehow wheedled an additional $2,000 out of the coach. Paul went back to the first guard, told him what happened, and awarded him a $2,000 boost in salary, too.

Paul was vindictive, they said, and they pointed to the Bill Bergey case. I tend to agree with that charge in connection with this one case, but it certainly wasn't reflective of a long-standing Paul Brown characteristic. On the contrary, Paul had a history of giving players a second chance. I cite the examples of Steve Chomyszak and Bob Maddox. Not until I crossed him—by criticizing the Tiger Johnson resignation—did I feel Paul's vindictiveness personally. It was chilling. Then again, I was the only one who went out on a limb against Paul, so maybe my action brought out this latent PB trait. Actually, I lost my job as exhibition season commentator on WLWT television because of Paul. The station told me it was because the Bengals had to approve the sportscasters, and the Bengals wouldn't approve me. In the papers, Paul said they approved another ex-Bengal to do the television coverage of pre-season games for WLWT because he wanted "to give someone else a chance."

That someone else was my former roommate, Bob Johnson.

Paul was not perfect. But with one or two exceptions he was recognized as the supreme head coach in pro football, rightfully so. The exceptions, the shortcomings, I have already mentioned. He did not motivate his players before a game, and he often coached by use of "the Threat." I still contend that, if a team mentally prepared itself one hundred percent before a game, it might nevertheless lose that game because the opponent was prepared one hundred ten percent. Head coaches must add that ten percent motivational factor. And Paul's threatening "if you can't do the job we'll draft somebody who can" was a patently negative approach to getting the best performance out of players.

But these were minor problems when you looked at the total picture and his total command. No one around, for example, was shrewder than Paul when it came to organization, drafting, judging talent and collecting good, head-smart players around him.

Another Paul Brown quality was unprejudiceness. It didn't matter what race or religion you were, if you possessed talent and kept your nose clean you could play football for Paul Brown. I think it may have been PB himself who broke the color barrier in modern professional football. It was during the early fifties in Cleveland and Paul took the boldly unprecedented, and often criticized, step of playing two black players—Marion Motley and Deacon Willis on his squad. On our team, of course, Paul drafted Jess Phillips, an ex-convict, and Tommie Smith, the disputed black power Olympian, when no one else would touch them.

As for compassion as a personal quality, Paul Brown possessed that, too. In 1971 we had a popular defensive safety named Ken Dyer. During a pre-season game played in Green Bay on October 3, 1971, Kenny hit Packer runningback John Brockington head on, and lost. Kenny injured his spinal column and became instantly and totally paralyzed; he came very close to dying on the play by gagging on his own tongue. Paul did everything in his power to help his player. He made sure Kenny had five months of the finest hospital services and accommodations he could get. Paul was obligated to pay Kenny his salary for the remainder of the year, but Paul went much further. First, he provided living space for Kenny's pregnant wife Pam at the Green Bay hospital; and, he paid her $400 a month as a "physical therapist." He also extended Ken Dyer's contract an extra year and paid him full salary.

Nor was Paul Brown too big a man to admit when he was wrong. We were playing Kansas City a few years ago and I was to "pick"—or brush block—their middle linebacker, Willie Lanier. I did a whale of a job, the best pick I had ever done. The official didn't think so, though, and he called offensive pass interference on me. It was a terrible call and when I got to the sidelines Paul was staring knives at me. "What's the matter with you," he hollered. "I could see that was interference from here." I knew that wasn't the truth, so I responded by saying, "You didn't see any such thing and you know it; don't tell me you did. That was one of the best picks I've ever made for you."

Paul looked at me with a red face. "Don't you ever talk to me that way," he snapped, "I simply won't have it."

"Don't you talk to me that way," I responded. "I know exactly what I did out there and you don't."

Now this was risky business, challenging the head coach this way. But I knew I was right. And, sure enough, on Tuesday, after viewing the films, Paul approached me and said, very sincerely,

"Bob, I apologize for my remarks. The films clearly show that there was absolutely no interference on that play. And it *was* one of the best picks you've ever done. I hope you accept my apologies."

How many head coaches would have bothered to admit such a mistake to a player?

Paul Brown did.

I suppose of all the qualities of Paul Brown, the one that stood out the most was his ability to teach and lead men. Look at the coaching staffs around the NFL—Pittsburgh's Chuck Noll and Miami's Don Shula, for example—all learned their football from Paul Brown. At one time a few years ago a third of the head and assistant coaches in the NFL grew up under Paul Brown's tutelege. That should tell you something.

There was one more misconception that Paul shattered. Some said not until they put him in his grave would Paul Brown step down as the Bengals' head coach.

Paul buried that allegation on the first day of 1976. I was at a Rose Bowl party when I received the news from a reporter: Paul Brown announced his retirement from football after forty-one years of coaching.

I went into shock. There had been so much speculation over the years. And now it had come to pass.

The announcement came in Paul's own unassuming way. He called Al Heim, the Bengals' publicity director, with his decision and told Al to "handle it." Then Paul took off for Pasadena to watch the Rose Bowl and left sports reporters dangling for a reason.

Was he in ill health? Had the loss to Oakland upset him to the point of resignation?

No, none of these, Paul was just *ready* to step down. When he took over the team in 1968 he said he would relinquish the head coaching reins when he felt the Bengals were "competitive." After our 11-3 season, it appeared that the Bengals were that. I really felt he wanted to leave the head coaching ranks in '75. But we suffered terrible injuries and finished 7-7. Paul was not the type of man to close a career with a mediocre performance.

And so Tiger Johnson was in. Then Tiger Johnson was out. The announcement came on October 2, 1978.

As I said earlier, I heard it while having lunch in a bar. After the people stood up and cheered, I just got up and walked out.

I walked over to Fountain Square and sat. My stomach was in knots, my mind spurting in flashes of faces, meetings and memories. What the hell was I going to do? Tiger's failing was so much Paul's fault, I felt. Did I owe it to my radio audience to give my opinion of the subject? Or did I owe my former employer—a man who had been my absolute idol, a man next to my father who I esteemed more than anyone else in the world—did I owe Paul Brown the courtesy of keeping my mouth shut?

For an hour and a half I sat there, devil on one shoulder, angel on the other.

Then it hit me. I *had* to tell what I knew. I owed my audience. It was a big, big decision in my life.

On my radio show, I presented it this way: "I pose you this question: If a team loses five games in a row, do you fire the man responsible? Do you fire the man responsible for selecting the team's draft choices, the man responsible for releasing players, the man responsible for hiring the coaches on your staff, the man responsible for you and when your team travels to away games? If your answer is yes to these questions, Tiger Johnson is not the man to be fired. There is only one man responsible—his name is Paul Brown."

I went on. "A football team at the professional level is eighty percent attitude. The attitude of the players comes from the people that hire them. If management approaches the game strictly as a business, the players will play as if it were strictly a business. This breeds an attitude by the players of looking out for your own best interests, and therefore, you have no unity on the football team, no spirit, no extra effort...and until the management of the Bengals can separate the running of the football team from the dollars and cents of the franchise, there will never be a championship team in Cincinnati. And with forty-thousand or whatever season ticket holders already paid each season, the organization will be very comfortable to keep their present attitude."

I concluded: "On the bottom line, Paul Brown put Bill Johnson in the same corner that Paul wanted to avoid when he came to this town—he wanted total control in Cleveland. He got it when he came to Cincinnati, but he didn't allow Bill Johnson the same control as head coach."

The words may seem mundane today. But in October, 1978, it was the first time that the tenets of an Ohio institution named Paul Brown had been publicly questioned.

The results of my tirade were staggering. That night the lights for the telephone lines in the studio blinked like the inside of a cockpit. There was newspaper coverage in papers from coast-to-coast. Actually, I didn't enjoy the phone calls on the program that night. People for the first time now had a springboard to launch every stored up criticism of Paul Brown they had carried around with them for so many years. That wasn't the purpose of the show. I simply wanted to give my opinion as a former player, someone who had been there, someone who knew.

At any rate, the die was cast.

I felt guilty. I didn't sleep an hour that night, knowing what I had to do.

I had to confront Paul Brown face to face.

The longest steps I ever took were those the next day into the Spinney Field Complex. I knocked on Paul's door. When he opened it, he looked up at me. His face turned scarlet. His first words were: *"I heard it. Mike heard it. My wife heard it, my daughter-in law heard it, and so did my grandchildren."* With that he went by me heading for the practice field.

Out on the field, we talked. "Paul," I began, "I wanted to make sure you knew exactly what I said on my show. I wanted to tell you face-to-face so you didn't think I was skulking behind your back." Then we started our conversation. Later, Bo Harris told me that Paul won in the threatening-finger waving contest 55-23. It lasted an hour and thirteen minutes, about every nine of which Paul paused, looked up and said, "Bob, there's something really wrong with you. You've lost your mental faculties."

We were getting nowhere. For example, one complaint voiced by teammates was the Bengals' habit of going to the west coast on the evening before the game, so our evening meal consisted of airline food. Some players didn't like the food and wouldn't eat it. Others were afraid of flying and were too nervous to eat. As a result, once they hit L.A., Oakland, San Francisco or San Diego, those guys would hightail it for the nearest fast food chain and fill up on nice greasy hamburgers. So, I suggested to Paul that each player be given a per diem meal allowance so, upon landing, he could go to a good restaurant and get a nice filling, carbohydrate-rich, steak and potato dinner. It went like this:

Paul: I didn't know you didn't like airline food. I like the food.

Me: That's not the point, Paul. Some of the *players* don't like it.

Paul: Why not? The food tastes OK to me.

Me: I know, Paul. But some of the players don't like it. Therefore, when they get to the west coast they load up on cheeseburgers.

Paul: I don't buy them cheeseburgers.

Me: I know, Paul. The players buy them themselves. They don't like the airline food.

Paul: We can't control what the airlines serve. Besides, you never told me you didn't like the food.

And so on.

When it was over, Paul instructed me to write down my complaints on a sheet of paper and submit them to him. Which I did. Nothing big, mind you. These were simple matters, things to help bring management of the Bengals closer together with the players of the Bengals. Before I submitted the list, I talked to several veterans on the squad to pick their brains. They loved the opportunity to express their opinions. Using this suggestion list they voiced to Paul Brown their beefs, something none of the players had ever done to Paul in person.

The list had thirteen suggestions, such as a "wives" night at training camp, certain travel considerations, helping new players in town with housing, that type of thing. As I said, nothing earth-shaking, but it was a start.

I sent Paul the list. But I never knew whether he followed up on the suggestions or not.

During my hour and thirteen minute Spinney Field conversation with Paul he told me: "I put a letter in the mail to you today. It's a copy of a letter your father sent me a year ago. I think you should read it."

Sure enough, next day the letter came. Here's what my father had written to Paul Brown on October 5, 1977:

Dear Paul,

For some time I've wanted to write you and say thanks for completing a job that Mrs. Trumpy and I could only begin.

As you know, because of his physical ability, it sometimes takes an outstanding athlete a little longer to mature emotionally. He is idolized by his classmates; his teachers often make exceptions for him; his coaches make certain that he remains scholastically eligible by steering him into the lower track courses. The news media constantly extol his athletic virtues, and the college recruiters convince him that he is a cinch to make it big in their program.

With a full-ride scholarship, spending money and other gifts from loyal alumni, he has no worries. All decisions are made for him. He does not have to think for himself, and often finishes college never having had to make an important decision on his own.

If he is truly a superstar he enters the professional field where doors are opened for him that are not open to most people. Because of the adultation afforded him, he lives in his own little world, always expecting others to cater to him, not understanding when they don't. He is often an immature child in a grown-up's world.

We sent you such a child in 1968.

As he began to absorb your teaching and your philosophy, he began to understand the meanings of responsibility, maturity, character and empathy.

He used to refer to things you said. He would quote you verbatim. He referred to your insistence upon character and commitment to excellence. More than once he predicted that a certain player would not remain a Bengal, not because he wasn't a good player, but rather because his character did not measure up to your standards.

Of all the contributions you have made to the

game of football, I believe the greatest to be the standards of quality you have adhered to throughout your coaching career. How many men, families, children and parents have benefited from the code you have so deeply believed in? There really is no way of counting how many have been affected.

So, from a mother and father who sent you a boy and can now claim a man as their son, we thank you . . ."

Sincerely,
Bob Trumpy, Sr.

Paul's sending a copy of this letter to me had the desired affect.

I felt lousy. What my dad had written was true. I knew then, and still do, that Paul saw me as a traitor, a turncoat. To PB that was the unkindest cut of all.

Do I regret what I had done?

No, not regret. But I felt bad. Paul was Richard Nixon, I was John Dean. But you know what?—I'd do it again.

I have taken a new career path now. The Bengals and Paul Brown are behind me. A whole future lies ahead.

But, oh, what times they *were*! Expansion. Division championships. The rush of victories. The football fraternity of teammate love. Bruce. Chip. Kenny. Johnson. Little Warren McVea. So many others.

Do I miss it? Yes. Who wouldn't? And no. Now, new challenges replace the old. That's the way things work.

Will the Bengals miss ol' number 84, fella named Trumpy?

Who knows. I hope in my ten years I at least contributed to some of those great wins, some of those memories for Bengal fans.

But I keep going back to something Paul Brown used to say alot to players. Said Paul, "You'd be surprised how well professional football will get along without you."

You know, Paul was probably right.

"I bet I'll miss him before he misses me."

Acknowledgments:

We would like to express special thanks to the following: Greg Nelson, Ms. Faye Woebkenberg, Fred Straub, the Cincinnati Enquirer, Cincinnati Photo Labs, Inc. and Mark Ackley. Photos courtesy of Fred Straub, the Cincinnati Enquirer and Cincinnati Photo Labs, Inc.